W9-ACG-069
A12900 251675

ILLINOIS CENTRAL COLLEGE
PN1948.U6Z4
STACKS
The American burlesque show.
A12900 251675

05974
PN
1948 ZEIDMAN
.U6 American burlesque shoe
Z4

WITHDRAWN

Illinois Central College
Learning Resource Center

THE AMERICAN BURLESQUE SHOW

THE AMERICAN BURLESQUE SHOW

by Irving Zeidman

Illinois Central College
Learning Resouce Center

HAWTHORN BOOKS, INC. / Publishers New York

05974

PN
1948
.U6
Z4

Copyright © 1967 by Hawthorn Books, Inc., 70 Fifth Avenue, New York City 10011. Copyright under International and Pan-American Copyright Conventions. All rights reserved, including the right to reproduce this book, or portions thereof, in any form, except for the inclusion of brief quotations in a review. This book was manufactured in the United States of America and published simultaneously in Canada by Prentice-Hall of Canada, Ltd., 1870 Birchmount Road, Scarborough, Ontario. Library of Congress Catalogue Card Number: 66-22317.

First Edition, 1967

Acknowledgment is made to Thomas B. Morgan for permission to quote from "Blaze Starr in Nighttown," which first appeared in *Esquire* magazine.

0295

To Henrietta, Woody and Cindy

CONTENTS

THE AMERICAN BURLESQUE SHOW

ACCENT ON SEX AND DIVIDENDS

THE trouble with the American burlesque show, from beginning to end, is either that it has been too dirty—or else that it hasn't been dirty enough.

Despite some original identification with travesty and vaudeville, and occasional timid divagations into the fields of talent, the American burlesque show has primarily been a commercialized sex show.

Nobody ever crusaded more sincerely or hopelessly for the anomaly of clean burlesque than Sime Silverman, founder and editor of the theatrical publication *Variety*. One of the few who took burlesque seriously, and also wrote about it honestly, he conceded (December 11, 1909): "Were there no women in burlesque, how many men would attend? The answer is the basic principle of the burlesque business."

The somewhat reluctant observation of Sidney Wire, commentator for the other outstanding theatrical guidepost, *The Billboard,* made it unanimous (March 22, 1913): "Ninety percent of the burlesque audiences go to burlesque theatres to see the girls."

The history of American burlesque, as a result, is the history of its producers' endless efforts to please both the censors and the audiences without ever actually achieving the impossible balance. When burlesque prospered, it did so by influencing amenable officials—thereby, in a way, fooling the censors and pleasing the audiences or, as in the case of the envied affluence of the hallowed Columbia Wheel, by pleasing the censors and fooling the audiences. Sex has been the main ingredient, controlled by the all-important factor of profit. "Burlesque," said Isidor H. Herk, burlesque magnate, in 1917, "is nothing more or less than a mercantile business."

Hence hilarity, frivolity, Rabelaisian ribaldry, have been conspicuously absent from the American burlesque scene. Brooks Atkinson, while dramatic critic for *The New York Times,* summarized it as follows:

> To those who seldom devote an evening to these less conspicuous theatres, burlesque suggests a riotous whirligig of clumsy entertainment, coarse and elementary, with intimate glimpses of immodest girls. . . . As a matter of fact, burlesque is generally dull.

Joseph Wood Krutch, in *The Nation,* deplored "the wearily mechanical antics of a group of underpaid and overworked performers." A foreign observer saw in American burlesque shows only an arena wherein "the performers sprawl and crawl and bawl their cheap obscenities."

Publicized for lavish and tempting and beautiful women, the chorus lines of burlesque have been among the more ominous spectacles of their times. The unheralded performers in burlesque are usually possessed of one understandable obsession—to get out of it into the more lucrative fields of entertainment. The female stars, the glamor "Queens of Burlesque," from the ample Lydia Thompson to the streamlined Hinda Wassau, from the wicked Millie De Leon to the respected Rose Sydell, from the rotund Lena Daley to the svelte Ann Corio, have been promoted and exploited as erotic sirens, and inviting Loreleis, by none other than—their own husbands.

Burlesque emerged in the 1880s and 1890s from its nebulous origins in musicalized European imports called burlesques such as *The Black Crook* and Lydia Thompson's Blondes. The evolving lady minstrel shows served as a bridge for the American-style burlesque show and the honky-tonks. Then came the large traveling organizations—the Eastern and Western Circuits, the Columbia and Mutual Wheels, finally stock (nontraveling) burlesque and then the end.

After 1905, when burlesque became established and entrenched, a remarkable uniformity and sameness were evident in every season, consisting of the following:

1. A handful of clean shows and the prediction that in contrast to prior periods of dirt and smut, burlesque had at last come of age and was now clean, specializing in slapstick and/or satire.
2. A preponderance of dirty shows which, inexplicably, made money.
3. Sensational newspaper articles alleging that in contrast to prior periods when burlesque was clean, specializing in slapstick and/or satire, current shows were dirty and smutty.
4. The inevitable police raids and cries for reform.
5. The burlesque producers promising to overhaul their shows, to institute their own censorship committees: "We will personally see to it that nothing offensive will henceforth be tolerated in any of our shows." Then, waiting out the storm for a few weeks, then proceeding as if nothing had happened.
6. Sime Silverman tearing his hair out.

From 1880 to date, burlesque has made a complete cycle, ending precisely where it began.

One of the first of its prominent queens, the robustly beautiful Pauline Markham, the "Venus" of Lydia Thompson's Blondes, was the mistress of a governor of South Carolina. One of today's most prominent strippers, the amply bosomed Blaze Starr, served in a similar capacity for an ex-governor of Louisiana. On a much lower level, the early soubrettes of burlesque often "hustled" customers in the saloons and honky-tonks. Now, seventy years later, the strippers often double as B-girls in burlesque nightclubs. Thus burlesque, emerging from nowhere, wound up in the same place.

What has sustained burlesque, more than any other feature, even up to the present, is none other than the old-fashioned hootchie-kootchie. Its female practitioners have been called, in part, Oriental dancers, classic dancers, Salome dancers, control dancers, interpretive dancers, shimmy shakers, tassel dancers, exotics—and still other names by the puritanical. But under whatever name and whatever the disguise, the bump and the grind, which to burlesque aficionados are physical representations of the sex act, constitute the essence of the dance. These cooch artistes maintained burlesque when it began, and maintain whatever is left of it now.

In the early 1900s, the reigning burlesque "classic" dancer was Millie De Leon, described by the *New York Telegraph* in 1909 as "a statuesque brunette, with large dark eyes suggestive of the Odalisque of the East." Her onetime husband and manager, Lew Rose, had her publicized, for less scholarly burlesque audiences, as the "Girl in Blue."

Millie De Leon, the "statuesque brunette with large dark eyes suggestive of the Odalisque of the East." *New York Public Library*

Millie De Leon's trials and tribulations have been duly recorded for posterity by the press of the day. She did not mind being arrested occasionally for neglecting to wear tights. On one occasion she was dragged out of the theatre by the scruff of her neck. This was routine. What bothered her was the perfidy of the male animal. Thus, the newspapers reported the following incident: While with the Kentucky Belles in 1904, she routinely tossed a garter into the audience, as was her cusom. This time, lo and behold, it was returned to her with a five-hundred-dollar bill and an invitation to dine. Millie De Leon did not hesitate. "I did just as any other girl would have done under the circumstances. I kept the garter and dined with him." Alas, as it turned out, his intentions were dishonorable. Whereupon, our virtuous heroine betook herself to the bank where he was employed as a teller and, surrounded by reporters who just happened to be there, publicly horsewhipped her betrayer.

The *New York World* in 1906 related this unfortunate incident, as told by Millie herself:

> "You see, I spent the night with my mother." . . . After which, she went for a harmless walk. Emerged a sinister figure from the shadows.
>
> " 'It's a lovely morning, isn't it? Where are you going, my pretty maid? May I go with you?'
>
> " 'I guess you've made a mistake, you don't know me.'
>
> " 'Yes, but I'd like to.'
>
> "With that I turned on him and hit him a terrible blow in the face."

In 1911, while playing in Chicago, creditors attached her salary for debts totaling five hundred dollars. With charming aplomb and frankness, she turned to the audience, pleading: "I am a poor hardworking girl who has wiggled twice daily all week for your amusement and edification, and now when the management has all the wiggles I had, they refuse to pay me my salary." Unfortunately, history does not record any concrete response to her appealing plea.

She symbolized the burlesque of her day, and the following review of her performance, in the Philadelphia *North American* in 1915, may give us some conception of what was considered consummate wickedness at the time:

> Slowly, and in a manner hardly noticeable even through the transparent net which constituted the middle portion of her gown, the muscles of her body took on a wave-like motion.

The undulations increased in rapidity. A purely muscular side to side movement, generally deemed the peculiar gift of horses, complicated the pattern and introduced a chaotic activity that probably lasted five minutes.

Finally, Millie De Leon became unspeakably frank. From knee to neck she was convulsive. Every muscle became eloquent of primitive emotion. Amid groans, cat calls and howls of approval from the audience, she stopped. Standing suddenly erect, with a deft movement she revealed her nude right leg from knee almost to waist.

A strut to the right, a long stride back, and the abdominal "dance" was resumed. The large pink rose in her belt nodded confusedly, and her hands clasped and unclasped spasmodically under the strain of the stimulated emotion. Streaked and sweaty, her face took on the aspect of epilepsy. She bit her lips, rolled her eyes, pulled fiercely at great handfuls of her black, curly hair.

Indescribable noises and loud suggestions mingled in the hot breath of the audience. Men in the orchestra rose with shouts. A woman—one of six present—hissed. Laughter became uproarious. And then, sensing her climax, Millie De Leon gave a little cry that was more a yelp, and ceased.

Moving towards a box where two women were sitting with their backs to the audience, she once more showed the white expanse of her limb, put her hand to her throat as if further to display her person, but instead snatched a gaudy flower basket from the hand of an attendant and began to throw tiny blue garters into the pit.

Then the glowing gaze of a youth in a left proscenium box caught her attention. In both hands she seized his blushing face and kissed him on the lips. In three bounds she was at the box immediately opposite, and burying her fingers in the black hair of an older man, kissed him audibly. Those women who showed only their back were in that box. They blushed. The audience howled.

"Here, Sailor, come here!" The sailor came forthwith down the aisle between laughing hundreds and up the stage to the dancer's side. He, too, was kissed.

"Here, you! Come on up! No, you with the bushy hair!" This to a youth of obvious refinement, patently out of his element, about halfway back in the left section of the parquet. He squirmed and dodged. She pursued unmercifully.

"I mean you in the end seat of the twelfth row," she insisted.

"Aw, go on!" supported the audience.

The boy might have been nailed to his seat.

The air with which De Leon turned away was meant to be imperial.

As the woman's watery eye ran over the audience, many a man took refuge behind the seat in front. Some ignorant boys, desirous but fearful, nervously twisted their paper programs into shreds. Others, of a totally different type, hopefully made themselves conspicuous.

It was one of the latter class, a light-haired strapping fellow, who went to the stage next. He received kisses and more—the rose which adorned the dancer's belt was tucked beneath his own waist-band.

For her final dalliance, the woman turned to a youth whom she had evidently marked from the beginning. He was tall and slight, not more than eighteen years, and had been watching her with the eyes of a child from a box at the right.

He answered her call reluctantly, stumbled to the stage in confusion, and was completely taken aback when she seized his hair, kissed him, held him off for a moment and then applied her lips fervidly to his forehead.

With a taunting laugh she thrust him from her and called to the lantern man in the gallery: "Put the light on him!" Her laugh issued again from the wings and was echoed to the audience as the spotlight revealed on the troubled brow of the youth the scarlet impression of her lips. Ten minutes later the boy left the theatre still troubled and still ignorant of the scarlet stains that seared his forehead.

As the chorus danced out for the final ensemble, the audience uproariously left the theatre.

In 1964 the routine of Blaze Starr in a burlesque nightclub in Baltimore is thus described in *Esquire* (July 1964):

The curtain parted revealing a long red couch, three electric candles on a small table, and a lamppost marked PASSION STREET. The band played *Pomp and Circumstance,* a customer shouted, "Go girl, go!" and Blaze entered. She wore a wrap and gown that she had made for herself out of real Somali leopard skins. On her gown, the leopard in front reached around in back so that his paws grabbed at her buttocks. In one hand, Blaze held a long cigarette holder trimmed in leopard. She smiled insouciantly until the applause died down. Then to a stripper's version of *Night Train,* she dragged her cape once around the runway. She switched on the electric candles and again minced up the runway, sans cape and holder, but now with a rose (her trademark) between her teeth. She bit off a mouthful of petals and tossed the stem and pistil to the deaf-mute. Then she bared one bulging breast and used it for a launching pad, flicking rose petals to a middle-aged barber with glazed eyeballs.

Blaze tripped to the microphone. Looking down at her exposed breast, she said, "What are you doing out there, you gorgeous thing?" Then she covered herself. "You got to tell them they're pretty," she said; "it makes them grow." The drummer whacked a cymbal and the boys laughed. "Strip, already," a youth shouted. He wore a red and white shirt with a black collar and an arm patch identifying him as a winner of the National Duck Pin Bowling Congress Triplicate Award. "You l'il evil ole tomcat," Blaze said and threw her pelvis at him. Then she flung herself on the couch and quickly stripped down to a transparent bra and black garter pants. She produced a powder puff and asked rhetorically, "Who's going to powder my butt?"

To the tune of *That's My Desire,* a volunteer leaned over the bar and did it. Another was allowed to dust her breasts. And a third received permission to peel off her pants. "You're fogging my glasses," he said. Blaze replied, "Oh, suf-fer." She returned to the microphone and shook out her pants. Powder flew: "That's not dust," she said, "it's r-r-r-rust." On the couch again, Blaze removed her bra, caressed herself, leaned over pendulously, and shouted "*Lunchtime!*" Then she lay flat, undulating, and pushed a secret button so that chemical smoke began to rise between her legs and shreds of red cloth stood on end rippling like fire.

As Blaze Starr has taken pains to point out, her act is not just a strip act. It contains, among other attributes, audience participation and comedy.

On every level and in every age, the pattern is the same. Anonymous, and usually arrested, the Cleos, Fifis, Zazas and Fatimas of burlesque have meant more to the steady patrons than any other portion of the entertainment. The difference between the "Oriental" dancers of yesterday and the "Exotics" of today are differences only of degree, not substance.

THE BLACK CROOK AND THE ENGLISH QUEEN

BURLESQUE, unfortunately, has never been any of the fancy or sentimental things ascribed to it—neither now nor then. It has never been a lusty form of folk expression or a national forum for satire or a showplace for knockabout hilarious slapstick. If burlesque ever became too talented, it ceased to be burlesque. It became vaudeville or musical comedy and even, as in the case of the E. E. Rice extravaganzas of the eighties, light opera.

The origins of American burlesque spring from nowhere and everywhere. Like vaudeville, burlesque owed much at the beginning to the circus, the minstrel show, the beer and dance hall, the honky-tonk. From the circus, particularly, came its first producers, managers and actors. From the minstrel show, burlesque derived its songs, its gags, the chorus.

Unlike vaudeville, burlesque was first associated with legitimate productions or travesties, on the one hand, and behind-the-barn tent or cooch shows, on the other. Burlesque wavered between these two extremes, eventually finding itself as an expanded hootchie-kootchie attraction.

In the very beginning, there were no burlesque shows, only burlesques. These were imported travesties from England, based on mythology and classical drama. They were slightly satirical and largely tiresome. Attractive women—without any hint of nudity—were often featured to bolster these feeble projections. Perhaps the most prolific writer of the legitimate burlesques was the Irishman Dion Boucicault; and one of the most popular of the female players, usually appearing in his productions, was his wife, Agnes Robertson, described as a "beautifully formed blonde," who was billed as the "Fairy Star." These burlesques were often set to music, and in 1859 appeared the most famous of them all, *The Field of the Cloth of Gold,* described as "a grand musical and terpsichorean burlesque." This production featured well-known legitimate players of the day: Morlauchi, Mme. Celeste, Fannie Ellsler and, later, the Worrell Sisters.

The Billboard's Sidney Wire traced the burlesque show to these legitimate burlesques and thence to the Gaiety Theatre in London whence they, in their turn, originated. This he called the original shrine of burlesque "when burlesque meant burlesque which consisted of regular works of literary fame." However, all that modern burlesque has garnered from them with any degree of permanence is the name "Gaiety," which has since adorned the marquees of numerous burlesque houses.

Variety and Sime Silverman came more directly to the point, ignoring with some accuracy any connection whatever. "Burlesque," he cried, "harks back to the tonks, back to the nondescript theatre, back to *The Black Crook,* a class burlesque show of its day."

The Black Crook is the acknowledged forerunner of modern burlesque because here, for the first time in the history of the American stage, female nudity was exhibited not as an integral part of the plot, but frankly and with bravado for its own crass and pleasant appeal.

There had been minor theatrical scandals before. In 1833, during a performance of the legitimate play *The Ice Witch,* at the Bowery Theatre in New York City, Mlle. Francisquay, appearing in decollette display, was hissed off the stage for this presumptuous affront to Colonial decency, while, it is recorded, the balcony and gallery went wild with delight. And, in 1861, occurred the deliciously infamous episode wherein the madcap Adah Isaacs Menken appeared as the Mazeppa of Byron's poem, strapped "nude" to the back of an untamed stallion. Though she was far from nude, her costume consisting of "baggy trunks . . . enough for three bathing suits," a sash and fleshings, the outcries of enraged reformers were loud and indignant.

The Menken episode was still rankling when on September 12, 1866, *The Black Crook,* a feeble dramatization by Charles M. Borras of some obscure German folk tales, was presented by William Wheatley at Niblo's Garden in New York City. Purely by accident, a ballet of

Some girls of *The Black Crook*. Culver Pictures, Inc.

"imported dances," imported by Jarret & Palmer for the opera *La Biche au Bois* at the Academy of Music, was independently interpolated into the production of *The Black Crook.* And a corps de ballet of one hundred diaphanously draped overweight Amazons in close-fitting, flesh-colored silk tights danced their heavy way into history. The results were sensational. The reformers shrieked, the "best people" boycotted it, and *The Black Crook* ran for sixteen consecutive months, the box receipts of sin aggregating over $1,000,000 for a profit of $650,000.

This financial bonanza was not lost upon the other showmen of the day. If this could coin money, then, legs up, it was everybody's race, with all thighs bared.

Thus originated and thus grew a profusion of female exposure which ultimately led to the modern burlesque show. The industry itself, giving credit where due, later labeled its shows with names like *Black Crook Jr., White Crook, Red Crook* and *Golden Crook.*

The development, however, was very gradual. The next phase demanded a Queen of Burlesque upon whose opulent and specific anatomical delights could be fostered and concentrated the aspirations of avid and eager males. And thus, opportunely enough, appeared Lydia Thompson and Her Blondes.

In 1868, still in the crinoline exterior of mythological satire, came the thigh-length tights and curvaceous postures of Lydia Thompson and Her Imported English Blondes. Whether, in truth, they were all really blonde, or otherwise, has been a subject of delicate academic discussion. But that they were English and imported, there could be no doubt. And to American appetites, already whetted by *The Black Crook* and succeeding extravaganzas of homemade and not particularly ingenious confection such as *Humpty Dumpty* and *The White Faun,* the Blondes were an exotic bombshell with indigo sparks.

Lydia Thompson had acted on the English stage all her life, usually playing boys' roles, and at the age of fifteen was already known in London theatrical circles. Under the guidance of Alexander Henderson, a London theatrical manager and her second husband, she migrated to New York with her bevy of beefy, comely blondes. Henderson skillfully exploited the troupe as the "British Blondes," and they opened at Woods' Museum and Menagerie on 34th Street, New York City, later known as Daly's Theatre, sharing the theatre with exhibitions of a live baby hippopotamus.

True to the mold set by *The Black Crook,* the play itself in which they first appeared, *Ixion,* by F. C. Burnand, was a feeble and humorless vehicle for the personality, charm and legs of its female protagonists. Unlike the anonymous ballet of *The Black Crook,* however, there were now specific female talents to excite the admiration of susceptible and even superior males. Lydia Thompson had, as her devotees, the distinguished critic, James Gibbons Huneker, and the younger Dumas. Ada Harland, who played Jupiter, married the theatrically academic Brander Matthews. The glamorous Pauline Markham, playing the Goddess of Love as a strapping Venus in tights, was the Venus of the wealthy and the influential. In the rest of the all-star cast, the clever Lisa Weber was Mercury; Alice Logan, of the Logan Sisters, was Juno; Harry Beckett, one of the few males in the company, played Minerva.

The legend of the burlesque and its mythological improvisations being fairly dull, Lydia Thompson was not averse to enlivening matters by an occasional song of delicate double entendre. And the hefty chorines, representing goddesses, meteors, eclipses, etc., spiced the production further by alternately displaying ruffled drawers—the perennial mark of the cancan.

As the reward for popularity, the Blondes were enabled to leave Wood's Museum and Menagerie where the disagreeable smells of the livestock on exhibition in the menagerie part of the theatre had been offensive to their refined nostrils. They ensconced themselves in the more pretentious Niblo's, presenting a new burlesque, *Forty Thieves.*

As the Blondes' popularity increased, they varied their repertoire and traveled over the country, a standard attraction for almost twenty years. Their success was founded on liberal unabashed girl displays, living tableaux, the ample revealment of ample legs exposed as diligently and as completely as legitimately possible. And Lydia Thompson continued, as always, to alternate psalms with ribaldry, the cancan with flowery curtsies, decorous poesy with costumes revealing the full arc of the thigh.

The Blondes were often condemned for their so-called unbecoming demeanor, but they were usually shrewd enough to exploit such incidents to their own advantage. In 1868, Wilbur F. Story, the venerable critic for the *Chicago Times,* suggested the possibility that considering their reckless antics on a public platform, Lydia Thompson and her girls might be lacking in the necessary maidenly virtues. In those days, burlesquers, naturally, were far from reconciled to the opprobrium to which they now so complacently resign themselves.

So, Lydia Thompson with, and according to another account without, the assistance of the formidable Pauline Markham, drew a cowhide whip from beneath the folds of her wrap and resolutely assailed her detractor. Verified details are scant, and it is altogether possible

Pauline Markham, "Venus of the wealthy and the influential." *Culver Pictures, Inc.*

Lydia Thompson of the Blondes in a pensive moment. *Culver Pictures, Inc.*

that the entire incident is apocryphal, but in any event, the Blondes' popularity and publicity increased apace—a circumstance that Millie De Leon may have recalled to her own advantage forty years later.

In time, Lydia Thompson's legs became as familiar and as unexciting to the professional reviewers as, it may be assumed, those of their own wives. In 1877, the *Times* critic thus condescended to yawn:

> There are half a score of pretty girls exhibited in an unending walk around, but they really have nothing to offer but their persons. As soon as you get tired of their bodies you yawn and want to get out. . . . It is simply nonsensical to object to the troupe or its performances on the score of morality. So far as decency of action and text goes, they are as pure as an unborn babe and quite as uninteresting. . . . Lydia's legs have been before the public so long, and have had so many commentators, that we may be said to know them by heart. It is sufficient, therefore, to say that they are now mature and have a repose they never possessed before. I think they would anywhere command the attention and respect due to age and respectability.

At this time, Lydia Thompson was almost forty years of age. She persisted as late as 1886, the *New York Clipper* remarking that she was then duplicating her success of eighteen years ago singing "It's Cockney, You Know" in a St. Louis theater.

Having at last become as old and familiar as any wife, Lydia Thompson became as respectable, abandoning the field of burlesque entertainment, before it became entirely disreputable, for minor parts in legitimate drama. As a comedienne, she played mild roles in plays such as *A Bad Penny, Uncle Dan* and *The Bric-a-Brac Shop.*

Thus, respected as well as respectable, she died in London on November 15, 1908, leaving a daughter by her first marriage, Zeffie Tilbury, a proficient legitimate and Hollywood actress in her own right.

TIGHTS AND SIGHTS

THE success of the Blondes, following directly upon that of *The Black Crook,* brought forth innumerable exhibits which were neither burlesque nor vaudeville, nor any other form of recognizable show business. A hodgepodge of every theatrical oddity, bolstered and buttressed by fat blondes, was the order of the day. And practically every title had the catchall "Blonde" in it. The New York *Spirit of the Times* summed it up as follows in 1870. This new "variety business" consisted of

> . . . music by the band, farce, beautiful ballads, performances of dogs and monkeys, stump oratory, character songs and dances, negroisms, Dutchisms, ballet, gymnastic feats and burlesque. . . . Blondes are in the majority and some of them very pretty. The audiences are large, mostly of the masculine gender.

The financial panic of 1873 lent further impetus to these developing burlesque shows. Burlesque thrives on depression. Prettier girls are obtainable at burlesque wages, and the unemployed or indigent male reverts to simpler and less expensive forms of entertainment. Sexy shows and blondes, imported and domestic, followed like camp trailers in the wake of the Lydia Thompson troupes.

Olive Logan, novelist and suffragette, decried the debacle:

> An army of burlesque women took ship for America and presently the New York stage presented one disgraceful spectacle of padded legs jiggling and wriggling in the insensate follies and indecencies of the hour.

Presaging the burlesque of the future, she added:

> . . . they do not either act, dance or mime, but they habit themselves in a way which is attractive to an indelicate taste, and their inefficiency in other regards is overlooked.

But the worst was yet to come. The impresarios of the day then took the minstrel show, the most popular form of variety extant, and substituted girls for the male chorus. From sheath dresses and skirts so cut as to reveal the legs, they progressed to the inevitable tights; and another large step was taken toward the establishment of the standard burlesque show.

Some of these female minstrel shows were substantial and somewhat talented. There were such as Blanche Selwayn's Red Riding Hood Minstrels, Mme. Rejane's Female Minstrels and May Fiske's English Blondes, Living Art Pictures and Grand Specialty Combination. But the majority of the female minstrel shows were shoestring productions whose main attractions were intimate glimpses of legs and curves at bargain prices. Tights did not protrude unnecessarily and did not extend below the curve of the hip. Since hips were wide, legs sturdy and thighs expansive, there was often more robust allure in a rollicking Amazon march than in a modern split-second flash of bare breast or buttock. The spice-seeking male of the seventies and eighties envisioned forbidden delights when he read of English Blondes and French dances, of "Zoe, the Flying Fairy" or the "Grand Ballet—Warriors of the Sun, Grand March by Fifty Young Ladies Around the Dress Circle." As Epes W. Sargent, theatrical commentator, remarked, it was "not so much the tights as the area of exposure."

A popular stunt in these lady minstrel shows was swinging out over the heads of the audience in trapezes and swings in midair, sometimes undressing in the process, and furnishing a closer erotic view of fleshy thighs. This device was appropriated from beer gardens and brothels and, it was rumored, was an added attraction in the private revels of Stanford White, the murdered playboy architect.

Vainly trying to stem the tide of these frankly sexual exhibitions was a legitimate producer, E. E. Rice, who valiantly combined the form and pattern of the old English burlesques with the talent and original-

It was "not so much the tights as the area of exposure." *Culver Pictures, Inc.*

ity of comic opera. His first production of this nature, *Evangeline,* was called by him "the first American opera bouffe." Acutely conscious of the new forms burlesque was taking, he attempted to present extravaganzas "free from all taint of uncleanness." The *Dramatic Mirror,* in 1879, paid tribute where due: "Mr. Rice has labored zealously to weed the garden of burletta and extravaganza of vulgarity and every other objectionable feature."

In *Rice's Surprise Party* appeared many talented performers, including the popular English comedian Willie Edouin; William H. Crane, the LeBlanc of *Evangeline;* Henry E. Dixie, the handsome Irish star of *Adonis;* Nat C. Goodwin, Jr., the Yussuf of *Corsair;* and Goodwin's wife Eliza Weathersby, among many other established performers. Lillian Russell started as a chorus girl under his regime.

Rice's productions were also bolstered by the "Living Pictures," prevalent in less worthy presentations, and his female stars were of equal weight with the beefy damsels of the cruder shows, though they had to possess singing voices as well. Vernona Jarbeau, a hefty New York girl of French parents, was a famous and sturdy Evangeline. Amelia Sommerville was another delicate little item weighing about 250 pounds. As Rosetta in *Adonis* she coyly sang:

I'm a Merry Little Mountain Maid
As o'er the world I rove
Eating huckleberries all the day
And learning how to love.

The Irish-born Amelia Sommerville had been a ballet dancer in *The Black Crook* and was truly proud of her lavishly awesome figure. But in 1909 when 250-pound chorines were Beef Trust freaks, and a shapely figure was in the 140-pound class, she went on an Herculean feat of weight reduction. And with her own deciduous body as Case History #1, published *Amelia Somerville's Rules for Weight Reduction and the Preservation of Youth and Beauty*. When she died in 1934, female burlesque stars were singing, not of huckleberries and mountains, but something like:

Take your pennies, put 'em in a glass
Save them up for a piece of—cake.

Eventually, however, Rice capitulated and abandoned burlesque entirely for comic opera. His "Surprise Parties" were the last of the transition burlesques that tried to combine the allure of legs so successful in *The Black Crook* and Lydia Thompson's Blondes with satirical lyrics and some authentic talent. But their day was ended.

The fervid eighties were not particularly receptive to delicate parody or airy fantasy. Lusty, uninhibited, knock 'em down and drag 'em out spectacles were more to the average masculine taste. With the arrival of these incredible melanges of excitement, there arrived in the eighties and nineties not only more provocative nudity, but double entendre, the crudest vulgarities, inelegant dancers, lady wrestlers and screeching, posturing chorines.

In short, the American burlesque show, as we recognize it today, had at last come into its flatulent own.

A NEW "ART"

"A MANIA for the grandiose began in the '70s and continued more and fruitfully in the '90s," wrote Thomas Beer of the Mauve Decade.

Then, as now, men yearned for some glamour, however false, some romantic tinsel, however gaudy. And the intimate suggestiveness of the cancan, the lifting of flowered skirts to reveal ruffled drawers, colored fleshings and rounded thighs, the beckoning prettiness of painted, smiling blondes—all were basic to the new burlesque shows which were rough and lusty in the eighties, unbridled and raw in the nineties. Above all, the keynote of the era was size, bulk, magnitude. So that the massivity of the burlesque female behemoths reflected not only the taste of the customers but the pattern of the times. They were years particularized by hustle and the bustle.

In such an atmosphere the first real burlesque shows developed—featuring elephantine girls, racial comedy, motley musical specialties, cooch dancers and blunt, often smutty afterpieces or ensemble finales.

The first standard or fairly reputable burlesque show of this type was the Rentz-Santley Novelty and Burlesque Company. This was the creation of Michael B. Leavitt, an energetic and leading showman of the day who had a penchant for replacing male actors with female performers. An admirer and follower of P. T. Barnum, Leavitt repeatedly went to Europe to import exotic attractions which might represent elaborate wickedness to simple souls in America. On one of his trips he became intrigued with a European tent show, called Rentz's Circus. The first successful minstrel show which he feminized went under the name of Mme. Rentz's Female Minstrels. In another of his productions, Adamless Eden, not only all the performers, but the ushers, doorkeepers, ticket takers and even the press agents were female.

Eventually, Leavitt conceived the idea of merging the lady minstrel show, vaudeville and musicalized travesty into one production which he called burlesque, and thus was evolved the first Rentz-Santley show, starring Mabel Santley, a typical Amazon of the period. There was a new Rentz-Santley edition every season, and with their continuing success, they provided the model for most of the reputable burlesque shows of the 1880s and 1890s. Many of the Rentz-Santley stars, notably Adah Richmond, "The Fair One With the Blond Wig," later formed their own burlesque companies. And the most enterprising and notorious of the later operators, Sam T. Jack, started his career as a manager of a Rentz-Santley show.

The format of the Rentz-Santley shows, also followed by other succeeding standard producers, was in three parts. First, the burlesque or comedy portion, then a musical melange called the olio, and finally a concluding comedy act with an ensemble finale, known as the afterpiece. However, musical and dance specialties often appeared outside the olio portion which roughly corresponded to vaudeville specialties in a modern burlesque show. Thus, one of the typical Rentz-Santley editions starred the enduring German-dialect comedian George P. Murphy, in "A Moonlight Dip," in the burlesque called *La Tosca's Reception*. Here, according to the playbills, were introduced many "clever and shapely women," and a "Nautch" dancer. According to the *New York Clipper,* this "elaborately rich" production was refreshened by "musical interpolations of the brightest." The concluding afterpiece was "Anthony and Cleopatra," some of the characters of which were Octobus Sweezur, Cheesi Hankipanki, and Hoctasuper. The story of Cleopatra has since been a favorite for burlesque comics, reappearing in 1964 at Ann Corio's *This Was Burlesque,* simultaneously with the movie premiere of Elizabeth Taylor's *Cleopatra.*

There were occasional, halfhearted attempts at satire, which never went too far. The 1895 Rentz-Santley show parodied the then current legitimate hit *Trilby* with its own "Twill Be Club." The characters and program were as follows:

Rosenblum Spingarlic, Harry Spongesoap, Reuben Hayseed,

Mabel Santley, star of the first Rentz-Santley shows. Culver Pictures, Inc.

Mrs. Astorbilt, Miss Nickelhouse, Mr. Taylormade.

Incidental to this scene will be introduced Songs, Dances, the latest Characterizations of the day, and a laughable satirical Burlesque on the latest Dramatic Sensation, Trilby.

Vaudeville—Living Pictures

Overture

Robin Hood, Jr.

3 Scenes Grand Spectacular Burlesque 3 Scenes

Other large established contemporary traveling units included Hyde & Behman's Combination, Reilly & Woods Troupe, Gus Hill's Aggregation, May Howard Burlesque Company, May Davenport Company, Night Owls Company, among many others. Some of these were more vaudeville than burlesque, and all of them featured some variety entertainment. There was no sharp differentiation between burlesque and vaudeville, and going into the 1890s, there were still a few English burlesques, straight variety units and some surviving lady minstrel shows, such as Madame Celeste's Female Minstrel Company, featuring "The Turkish Bathers" and "The Turkish Harem."

Even at this early stage, the more pretentious burlesque productions were acutely self-conscious of the name "burlesque." The Reilly & Woods show, modestly entitled "Glory Crowned Diadems of Both Hemispheres Specialty Company," starred Pat Reilly's wife, Florence, "the handsomest formed woman on the American stage." It proclaimed that its "farce comedy, *Hades and the 400* is not a burlesque and cannot be classed with the so-called Leg Shows, but a strictly musical farce comedy with spectacular effects including the Barometrical Laughtometer (Patent Applied For)." And "Hattie Leslie's Lady Athletics" beseeched their admirers to "bear in mind this is no leg or burlesque show," but rather "a perfect legitimate lady athletic company."

In general, the ingredients of a reputable burlesque show would try to include the following, as heralded by Mabel Snow's Spectacular Burlesque Company in 1891: "New wardrobes, bright, catchy music and pictures, Amazon marches, pretty girls and novelty specialty acts." Naturally, the Little Egypt furore at the Columbian Exposition of 1893 found its echo in many burlesque shows. The Night Owls opened with a "new and novel operatic burletta entitled *Society Crushed,* starring Alex Zanfratta, 'The Grotesque Comic,' La Petite Aimee and her 'Artistic Songs,' Dollie E. Howe 'the cleverest character soubrette,' and introducing "Songs, Dances, Medleys, and the

Supper Scene, concluding with the great Clown Chase."

For the second act, there was:

> A bright and spicy program always concluding with a novel Burlesque up to the times, entitled Liberty's Reception to Uncle Sam with much females.
>
> P.S. During the Burlesque there will be introduced Songs, Dances, etc., also the latest novel craze from the Colombian Exposition, entitled
> THE PLAISANCE DANCERS.

Prices for this tremendous array of pageantry were 15 cents, 25 cents, 35 cents and 50 cents.

From New York to St. Louis, a wide range of traveling troupes, standard burlesque shows and variety units, "turkey" shows and "lady athletic exhibitions" toured the cities and the hinterlands to mounting popular acclaim and approval. Talent and comedy were submerged among a profusion of vigorous and indecorous "Blondes" with hair of every color, who, augmented by "Oriental" cooch dancers, swayed tortuously and pranced heavily on the boards of the London Theatre and the Miner Houses in Manhattan, the Star, Empire and Hyde and Behman's Theatres in Brooklyn, the Trocadero, 14th Street Opera House, Arch, Lyceum and Kensington Theatres in Philadelphia and the Howard Athenaeum, Lyceum, Palace and Grand Theatres in Boston. Theatres in every city, every locality, were besieged by the onrushing new spectacles.

And legitimate burlesque of the old school such as *Blue-Eyed Susan* was left to the sedate Academy of Music where it was presented by the Columbia Dramatic Club!

DIVES AND DIVAS

THE bane of the reputable burlesque shows was the mushrooming of innumerable "turkey" shows and "behind-the-tent" companies. These had a tiny cast of two or three coochers, a comedian or two, little if any scenery, practically no wardrobe, and were devoid of the usual accoutrements of even the cheapest theatrical exhibits, such as a spotlight. Their main investment consisted of lurid posters of salacious invitation. They roved around the rural centers, settled in dubious locations, presented a scene or two, generally based on the phallic insinuations of pickles, bladders or frankfurters, all the time keeping a sharp eye open for any officious stranger, whispered out the cooch dancers at the finale—and they were gone, anxiously counting the profits, to repeat at the next town. Their nearest modern equivalent is the troupe in a skid row theatre, a small groveling cast which gets paid only if the meager receipts exceed the rent. This is known as scratch burlesque.

They gave burlesque its early bad name, just as the small stock shows, decades later, smeared the reputation of the responsible traveling Wheel or Circuit shows. These one-night "turkey" troupes, in turn, had to compete for sensationalism with the orgiastic pleasures of country fairs and carnivals, a great many of which were completely uninhibited. The Christian Endeavour Society dejectedly catalogued the more popular of such fair and carnival attractions as

> A Petrified Woman, a Circus with Oriental Dancing Girls, Oriental Dancers, He, She or It (with nude views for 10¢ extra) "purely for scientific purposes," Lady with the Horse's Mane, Living Pictures, Wild Double Woman, for "Men Only." "Barkers" called, "Hot Stuff—nothing tame like the women and children are permitted to see in the opera houses." And the worst of it is that these "barkers" told the truth.

Other normal ingredients were:

> . . . the nigger babies, the cane rack, the silk handkerchief and pewter-spoon fakers, the educated pig, the museum of anatomy, the living pictures, the petrified lady with the snake lady that ought to be petrified . . .

With a public avid for such displays, and little money needed to present them, small barnstorming burlesque troupes, of all types, sprang out over the East and Midwest.

One of the very first respectable burlesque shows, vying in priority of time with the Rentz-Santley companies, started as a small family affair, headed by "Pop" Siddons, his daughter, Ida, and her comedian husband. Ida had been a rope skipper and fire dancer in lady minstrel shows. She now emerged as a "serpentine" dancer, and added another comic. A few girls in tights were huddled together in tableau settings and "living pictures," and thus in 1883 another "first" burlesque show was born. This eventually became known as the Ida Siddons Burlesque & Novelty Company and played the Miner Theatres in New York City. Ida Siddons died in 1933, at the age of seventy-six. Burlesque was born, buried and resurrected in the span of her lifetime.

But very few of these makeshift troupes attained any status or reputation, even among themselves—with the conspicuous exception of Sam T. Jack, the Billy Minsky of his day.

Sam T. Jack emphasized the basic crudities, the cancan, tights, living pictures, cooch exhibitions, made them even rawer and spicier, yet withal disdained to run away, as did the "turkey" show promoters. He not only stood his ground, but proclaimed burlesque to be "that fairyland of lightness and alacrity, animation and vivacity, where the muses linger in a languor of love."

His Lilly Clay's Colossal Gaiety Company was heralded with the following magniloquence:

A "living picture" in a one-piece union suit. *Culver Pictures, Inc.*

50—Tropical enchantresses in tantalizing and pleasing play—50

> 30 olive-hued nightingales in sweet and soulful songs, artistic poses, lovely costumes, fairy-like forms . . . the greatest stellar attraction since Hipparchus numbered the stars. A show of novelties from a cornucopia full of splendors.
>
> All the glories and beauties of the tropics under the mottled mantle of hilarious burlesque.

Under this mottled mantle he presented at Sam T. Jack's Theatre, at Broadway and 29th Street, New York City, self-styled "Home of Burlesque," such tidbits as *Oriental Sensations, Moulin Rouge,* and *The Model.* The star was Jennie Yeomans, who in earlier days had been billed as "The Little Comedy Sunbeam" in a comedy-drama, *Our Jennie.* Now she was, rather starkly, presented as "Jennie Yeomans in Tights."

New York, however, was at times a bit too effete for his Sam T. Jack's Tenderloin Company, which, on one occasion, had to cancel the performance of the featured dancer, Karina, at the London Theatre, after its first showing at the Monday matinee, because it was too "realistic."

Jack found a more receptive climate in Chicago, where he popularized stock burlesque, in which the cast remained more or less intact at the same theatre, instead of traveling from theatre to theatre in a circuit arrangement. However, each week a different production (except for the cast), with new costumes, comedy, production numbers, etc., was presented. Since a performer's tenure was usually based on the continuing approval by substantially the same audiences from week to week, there was always the tendency to exceed the previous week's off-color sensationalism, so as not to grow "stale" with the audiences.

Sam T. Jack was so successful and so notorious that, more than any other producer, he was denounced regularly from the pulpits as an unscrupulous harbinger of sin. This he may have been. He was also the prime burlesque showman of his day.

Another facet of disreputable burlesque at this period was the preponderance of saloons and beer halls, honky-tonks and so-called Concert and Music Halls, where burlesque performers were hired as entertainers. Although such performances were not really burlesque shows, they were included in the general category of burlesque and undoubtedly did much to lower its reputation to a point where many talented players found it expedient to abandon burlesque for other fields.

Such honky-tonks were owned and operated in many cases by local political bigwigs, and unlike the "turkey" shows were not hampered by police interference. In the Midwest and West, particularly, where standard burlesque shows had as yet not penetrated, famous-to-be comedians plugged away for the delectation of their raucous clientele, while their wives, in full view of their Pagliacci husbands, entertained the sourdoughs in the boxes, on the orders of the management. This was on a par with some of the cheaper burlesque troupes which would send their girls out to solicit customers for their performances by promising richer rewards after the show.

Some of the honky-tonks, particularly in the East, expanded into legitimate theatrical emporiums. The first theatre chain in New York City was an outgrowth of beer gardens where the waiters doubled in brass as comics and plump wenches Ta-ra-ra-boom-de-ayed as they flounced the rear of their raised skirts toward the drinkers. The Miner chain of theatres, established by Henry Clay Miner and Thomas Canary (Miner's Bowery, Eighth Avenue and Bronx) and subsequently managed by Miner's four sons, was developed in this manner.

Of a different stripe was Koster & Bial's Concert Hall on Sixth Avenue and 23rd Street in New York City. Koster & Bial's began as a simple honky-tonk with prostitutes for customers and entertainment to suit. It was raided on at least one occasion when two female performers stripped to the waist, thereby anticipating burlesque by about thirty years. As it grew affluent, it yearned for respectability—an occupational disease of burlesque operators—and switched to a policy of vaudeville, crude novelty acts and some girlie entertainment. Competing with the successful and comparatively genteel Pastor's showplace, which featured straight vaudeville, Koster & Bial's then went all out for the good life, eliciting the following tribute from the *New York Clipper* in 1892: "The order of entertainment at this popular resort is now as clean and as meritorious as the most fastidious vaudeviller could desire." Whereupon Koster & Bial's declined into a benign and fading apathy.

Coney Island abounded in scabrous entertainment of every description, nearly all of it called "burlesque." Just as, in later years, supposedly spicy entertainment was labeled "Paris After Dark," the afterpieces of many burlesque shows were named "Naughty Coney Island." Eventually, such showplaces as Connor's, Kojen's and Wilson's gave way to more substantial theatre restaurants such as Inman's Casino and Henderson's Walk.

In spite of itself, burlesque grew and flourished. It penetrated even up to Canada where the City Sports show at Montreal "jammed the house with a rattling good burlesque show." With the turn of the century, legitimate burlesques and the lady minstrel shows were all but obsolete. The old fear of outlawry that had menaced the first burlesque managers was replaced by a realization of their permanent status as theatrical impresarios. Prizefighters and champion wrestlers joined burlesque shows as added attractions with the cooch dancers. Tights, by this time, were no longer a sensational novelty, but a commercial expense. Silk tights cost all of $2.50 a pair. They were replaced in most shows by cotton tights.

Blondes were supplanted by the vogue of "Oriental" dancers. Little Egypt was followed by Little Africa. The capacious May Howard, one of the first Queens of Burlesque, was succeeded by a more gossamer though still substantial type of beauty, as exemplified in a new favorite, Truly Shattuck, extolled in 1898 as "the handsomest woman possessing the best voice and most perfect figure."

It was quite a confused and horny and tawdry era in which the first burlesque shows took shape, side by side with variety entertainment. But while variety became vaudeville and aligned itself with talent, burlesque became itself and aligned itself with dirt. Burlesque of this period was thus castigated by Fred McCloy, the super press agent for the Columbia Amusement Company, in 1915:

> They called their shows burlesque, but they were not burlesque at all. They were a conglomeration of filthy dialog, libidinous scenes and licentious songs and dances with cheap, tawdry, garish and scant scenery and costumes. The "theatres" in which they played were invariably located in or near the slum spots in the larger cities, and were dirty and unkempt, dismally lighted, and with no attempt at ventilation. They were allowed to exist without police interference along with the bawdy houses that infested the neighborhoods. No woman ever crossed the thresholds of their doors, and male patronage was confined to shameless degenerates and to that other species of degenerate that sneaked in with concealed faces. This describes 90 percent of the burlesque business up to about 1900.

Nevertheless, from such shows were spawned names of which even the Columbia Amusement Company could well be proud. It had to be, for those same names founded and fostered that mighty burlesque dynasty. Sidney Wire admitted as much in 1911:

> From where did the present burlesque industry, for an industry it is, spring, if not from the one-night stand or "turkey" show. And it is not so far back that the bigger percentage of the managers and owners of the present Empire and Columbia systems, were to all intents and purposes, vagabonding through the country in practically the same "wildcat" manner as the "turkey" show manager of today.

NAMES FORGOTTEN AND REMEMBERED

MANY talented performers, mostly comedians, were developed in this welter of foaming theatricalism. Significantly, those whose names have endured and are most widely known to the theatregoing public and the critics are precisely and only those who abandoned burlesque early enough in their careers for other forms of entertainment, usually vaudeville. These performers undoubtedly represented superior talents. But the possibility exists that had they remained in burlesque, they might have become stultified into comparative nonentities. Conversely, it is conceivable that many talents virtually unknown outside burlesque might have achieved the proverbial fame and fortune had they entered more satisfying forms of show business early enough in their development.

Of those who did desert burlesque about 1900 Weber and Fields are the most prominent. Weber and Fields had cavorted in Adah Richmond's Burlesque Company and with Gus Hill's Stars. But their reputation was earned after they left burlesque, never to return to it. There has been some confusion among the naïve that Weber and Fields represented the best of burlesque in that they presented real satire, or as they called their productions in later years, "travesties." Actually, neither they nor their audiences considered these performances "burlesque shows." Weber and Fields themselves are quoted in

Bernard Sobel's *Burleycue* as saying, "Once we were started in travesties, we never went back to burlesque."

The early defection of Weber and Fields was a double blow to burlesque talent because they attracted to their renowned Weber & Fields Music Hall such personalities as Harry Morris, the comedian husband of May Howard, as well as May Howard herself, Sam Bernard, the comedian of the Night Owls and the French Folly Company, Peter F. Dailey of *Evangeline,* Harrigan & Hart, David Warfield, Lillian Russell, William Collier, Louis Mann and Fay Templeton, among others. In return, all burlesque got from the Weber & Fields Music Hall was Frankie Bailey of the shapely legs, in her later years at that, and all it got from vaudeville—from Tony Pastor's Music Hall—was Mother Elm, the wardrobe mistress, forty years later, at Minsky's National Winter Garden. Burlesque was left with its girls and dirty afterpieces. As a final sign of the times, the discriminating James Gibbons Huneker transplanted his personal affections from the burlesque blonde Lydia Thompson to the vaudeville hoyden Maggie Cline, who was then giving out with "Throw Him Down McCloskey" at Pastor's Music Hall.

Among the comedians who did remain in burlesque at this time, the most widely known is probably Billy (Beef Trust) Watson. Born Isaac Levie on New York's lower East Side, he entered show business as a singer at the Chatham Square Museum. His name then was Billy Buttons. He found himself as a comic in burlesque with co-stars Harry C. Bryant and Billy B. Van in *The Bohemians.* Later, he was a member of Ida Siddons' troupe. His fame in the nineties was based on the salty afterpiece popularized by him and his partner, Billy (Grogan) Spencer, "Krausemeyer's Alley." Portraying a newly arrived German immigrant, fenced in by alley cats and garbage cans, Billy Watson would yell blasphemously, belch heartily, grimace ludicrously, belabor Billy Spencer with brickbats and wet towels and, as the pièce de résistance, slobber all over him. Gross and vulgar, but not smutty, "Krausemeyer's Alley" was a standard burlesque act for over forty years. Accustomed to padded, upholstered soubrettes, Billy Watson shrewdly burlesqued their type in the 1900s as a comic gesture, adding his "Beef Trust" exaggerations to those of "Krausemeyer's Alley."

Billy Watson has often been cited, usually by himself, as an example of "clean" burlesque. Ironically, he was often censured and, at one time, expelled from the Columbia Wheel shows, operated by the Columbia Amusement Company, for using offensive language and for pinching the posteriors of his hefty chorines.

Two notable stars and producers, who influenced burlesque con-

Billy "Beef Trust" Watson.
Sy Seidman

"Mr. Burlesque": Al B. Reeves in blackface with his gold-encrusted banjo.
Culver Pictures, Inc.

siderably in later years, were Fred Irwin and Al Reeves, the first more or less the prototype of "clean" burlesque, the other, of burlesque as it was and became. A former circus manager, Fred Irwin was the star, before 1900, of Irwin Brothers' Comedy and Vaudeville Company, advertised as "A Powerful Organization of Clever Specialty Artists. It featured "A Good Bum Juggler—Harrigan" and starred, above all, MR. FRED IRWIN. As a manager and performer on the Columbia Wheel for many years, he, like Billy Watson, also had his differences with the executives of the Columbia Amusement Company, though for different reasons. He never really made the "big time," despite his long duration in show business. Primarily a vaudevillian, he might have fared better outside burlesque.

Al Reeves was a product of Coney Island beer joints, medicine shows and Ida Vernon's Female Minstrels. Not too subtle, and far from clean, he finally found his way to burlesque, his congenial and natural habitat. In fact, he was Mr. Burlesque himself. His Al Reeves' Big Burlesque Company in the 1890s starred himself, "The World's Greatest Banjoist and Comedian." He sported the most splendiferous banjo in activity, encrusted with gold and diamonds, but his ability to play it was never phenomenal. Like Billy Watson, he changed the name of his show, later on, to Al B. Reeves' Beauty Trust. A thorough extrovert, he delighted himself and his audiences by discoursing on the curvy contours of the chorus girls he had personally selected, expatiating to all and sundry on their specific outstanding anatomical attainments. After the applause, he invariably exclaimed, "Give me credit, boys!" A prominent figure in the Columbia Wheel, he was often in disfavor with its censors because he would not countenance their emasculation of lusty scenes, their occasionally sanctimonious fear of the feminine figure, all of which was dear to Al B. Reeves, for which, indeed, he deserves credit. He was finally disenfranchised by the Columbia Amusement Company in 1920 after twenty-nine years of solid trouping, but readily found a haven in the raucous Mutual Circuit.

The Sam Devere Show was another well-known troupe with a similar format. Sam Devere also played the banjo, more or less indifferently, while warbling off-color ditties. His girls were loud and luscious, his entertainment coarse and popular.

Gus Hill, the star of his own "Stars" show, was another notable producer and actor of the Fred Irwin type, whose shows were as much vaudeville, in the early days, as they were burlesque. Unfortunately for himself, he chose to remain in burlesque. Many famous stars subsequently appeared under his tutelage. Practically unknown outside burlesque, despite his many years in show business, he received some publicity in 1929 when he asserted himself as the owner of the original production rights to *The Black Crook,* then being revived in Hoboken fashion by Christopher Morley.

George P. Murphy remained in burlesque all through the days of the Columbia Wheel, and in 1924 went right on into the Mutual Circuit. His "Well, I'm a Son of a Gun" and "Oh, for Goodness Sakes," were standard in the repertoire of every German comic.

Will H. Cohan entered burlesque in 1893. His delivery was that of a good small-time vaudevillian, and whenver there was a campaign against burlesque in later years, he was usually recalled to active duty as an example of clean comedy. He and Charlie Case, a blackface performer billed as "Charlie Case the peculiar and entirely different Comedian," were often cited as exemplars of the best in old-time burlesque comedy. They are practically unknown today.

Pat Reilly and his shapely wife, Florence Miller, continued in burlesque with the same type of show they had popularized before 1900 in the Reilly & Woods Burlesque Company, later presenting "pictured melodies, acrobats, and a well-balanced chorus of pretty girls making a feast of fun and music." Pat Reilly was Simple Simon in one of his widely known comedy sketches, "Simple Simon and Simon Simple." On his death in 1915, he was eulogized as a cartoonist, and a student of the Bible and Shakespeare.

Billy K. Wells, comedian and producer for the Columbia Wheel, and writer not only for burlesque, but for musical comedy and Broadway revues, started with one of the Rentz-Santley shows. Continuing in burlesque well after 1900, he wrote the gags for the shows of James E. Cooper, a top Columbia producer, who had himself begun his career in Coney Island concert halls.

The female principals, whose appeal was based on youth and beauty, were replaced quite quickly and did not, for the most part, become part of the new era of burlesque. Stalwart feminine perennials of early burlesque, like Pauline Batcheller, Fannie Bloodgood, May Davenport and others who had barnstormed with Mme. Rentz's Lady Minstrels, Ida Siddons and Mabel Santley, were succeeded by newer and younger faces who were the burlesque headliners of the future.

Rose Sydell and her husband, W. S. Campbell, started their London Belles show just before 1900. Other burlesque shows which retained their appeal for decades thereafter came into being at this time. There was, for example, The Knickerbocker Burlesquers of Louis Robie and T. W. Dinkins, starring Mae Taylor, the "Sunbeam Soubrette." The White Crook Burlesque Company acclaimed Agnes Behler, "young, pretty and vivacious chansonette." In 1898, Jules Hurtig and Harry Seamon produced their *Bowery Burlesquers,* another hardy long-term show. It presented at the time Vinny Henshaw as Mussy Liz, Queen of the Bowery, and featured Loney Hascall, who impersonated a "Hebe," a "Chink," and a French count.

Veteran producers like Sam T. Jack and T. E. Miaco of the May Howard Company were being supplanted at the turn of the century by the future titans of the industry—Samuel Scribner, J. Herbert Mack, Rice and Barton, among others.

The very first comics of burlesque, who had become famous in the 1880s, such as Dan McAvoy, Matthews and Bulger, and Bert Leslie, were replaced by younger performers who grew up in the honky-tonks, the "turkey" shows, the Coney Island and Bowery music halls—the Vinnie Henshaws and Annie Ashleys, the Al B. Reeveses and Billy Watsons, the Fred Irwins and Gus Hills, who stayed with burlesque all their lives.

There were dozens upon dozens of others who got in on the bottom rung of burlesque, and as actors or producers or both, climbed to the top of the ladder, which was the Columbia Wheel. They progressed together with burlesque, which advanced from a polyglot behind-the-barn afterpiece to a national institution that was to appeal to men from coast to coast for its elemental and primitive and sensual rawness. What had begun with foreign importations, had become solidly native. By 1900, it was in truth the "American" burlesque show; and deplored, boycotted, bowdlerized and exploited, it literally grew into the core of the cities eventually outlasting its rival, vaudeville, to the consternation of its critics and the surprise even of itself.

CIRCUITS RISE

In 1900, burlesque took time out to think. Everybody had been too busy, before, scrambling in on the profits of a booming business, grabbing the right theatre before a rival troupe could get there, organizing, expanding and reorganizing. Burlesque was here to stay; it was no longer a fly-by-night adventure. The lucky ones who had come out on top during the adventurous 1880s and 1890s were concerned in 1900 with consolidating their gains and aligning themselves with their former competitors so as to eliminate the ruthless and often unethical competition bound to result from having more shows than theatres. Having progressed from the "turkey" stage themselves, the currently established operators did not want their gains jeopardized by new gimcrack outfits.

The immediate result was not a betterment of the shows, but an improvement in the mechanical and commercial aspects involving traveling arrangements, allocation of theatres, territories, etc. The elementary correspondence system of theatre booking, then prevalent, was all but eliminated with the formation of the first real cooperative venture in burlesque—the Travelling Variety Managers' Association—combining in one organization the established producers of the shows and the theatre owners.

The "wheel" or "circuit" arrangement was standardized, a procedure for traveling burlesque units that has lasted to the present day.

Each show was given a specified tour of so many weeks from theatre to theatre, and from city to city, following its preceding show regularly and in turn being succeeded by another production in rotation. As expounded by Walter K. Hill, press agent of the Columbia Amusement Company, "Shows follow their leader as the spokes of a wheel revolve around its hub."

This arrangement was of immeasurable benefit to the performers in burlesque, who were now assured of permanent employment for an entire season lasting as much as forty weeks—the one advantage burlesque employment has had over all other forms of show business. The wheel system also decreased considerably the hazards of a burlesque troupe, hitherto totally dependent on the whims and resources of the company manager, from becoming stranded without funds in some remote exile, a commonplace of theatrical life.

Many problems still were unsolved. There was still too much rivalry, not to mention outright skulduggery, between the theatre owners on one side and the show producers on the other. In 1905, the managers and producers started to book their shows independently of the Association. Finally, two circuits or wheels were evolved, each bitterly competitive with the other. An intricate maze of leases, subleases, franchises and options was thereby precipitated, which produced its own complement of vicarious rivalry, jealousies and double-timing. But the hatreds were now focused on specific quarters, and a manager could at least expect some cooperation from his colleagues in the same circuit.

The theatre owners combined under the name of the Western Wheel, or Empire Circuit. The leading figures were a number of boys called "Jim." There were James E. Fennessey (the discoverer of Millie De Leon), James J. Butler, James Curtin and James L. Kernan. These men represented typical moustache-twirling politicos who owned and operated theatres as a profitable addition to other financial interests. They were real estate operators first and showmen second. In the East, the leading theatre owner, George Reif, was included in the Western Wheel. Also, Big Tim Sullivan, Tammany power, took over the operation of the Dewey Theatre, aligned himself with the Miner boys and their theatres, and the entire group joined the Western Wheel, or Empire Circuit.

The Eastern, or Columbia Wheel, under the auspices of the Columbia Amusement Company, comprised the authentic showmen of burlesque. They had whatever talent and originality there was in burlesque, but not nearly enough money. The dominating figure was Samuel Scribner who lent the name of his 1898 show, *Scribner's*

Columbia Burlesquers, to the parent organization of the Wheel. He was president. He was flanked by his crony, J. Herbert Mack, a veteran of the old minstrel shows, and by the sophisticated L. Lawrence Weber, a former secretary to the British Minister to Japan. An imposing array of producers, managers and comedians joined the Columbia Wheel, including most of the independent and established productions. The Eastern Wheel also had its own impressive political connections in the person of Rud K. Hynicka, political lieutenant to Mark Hanna.

In the hectic rivalry between the two circuits, every city in the East was tapped for possible theatres. But neither of them went beyond the Midwest. The West Coast, San Francisco, was exceeding the wildest burlesque imaginings with its Barbary Coast dives. Burlesque there could only be anticlimactic. Furthermore, a few short-lived ventures to the Far West found the lack of suitable railroad connections an insurmountable obstacle for traveling companies.

But in the East, burlesque was now ready to take its place as a standard, accepted form of American show business. As Sime Silverman put it:

> Burlesque, an offshoot from the varieties with a dame ensemble backing the comics, was just about breezing in as a substitute entertainment halfway between the variety shows and the more heavy legitimate melodramas in 1905.

And burlesque was dignified and elevated to a point where it was treated just like any other theatrical amusement. *The Billboard* of January 11, 1908, remarked that the current week was one of the most interesting of the season, consisting of "a new drama, a new burlesque and a new musical comedy."

Burlesque had arrived!

THE EASTERN AND WESTERN WHEELS

THE wheels not only stabilized burlesque, they further routinized it and made it repetitious. Henceforth, the shows and seasons turned out to be replicas of each other. With each succeeding year, the humor got staler, the chorus girls older, the productions shoddier. Fresh comedy, inventive production settings, found more lucrative rewards in vaudeville and musieal comedy. Old soubrettes, commanding fair salaries, could be replaced by younger ones. But chorus girls were very hard to get—a perennial shortage never overcome. Typical was Sime Silverman's observation of a chorus line in a Columbia show in 1908: "Their work shows a lack of discipline . . . one tall good-looking blonde might fall asleep standing up from her bearing." The bane of slovenly chorines was not unnoticed by the managers, but tolerated out of sheer necessity.

The operators made up for these shortcomings by spicing up the shows with double entendre, cooch dancers and audience mixing. The Eastern or Columbia Circuit did so rather shamefacedly. The Western Wheel made no bones about it. It simply continued the financially profitable trend of the 1880s and 1890s. Absolutely indifferent to good manners, the Empire Circuit gave its rowdy patrons what they demanded. And, as *Variety* stated in 1906, ". . . the gang wants it as raw as it will come." The shows in Miner's Bowery were, in Sime

Silverman's words, "frankly profane." The burlesque-olio-afterpiece arrangement was also being discarded. The Western Wheel shows paid little heed to coherent scenes or a logical framework. A cooch dancer squared a lot of non sequiturs.

Faced with this competition, the Columbia managers, well-intentioned men, anxious for kudos as well as riches, nevertheless had no choice but to follow suit, investing the coochers, however, with fastidious misnomers and titles worthy of more ambitious undertakings. In one respect, at least, the owners did make substantial progress—in the field of public relations and self-serving declarations of noble intent, which in the later years of the Columbia Amusement Company reached unprecedented heights.

There were two outstanding shows at this period, M. Mortimer Thiese's *Wine, Women and Song,* and L. Lawrence Weber's Parisian Widows Extravaganza Company.

Wine, Women and Song starred Alex Carr and Sam Howe as "Hebe" characters. "Wine, Women and Song," the program announced, "are the Joys of Life." The preface continued:

> The performance will commence with an exaggerated musical comedy in one act introducing a bevy of Comely Girls and Clever Comedians in a Potpourri of Humor, Song and Fun.

The opening burlesque and its cast were:

> What Married Men Do
> Mr. Hans Hofbrau, caught with the goods—Sam Howe
> Leonora Footlight, an actress and homebreaker—Bonita

There was a substantial olio and an afterpiece entitled "Fun in the Subway." This was, in effect, a minor musical comedy, and the producer took the precaution never to repeat in burlesque. *Wine, Women and Song* was his one and only burlesque production.

The Parisian Widows Show lasted longer. It starred Ben Welch, who epitomized the "Hebe" pattern of slouched shoulders, screwed-up face, gesticulating mannerisms and singsong accent. The characters in this show consisted of the following:

> Barney McCann, alias Isie Smooth; Tony Sparrario, alias Isie Rough (played by Ben Welch); Barking Dog, King of the Grafters; and Sure Lock Holmes, a real detective

There was also an olio, an afterpiece entitled, "A Day at West Point," and chorus girls with names like "Miss German," "Miss Irish," "Private Cannon," "Private Pistol," etc.

The 1904 Parisian Widows Company was entitled *Roses and Onions,* anticipating a more recent musical comedy with the name *Corned Beef and Roses.* It starred at that time Bert Leslie and Marie Richmond.

"Hebe" comics predominated on both circuits. Joseph K. Watson (The Little Hebrew Gentleman) was co-starred with Harry Keeler in the highly regarded *Bon Ton Burlesquers,* produced by Weber & Rush. Abe Reynolds was a hit as a Jewish sultan in "Pete" Clark's *Runaway Girls.* Billy Watson was now Julius Levy, a wandering peddler, in "A Japanese Honeymoon," or "Levy Lost," the feature of Charles H. Waldron's *Trocadero Burlesquers.* His co-star was Agnes Behler, as "Henrietta, a French chansonette." One had to agree with the title of a skit in the *Bowery Burlesquers* that there were "Too Much Isaacs."

One of the few pretentious Empire shows, produced in collaboration with the Miner Boys, was Dave Marion's *Dreamland Burlesquers* of 1908. It presented a new type of comic in Dave Marion's characterization of "Snuffy, a harelipped cabman." "In no point does it show its unconventionality more than in the entire absence of dialect comedians," wrote a reviewer. The show had twenty chorines, about half a dozen more than the usual burlesque production. To add to the novelty, the framework of the show consisted of separate and distinct sketches, hereafter known as "bits," rather than the customary interrelated scenes of an act. The olio was discarded. Another heralded feature was a chorus of seven men in evening dress, who sang as a choral unit. This nonsensical innovation was copied almost thirty years later by the Irving Place Theatre on 14th Street in New York City, which used a similar chorus of ugly men in faded tuxedos, singing innocuous melodies as a respectable prelude to an impudent procession of bare-bosomed, bare-buttocked chorines. Unlike the Irving Place show, however, the finale of *The Dreamland Burlesquers* was a dog circus.

The *Baltimore Beauties* in 1905 elicited the following praise:

> From opening chorus to finale there is not a line at which anyone could possibly take offense, the offering being a demonstration of the sometimes disputed idea that burlesque audiences cannot be made to laugh except by talk verging on the suggestive.

But Leon Errol was the star of this show, and where could the Wheel find seventy-five Leon Errols?

The false promise of these better productions deceived some ob-

Dave Marion as Snuffy the Cabman, one of the few nonracial comics.
New York Public Library

servers into the barren belief that burlesque might amount to something after all. But even these shows, tops in the field, could not maintain their popularity for more than one or two seasons without the intrusion of the familiar risqué clichés of the less talented exhibits.

Alas, already too obvious was the inherent incapacity of burlesque to rise above itself. If a good, clean show remained on the Wheel, it inevitably was dulled by repetition. New witty dialogue, new costumes and fresh comics every year were too expensive for burlesque. *The Billboard* lamented as early as 1907 the ever present weakness of the entertainment:

> The greatest trouble that the managers have to contend with is the fact that as soon as they develop a good performer, the higher priced managers offer their people all kinds of money to go "on Broadway."

Similarly, Casper Nathan, theatrical observer and writer, observed in 1912: "How many changes in form and policy could burlesque afford to make under pressure and still remain 100 percent burlesque?"

Fred Irwin, for example, was generally considered one of the most inventive producers in burlesque. His *Majestics* show was hailed by *Variety* in 1909 as "tops" in the entire Eastern Wheel. But in 1910, *The Big Show* by the same producer could not make the grade. Though pretentious and expensive for burlesque, its musical numbers were

> . . . all good, well staged and elaborately and cleanly costumed, but despite the large company there is no exhibition of merit or ability, except perhaps in the pantomime. . . . The book is probably responsible for the poor showing of the comedians.

This precise criticism could be leveled at the heart of over 90 percent of the shows in this period, and certainly in succeeding years.

The disillusionment was practically unanimous as well as prophetic. So prosaic and practical a theatre owner as Thomas W. Miner, the most active of Henry Clay Miner's sons, complained: "The same old stuff; when will burlesque managers get wise and give us something new?"

Sidney Wire exclaimed in 1912:

> What a relief it is to hear a successful number that is not a worn out and whistled to death nuisance, that you have not heard at every burlesque show you have sat through this season!

Sime Silverman, caught between clean dull shows that were elaborate and nothing else, and the usual "dirt" shows, which he despised even more, did not know which way to turn.

> What is needed [he angrily wrote in 1905], is a comedian or comedians and a stage manager with some idea of humor which hasn't been stored up in his thinking since he visited his first burlesque show or saw an afterpiece.

Yet, aware of the fundamental weakness of the Columbia shows when they tried to be better than burlesque, he accurately pinpointed their failure:

> The productions are neither "musical comedy" nor "burlesque." They are just between, as far removed from one as the other, with the result of an unsatisfactory show . . . the attractions . . . are overproduced. Nearly all of the pretentious shows are just "production."

In the long run, for better or worse, burlesque could only be itself. Dan Dody, prominent ensemble and stage director for Columbia, came down to essentials, repeating in 1910 what has been said every season before and after him: "Girls are the answer to the burlesque show of today."

The girls varied. The Red Raven Cadets advertised acrobatic chorines: ". . . twelve handsome young women, headed by Madame Hilda Carle . . . nearly raising the roof with volleys of rifle fire, and conclude by scaling a high wall in true army style." But more usual were the time-honored hootchie-kootchie dancers, now known as "Salome" dancers and employed to bolster the cleanest productions. Millie De Leon was an added attraction with Fred Irwin's *Majestics* and his *Big Show*. Her services were deemed necessary for other top Columbia shows, too. She appeared in L. Lawrence Weber's *Parisian Widows,* Hurtig & Seamon's *Bowery Burlesquers,* Al Reeves' *Beauty Trust* and "Pete" Clark's *Runaway Girls.* The Western Wheel's most elaborate and most talented showpiece, Barney Gerard's *Follies of the Day,* succeeding Dave Marion's *Dreamlanders,* was graced by her presence in 1911 as "Lola" in the "Danse du Vengeance." Dave Marion took the precaution of adding a bare-legged "Salome" dancer to his show, Louise Rice, described as "an extremely nice-looking young person." Louis Robie's *Knickerbocker Burlesquers* on the Columbia Wheel featured a luridly exploited "Cleo, the Girl in Red." Even from the sedate new Star and Garter Theatre in Chicago, pioneer in the solicitation of women patronage, came the strange news that in the *Marathon Girls* "Petite Babette presented her sensational hula-hula dance, and it is one of the most startling exhibitions yet interpreted on the burlesque stage."

When Catherine Devine, who claimed to be the "Only and original Little Egypt," died in 1908, her successors swarmed all over burlesque. Then, the "Salome" dancers gave way to a new vogue, "Venus" dancers—Zallah the Dancing Venus, Jessie Keller the Venus on Wheels, Carmelita D'Eclidere the Animated Venus, etc. There was even a headlined lady wrestler, Cora Linn of the Yankee Doodle Girls.

Though there was no nudity, there was considerable audience mixing. The chorus girls regularly paraded up and down the aisles in tights. In the Jolly Follies show a Miss Maurice Wood sang "Tickle My Fancy" and grabbed a handy male from an aisle seat to dance the Turkey Trot with her, a procedure damned by Sime Silverman as "nasty." In the comparatively refined Bon Tons show, Frances Clare, a leading Columbia soubrette, sang "I'll Do Anything in the World for You." A customer took her at her word, and insisted on at least a kiss. This plaintive plea to a supposedly wicked vamp, who happened to be the wife of the show's comedian, Guy Rawson, led to a riot, and "A frightened Miss Clare had to be escorted to her room by police." One theatre was sued for sixty dollars when a customer, instead of relishing the contact of his coat sleeve with the cheek of a chorus girl, complained that his suit had been ruined thereby.

Charmian, billed as "the only headliner that has never failed to make good," did a Millie De Leon, exhibiting her curves, while distributing garters and photographs to an "excited" audience. And in the Parisian Widows show of no less a personage than L. Lawrence, Weber, Millie De Leon was succeeded by Julia Sinclair, who "not only gives a view of bared limbs and finally pulls a mild cooch," but also "does an audience number in which she takes liberties with willing subjects." Shortly thereafter, in June 1911, L. Lawrence Weber left the Columbia Wheel and burlesque permanently and finally. Gus Hill and John G. Jermon were added to the executive board in his place.

So, as far as talent and creativity went, burlesque even under the aegis of the Columbia Amusement Company failed to make any headway at all. "One doesn't expect much in the line of burlesque after the season just passing," Sime Silverman wrote rather dejectedly in 1908. "Burlesque this season," he repeated wearily in 1912, "has not advanced."

That just about summed it up.

OVERTURE TO REFINEMENT

In the early 1900s, there was a series of censorship waves and accompanying raids, in and out of burlesque, which the experienced Wheel managers took adroitly in stride. In 1905, Olga Nethersole, as Sappho on the legitimate stage, permitted herself to be kissed on the mouth and dragged bodily and pantingly to a theatrical bedroom, in an episode not unlike the afterpiece of many a burlesque show—or so it seemed to the police, at any rate, who arrested the cast.

Burlesque responded by instituting censorship committees of its own, which were supposed to investigate delinquent shows that failed to measure up to Wheel standards. These committees were usually dormant, but revived with noisy alacrity whenever there was a "vice" raid or one of the periodic newspaper scandals.

The most serious scandal occurred in 1907. Eva Tanguay, running wild, was the primary cause. She never was a burlesque performer, though as a burlesque "natural," she indicated her affinity to it by occasionally appearing as a "guest artist." However, her imitators in burlesque were legion. Millie De Leon, for one, accompanied her own uninhibited convolutions with an "I Don't Chair" parody. There were endless newspaper critiques on the "art" of "Salome" dancing, and the public hullabaloo excited the reformers and stirred the police to action. With their customary ineptness, they raided, of all places, the

Metropolitan Opera House, in February 1907, alleging that the "Salome" dance in the opera then being performed was "indecent."

The Metropolitan Opera House survived, but the raid and the publicity precipitated a further influx of "Salome" dancers in burlesque and vaudeville, the introduction of a bill in the Wisconsin State Legislature to prohibit the wearing of tights, and sociological treatises such as "The Morals of Tights from the Wearers' Standpoint," which arrived at the dismal conclusion that "They do it because they have to." This, in turn, was bitterly refuted, particularly by Mlle. Florine, a happy tights wearer at the Star Theatre in Brooklyn, who came right out with her own conclusion at first hand: "It has often been said the women who do not like to wear tights on the stage are those who have not been blessed with the charms which would make them delight to display them."

Nevertheless, the furore on decency so afflicted a patron in a Toronto burlesque house that he seized a chorine parading down the aisle in tights and proceeded to give her a spanking. This moral vigilante was fined thirty dollars. And, a few years later, a chorus girl, Henrietta Lee, secured a court judgment against Hurtig & Seamon on the ground that she had been discharged unjustifiably for refusing to strip down to tights.

In 1908, the chief executives of the Eastern Wheel, Samuel Scribner, L. Lawrence Weber and Gus Hill, foreshadowing the later excessive caution of the Columbia Wheel, banned a mainstay of burlesque since the nineties, namely wrestling and prizefighting bouts. These, they claimed, provoked the galleries into unruly behavior. This was appeasement at its most abject, but it failed to satisfy the reformers. Another "Girl in Red" had been arrested in Chicago, and all the newspapers were dwelling deliciously on the return of the "old days of lawlessness," referring, perhaps, to Sam T. Jack. The tempest was still raging when Chooceeta, who cooched according to the instructions of her husband and manager, Fred M. Barnes, was arrested for indecent wiggling. When Chooceeta had been similarly apprehended a few years earlier, she had escaped with a judicial determination that her dance was "cute, graceful and artistic." In the current scandal, however, she was found guilty and fined ten dollars, and there were more indignant outcries by the righteous.

The public relations machinery of the Wheels immediately went into action. Columbia issued an edict and a warning. There was a difference between spice and smut, it averred, and a manager who forgot the difference would not be tolerated on the circuit. In Chicago, the Star and Garter Theatre advertised that it now featured "Censored

Burlesque" and "Clean Entertainment for Self-Respecting People." In Toledo, pledges were secured by the local churches against the shows of the Empire Circuit, prompting one of its officers, James H. Curtin, a Texan sheriff, to deliver himself of an article, "The Typhoid of Morality," which stressed the need for charity in the hearts of men, but otherwise offered no concrete suggestions. As for Chooceeta, it was gravely announced that she "has abandoned her wiggle" and had taken to a "Spanish" terpsichorean gyration.

Some burlesque shows tried to crawl out from under, disdaining the "burlesque" label. "Pete" Clark's *Runaway Girls* now called itself "a first class comic opera." The Trans-Atlantics, starring Ida Emerson, publicized that it was "better than burlesque." In the current reform wave, however, even vaudeville was condemned. It had been giving burlesque competition not only with Eva Tanguay, but with such headliners as La Deadima and "Animated Visions of Art." The *American Magazine* called vaudeville "decadent." But it reformed quickly enough, relegating Jack Johnson, the pugilist, to burlesque, alleging he was not dignified enough for vaudeville. Whereupon, the Columbia Wheel, not to be outdone, banned the use of "hell" and "damn" in its shows. The Western Wheel, dragging its feet in this great crusade, finally came to life with a pronouncement by James H. Curtin, the most literate of its operators:

> The featuring of wrestlers and pugilists has been eliminated and at none of the theatres on the Empire Circuit can be found the so-called Oriental or cooch dancer . . . the days of suggestive books and songs are fast declining . . . the cheap slap-stick comedian with his careless and dirty make-up is an objection of the past.

Simultaneously announced, unfortunately for this beatific report, was the addition of extra-special coochers in the Standard Theatre in St. Louis by James J. Butler, who was none other than the President of the Empire Circuit. This precipitated a tempest between the old-line producers on the Western Wheel and the New York contingent, headed by the Miners, Barney Gerard, and a new aggressive youngster, I. H. Herk. However, the reform waves receded as quickly as they had come, the operators were reconciled quickly enough, the public's attention shifted to weightier matters, and burlesque continued as before.

Financially, the industry prospered. In 1906, a Wheel season consisted of forty weeks, including thirty-three theatres and seven return engagements. There were two thousand performers and another two thousand "house people" connected with the operation of the theatres and shows. In 1908, the Columbia Amusement Company, originally capitalized at $200,000, now boasted assets worth $600,000. Prices were as low as fifteen cents in the gallery and as high as one dollar in the boxes. Yet, the newer burlesque houses could boast weekly grosses of $6,000. By 1912, there were about seventy shows, a hundred burlesque theatres and total personnel in burlesque of five thousand. The cost of a burlesque production in a season could range from $5,000 to $10,000, for a cast of thirty-five to forty people.

Columbia paid dividends of 27 percent on its stock in 1911, the Empire Circuit 24 percent. "Next to Standard Oil interests, give me a slice of burlesque and never mind which wheel," exulted Sidney Wire. And Wire, true to his word, remained part and parcel of burlesque activity until his death in 1922. A former advance agent for Buffalo Bill and Barnum & Bailey shows, he switched to burlesque as publicity man for numerous troupes and continued as such, while writing for *The Billboard*.

When the Wheels were in full turn, the value of a franchise on either circuit was valued in the neighborhood of $100,000. L. Lawrence Weber and Fred Irwin, following their exits from the Columbia Wheel as a result of serious disagreements with the Wheel moguls, sued for damages of $100,000 each.

The theatres multiplied with the advancing prosperity of burlesque. In 1908, the first class theatre ever built solely for burlesque productions was opened in Chicago—the Star and Garter, dedicated to the shows of Columbia. In 1911, the Columbia Theatre in Chicago was unveiled. In the same year the New Empire made its debut on Quincy Street, Brooklyn, with pomp and politicians at its pretentious premiere. This was followed by the Casino Theatre in the same borough, giving the "City of Homes and Churches" also five burlesque houses, including the Star, the Gayety, and Hyde & Behman's Olympic. In Manhattan, Hurtig & Seamon's Music Hall on 125th Street transferred from vaudeville to burlesque. Tony Pastor's Theatre, on 14th Street, the shrine of vaudeville, also became a burlesque house, known as the Olympic. On the other hand, the Dewey and Gotham Theatres were wrested from burlesque by a young, inexperienced newcomer who virtually wheedled away these desirable houses from their supposedly worldly owners. Law suits could not thwart him, and this brash beginner victoriously installed movies in the two theatres. His name—William Fox.

The Miner boys, operating the Bowery, Eighth Avenue and Bronx houses for burlesque, let their Eighth Avenue theatre desert burlesque for the movies. In replacement, they opened up a brand new theatre for Empire shows in Newark—the Empire. The Miner Theatres introduced Amateur Nite during this period, and the notorious "Get the Hook" shenanigans at Miner's Bowery served one useful purpose for the harried performers of the regular burlesque show. It enabled the "gang" to vent its raucous energies on the amateurs, rather than on the professional actors. Another contribution to burlesque made by the Miner Theatres, and more lasting, was the gradual elimination of the distinct olio portion, resulting, eventually, in its complete disappearance.

Inevitably, the Columbia Amusement Company decided to open its own special theatre in New York City, the headquarters of the Wheel, to outdazzle the Star and Garter in Chicago and the Empire in Brooklyn. In January 1910, the Columbia Theatre on 47th Street and Broadway, erected at an estimated cost of $300,000, was formally opened. The same year, with Scribner, Weber, Hynicka and J. Herbert Mack as top officiating executives, the Eastern Wheel designation was dropped permanently—it was now the Columbia Wheel for all time.

The opening ceremonies of the New York Columbia Theatre were carried out with consummate showmanship. Again, prominent public figures graced its august premiere. The ushers were not the tough bouncers customary in other houses, but Japanese college students. Charitable eulogies were spread all over the place. Even the Empire Circuit was included: "Success augurs much for the future of clean meritorious burlesque which has been the keynote of this season's productions on both the Eastern and Western Wheels."

The house had a capacity of 1,500, and prices ranged upward to a one dollar top. Actual management of the new showplace was entrusted to J. Herbert Mack, who immediately issued an edict that henceforth all hosiery worn by the chorines in his theatre must be of silk. Unfortunately, for all this fanfare and the congratulatory predictions of success for "clean" burlesque, the Columbia Theatre was a flop until, according to Weber's statement quoted by Bernard Sobel, A. H. Woodhull's show, The Highrollers, "one of the dirtiest, smuttiest, toughest shows we had," played there.

This prosperity seeped down to the performers, not in higher wages—chorus girls earned less than sixteen dollars weekly—but in steady employment, which, to a great many, compensated for all other disadvantages. When Frankie Bailey, "The Girl with the $1,000,000 Legs," who had played one season in burlesque (The Boston Belles in 1906), reentered the field at the end of her career in 1912, singing

05974

her featured specialty, "I'll Do as Much for You," she admitted frankly enough:

> I am glad that my reception in burlesque has been so warm, and I feel that I shall be more at home here than in any other branch of theatricals. I know that the work is hard, but it will be a greater pleasure to work when you feel that your work is appreciated and that your engagement is secure. After all, I believe that the burlesque game is the only sure end of modern theatricals, and forty weeks work at a sure salary is far better than spending half of your life rehearsing shows that half the time are no sooner on than they are off.

In the same vein, the following poem by soubrette Louise Dacre accurately summed up the practical burlesquer's attitude:

Me for Burlesque

Give me burlesque with its perhaps dubious frame
Where a man's called a "guy" and a woman's a "dame"
Where "props" is a "stool pigeon" and the girls are in debt
Where, maybe, the soubret is the manager's pet,
Though the straight is a souse and the leader's a crank
At the end of the season I have coin in the bank.

To make sure she had the coin, Louise Dacre drew repeated encores in her act. Her specialty was a comparatively spicy feature in which she cast the reflections of a mirror on some blushing male and sang intimately to him—a standard number in future burlesque. At this time, however, it drew a reprimand from *Variety*: "Of course, Miss Dacre was recalled time and again, but everyone knows that it requires no special talent to gain a recall with the stuff she is using."

Soubrettes, as distinguished from the cooch dancers, could attain some prominence and respectability on the Eastern Wheel. Coyly competitive, Rose Sydell, wife of one star comedian, W. S. Campbell, and Jeanette Dupree, wife of another, Billy Beef Trust Watson, vied for superlative honors in the early regime of the Wheel. When Jeanette Dupree divorced Billy Watson and turned to vaudeville, her place was taken by Mollie Williams, who, emerging from the chorus ranks, first attracted attention in 1910 by dangling from a stage airship in a showy production number in Jack Singer's Great Behman Show. She then held her rank as a principal with surefire imitations of Anna Held.

In those days, the leading soubrettes, such as Rose Sydell, Mollie Williams and Ida Emerson, were noted, not for their skill in undress-

Rose Sydell, star clothes horse of the Columbia Wheel.
Culver Pictures, Inc.

ing, but, on the contrary, for their competence as clotheshorses. Lacking the authentic talent of vaudeville and Broadway stars, the soubrettes were faced with the usual Columbia dilemma of being entertaining without becoming too risqué. Hence, they often resorted to the spectacular and bizarre. Rose Sydell, for example, a Kentucky girl, who claimed to have studied for her art at the Royal Academy of Music in London, scrupulously avoided any off-color reputation. In preference to tights, she wore expensive long dresses which were embellished by ostrich plumes, jewels and a diamond butterfly attached to her breast.

In contrast to these soubrettes' durability in burlesque, such talents as Sophie Tucker and Fanny Brice, who made their debuts in burlesque about 1909 and 1910, left burlesque almost as soon as they entered it. Though the stay of each in this field was extremely short, the fact that they were there at all seems to be the one item most recalled about their pasts. Sophie Tucker was in Hill & Manchester's *Gay Masquerader* show for one season, and then went into vaudeville. Fanny Brice was somewhat more prominent in burlesque. In April 1910, singing "Sadie Salome" and "Wild Cherry Rag" in the College Girls show, she attracted immediate attention. "What a truly clever girl!" raved Sidney Wire. She was only eighteen, and already one of the bigger hits in burlesque, he added. She snared the interest of other and more influential connoisseurs at the same time, and two months later she was in the *Ziegfeld Follies*. Lasting a little longer was her brother, Lew Brice, who specialized in an imitation of Bert Williams.

Also mugging her way to fame during these years was a youngster, Mae West, who, as irony would have it, never appeared in burlesque. In 1912, *Variety,* reviewing her performance at the Hammerstein Theatre, advised that "Miss West should be coached to derive the full value from her personality," an admonition which, it may be assumed, Miss West took seriously to her bosom.

The female representatives of burlesque in the Actors Fund Fair during this period were Mollie Williams, Louise Dacre, Frances Clare and Frankie Heath. Frankie Heath, one of the first and most proficient "talking women" in burlesque, was a comedienne adept in double entendre. She was finally graduated into vaudeville and Earl Carroll reviews in which she advised girls in song, "Don't Say Yes, Don't Say No, Just Say Maybe."

Tastes in girls varied from the type of Vera Hearte, who "stands well up in the air and takes a great deal of room sideways," to Maryland Tyson, over whom *The Billboard* rhapsodized: "The prettiest, daintiest and most unusual little girl on the burlesque stage."

The most prominent male talent developed at this time was probably Leon Errol. After his stint as producer and comic for the *Jersey Lillies* show, he, too, left burlesque in 1912 for the *Ziegfeld Follies.* However, he remained active in burlesque as a producer and owner of lucrative franchises on the Columbia Wheel.

Burlesque then was the training ground for talent. Scores of performers were in burlesque for a season or two and then left it for brighter fields. Some entertainers who tarried longer, enriching burlesque for a while, included, among others, Roger Imhoff, Sim Williams and Margie Hilton of the *Dainty Dutchess* show; Ruby Leoni as "Dolly Dimples from the Tenderloin," co-featured with Lilly Vedder in *The Crackerjacks;* Solly Ward as Herman Housebuilder and Brad Sutton as Ignatius Mahoney in "A Mix-up at Reno" from James E. Cooper's *Roseland Girls*; and Jean Bedini.

Jean Bedini's original juggling act, known as Bedini & Arthur, included Eddie Cantor for a short time, and Bedini, a product of the London music halls, was an associate and part discoverer of other show business greats. One of Columbia's most successful operators and franchise holders, he persisted, rather pathetically, as a burlesque straight man long after the end of the Wheel.

Most of the superior talent was on the Eastern or Columbia Circuit. The Empire Wheel, devoid of the need for inner uplift, and not given to soul-searching, was also thriving, but the younger and more enterprising managers and producers, with the exception of Barney Gerard and Isidor H. Herk, had attached themselves to Columbia. The real estate operators, politicians and saloonkeepers who had dominated the Western Wheel were dying off, or getting tired of it all. The young men of Columbia were too much for them. As it was, the Empire Circuit had flourished beyond reasonable expectations, after the coup engineered against it in 1905. Its rawness was a perpetual reminder that burlesque was still burlesque, a leering rebuttal to Columbia's vaunted posture of decency. And as long as Empire shows were successfully competitive, Columbia managers had to dirty their shows if they were to survive.

The inevitable happened in March 1913, with Herk and Gerard acting as the liaison agents between circuits. The Western Wheel or the Empire Circuit capitulated, and was taken over and absorbed by the Columbia Amusement Company. The Empire Association was not dissolved. It continued to exist as a corporate and solvent organization. But its members either joined Columbia or left burlesque and retired to nurse their accumulated fortunes. The Columbia Wheel, with

Leon Errol. *New York Public Library*

forty-four of the most prosperous shows on both Wheels, now exercised a virtual monopoly over the entire field of burlesque.

The end of the Western Wheel turned a page in American theatrical history that few have cared to remember, and fewer to regret. There had been a time when a *Variety* reporter who had inveighed against the rawness of the Empire shows was singled out from the audience by a cooch dancer in the middle of her performance. After demonstrating her art before the reporter with wild and defiant abandon, she topped off her writhings with a particularly portentous bump, exclaiming, "And stick that in *Variety* and see how they like it!"

That was the Empire Circuit.

Burlesque was all Columbia now. Those days would never be seen again.

So it was prophesied—erroneously.

THE TITAN—
SAMUEL A. SCRIBNER

THE Columbia Amusement Company ruled burlesque, and the company, in turn, was governed autocratically, even imperiously, by the most determined personality in burlesque—Samuel A. Scribner.

His beginnings were as humble as most of the operators on the old Eastern Wheel. He came to burlesque from medicine shows, a circus sideshow, and minstrel entertainment. His biggest production as an early independent producer was his *Morning Glories* show, hardly to be distinguished from other exhibits of its ilk—with Lady Godiva scenes and acts like "Oh, You Woman," calculated to appeal, as Fred McCloy would have put it, to "baser interests."

As the head of Columbia, he was determined tc make burlesque both clean and profitable. That he was able to do so for a time is a tribute to his power and energy and force of will. But as his long and turbulent years are reviewed in retrospect, it must all be considered an unfortunate experience both for burlesque and for Scribner.

Financially, he profited. With some of the profits, he returned to his home town, Brookville, Pennsylvania, and with other Wheel associates bought the coal mine there. When Columbia burlesque was no more, driven out by the shimmying wenches of the Mutual Wheel and the strippers of stock burlesque, Scribner was far from impoverished. According to Fred McCloy, in 1935, ". . . when he was not on the golf links, he was motoring around the country and generally living the leisurely life of a retired gentleman."

Though not widely known by the general public, he was lavishly honored in show business, as Treasurer of the Actors Fund, President of the Theatre Benefit Authority and of the Vaudeville Managers Protective Association. Even after his supposed retirement, it was Scribner on whom the operators called whenever they had license trouble. And Scribner, "whose political connections are perfect" (*The Billboard,* October 22, 1932), always commanded the respect of every city official and usually got what he wanted.

In his efforts to present burlesque shows as he and he alone wanted them to be, he brooked no interference. In his struggles for power with other dominant figures, L. Lawrence Weber, Gus Hill, I. H. Herk, it was always Scribner who remained and the others who withdrew. "He only knows how to give orders and has never taken any," commented *Variety* in 1928. At that time, his personal dictatorial approach in the face of impending financial disaster for the Wheel precipitated a wholesale exodus from Columbia of many of its most prominent producers, thereby sounding its death knell.

Yet, the sum total of all his fierce energy and tyrannical powers ultimately dwindled into nothingness, as clean burlesque collapsed with disheartening finality. Before the end came,. he was forced to retreat, step by step, in an agony of personal frustration. And as he did so, it became evident that despite his unquestioned sincerity, underneath the sanctimonious exterior there still lurked the cunning self-interest of the carnival grifter.

When it was obvious in 1925 that his emasculated productions could not survive the competition of the Mutual Wheel's bouncing bumpers, he renounced the efforts of a lifetime. "There is nothing musical comedy about our shows," he cried with defeatist despair. In December of the same year, the hitherto chaste Columbia Theatre in Cleveland advertised "That Extra Special Feature, Francee, the Dancer All Paris Went Wild About," causing *The Billboard* to remark: "Sagacious Sam has evidently relegated his would-be intellectual advisers to the background and is now out in the open with an indorsement of old-time burlesque including classic dancers." In 1932, he allied himself with the Minskys and Wilners, whose specialties were the cooch and the strip.

Behind the piety of the Columbia Amusement Company, there hovered always a secondary, if obscure, circuit to take the cash of the customers who preferred rowdier entertainment. Outwardly, there was no connection, but pulling the strings of the puppet wheel was "Sagacious Sam." When the Columbia Wheel found itself involved too deeply in censorship troubles, as had to happen occasionally, he at once disclaimed any responsibility for its shows, though he was the czar of the industry. "The Columbia Amusement Company," he whimpered in 1915, "is simply a booking agent for the different burlesque managers who hold franchises."

As for burlesque itself, what might conceivably have become a lusty and vigorous entertainment lost forever the sparkle and authenticity that were at least possibilities in the old racy shows, before Columbia invested them with synthetic refinement and acute self-consciousness. When the Columbia Wheel collapsed, and with it the false gaudy shell of "refined" burlesque, the reaction produced a precipitate, awkward backsliding into dirt, from which burlesque never recovered.

At Scribner's death, July 9, 1941, his funeral was attended not by the rank and file of the industry, but by such distinguished outsiders as Ex-Governor Alfred E. Smith, Ex-Acting Mayor Joseph V. McKee, George M. Cohan and similar eminent figures. No, the strippers and coochers, the comics and chorines were not there. But Paul Moss, the License Commissioner who outlawed burlesque, was.

It took just such a man as Samuel A. Scribner to make burlesque clean. His ultimate failure was prophetic. If Sam Scribner couldn't clean burlesque, nobody could.

WHEELS WITHIN WHEELS

COLUMBIA Wheel shows were a shrewdly concocted amalgam of 25 percent talent, 25 percent sex and 50 percent exploitation. They were able to fool most of the people most of the time for about three or four years. Then World War I and its aftermath gave Columbia a few more years of financial prosperity. Finally, it folded in 1927.

All in all, Columbia had seven fat years followed by seven lean years.

Sam Scribner and the Columbia Amusement Company were dedicated to the proposition that burlesque shows could be clean as well as profitable. But in the face of the talent and opulence that musical comedy and vaudeville offered, clean burlesque could attract audiences only on the appeal of lower prices. Such patronage could never be large enough to sustain the industry.

That the Columbia Wheel was nevertheless able to parlay a forlorn hope into at least seven years of unprecedented prosperity was mainly due to the remarkable talents of three men: Samuel Scribner, the boss with the drive and connections, I. H. Herk, who did the dirty work, and Fred McCloy, public relations expert extraordinary.

In 1913, upon the consolidation of the Eastern and Western Wheels, and the supremacy of the Columbia Amusement Company, the property values of the Wheel represented an investment of $15,000,000. In New York City alone there were nine theatres devoted to Columbia burlesque. By 1914, there were eighty-one theatres and seventy-three shows, and an estimated 700,000 Columbia fans from New York to Omaha. Columbia burlesque was big business, and it was run like big business.

Fred McCloy, Columbia's diligent press agent, formerly with Barnum & Bailey, Klaw & Erlanger, editor of the *New York Morning Journal,* and part owner and publisher of the *New York Dramatic News,* gloated with his usual superlatives: "The Columbia system moves like clockwork. . . . Today there is not a more perfect business organization in the world."

Its directors at this time were Samuel Scribner, Jules Hurtig, John G. Jermon, Gus Hill, Charles Barton, J. Herbert Mack, Rud K. Hynicka and Charles H. Waldron. Two immediate objectives were envisioned by the "establishment": (1) To improve the image of Columbia as clean burlesque. (2) The formation of a subsidiary circuit to absorb the cheaper shows, which would also cater to audicences clamoring for rougher entertainment. The second objective was found necessary because of the success of a new competitive circuit called the Progressive Wheel, which had come into being when the Western Wheel went out of existence. The Progressive Circuit lasted one year with shows like Panama Pansies and headliners ranging from Millie De Leon to Bob Fitzimmons. The No. 2 Circuit, an admitted Columbia subsidiary, was founded, and that put the Progessive Wheel out of business. The No. 2 Circuit lasted another year, and then the correct formula was established with the American Burlesque Association which lasted from 1915 to 1922.

Herk was appointed a director of the American Wheel and, as its directing genius, guided it tortuously between the pietism of Columbia and the rawness of the stock burlesque houses that were now beginning to take shape.

As the bright young directors of Columbia put it, the Columbia Wheel presented "Approved Burlesque," the American Wheel "Standard Burlesque," which meant that the American Wheel could have the coochers and the extreme double entendre; it could also have the runway in its theatres. The Winter Garden on Broadway, Shubert temple of music comedy and revues, had experimented successfully with these platforms extending out into the audience, but for Columbia theatres they were considered too brash. The headquarters for both circuits were in the spacious offices of the New York Columbia Theatre Building, and whether the shows were clean or dirty, the profits in any case ultimately went to the Columbia Amusement Company.

The diplomacy and public relations finesse, which were Columbia's forte, were given a severe test when, through no fault of its own, its good, clean image was blemished, and another periodic newspaper "scandal" brought out the censors in full regalia in 1915.

It started with a minor raid on Daly's Theatre, which had just been opened for stock burlesque. One of its operators was Jerome Rosenberg, who incidentally was financially affiliated with the Columbia Theatre Building and whose brother, Walter Reade, was Vice-President of the Columbia Theatre and Building Company. On the hallowed stage of Daly's, where once Lydia Thompson and Her Blondes had cavorated, now Millie De Leon wiggled incessantly, and then permitted the customers miscellaneous liberties with her garters, while she was still wearing them.

When the press blew this up as a shocking blow to morality, Columbia wasted no time. One hundred managers held a solemn conclave at the Hotel Astor, and duly dignified and publicized pronouncements were issued therefrom, enunciating a new campaign of purification. Not publicized, but more important, was the immediate change in name of the No. 2 Circuit, also known, unfortunately, as the Columbia Annex Wheel, to the American Burlesque Association. Come what may, the name "Columbia," at least, would not be sullied.

This move was none too soon. In the same year, a small burlesque company at the Garrick Theatre on 35th Street and an American Wheel show, playing the 14th Street Olympic Theatre, were simultaneously raided. Apparently, there was nothing of great importance to divert the press and the public at the time, and the two raids provided a titillating field day for all. As a matter of fact, the delinquent Wheel show, managed by Sim Williams, boasted some highly proficient performers, headed by the later vaudeville and musical comedy comedian Billy Gilbert, and including Beulah Kennedy, Sadie Rose and Murray J. Simon.

Nonetheless, the Commissioner of Licenses, George H. Bell, insisted in *The New York Times,* "Reports of my inspectors reveal instances that seem almost unbelievable."

This was an occasion that warranted the personal attention of Sam Scribner himself. At first he took the position that Columbia merely served as a booking agent. When this fooled nobody, he took strenuous action. He outcensored the censors: "You may rest assured that this will be the last year of offensive burlesque. Personally, I advocate the imprisonment of performers, producers and managers who resort to smut in their shows." And then in effect still smiling, but clawlike, he added: "The managers of those theatres where indecent shows are given have the effrontery to believe they are protected by political influences, and this is undoubtedly true."

The License Commissioner then retreated somewhat. Disregarding the actual ownership of the raided American Wheel show, he conceded: ". . . in the houses of the Columbia Burlesque Circuit such performances as came under the ban are never given."

Following this exchange of courtesies, it was to be expected that all would end well. The managers tabulated, with a discerning accuracy, all the offensive items: "Cooch and Oriental Dances, Bare Legs, Smutty Dialogue and Vulgar Jokes and Action." All these, they promised, in a contrite letter to the Commissioner, would be eliminated henceforth and forevermore. The Commissioner then forgave everybody, and licenses were renewed all around. Not only did the Garrick and Olympic Theatres reopen, but Daly's, sporting a new runway, also reappeared; and another stock aggregation, the Union Square Theatre, joined the Olympic and 14th Street Theatres, composing an unholy trinity in that sinful sector.

"Commissioner Bell feels his crusade has accomplished good results," reported *The New York Times*. In December, Fred McCloy had found his bearings, and the annual Christmas pronunciamento on the advanced state of burlesque was released. Quoth he: "Today there is not an indecent burlesque performance being given on any stage in America."

Again, Columbia tact and diplomacy and connections had prevailed.

The directors of the Columbia Amusement Company were serving their stockholders and themselves efficiently and lucratively. They were not out to pollute the theatre with American Wheel shows, nor to reform it with Columbia productions. Profits were the sole motive. Sime Silverman accurately called the turn back in 1910: "When the managers reached the conclusion that 'clean shows' were the thing—not for the good of burlesque as much as because they thought there would be more money in it—the 'clean show' arrived."

The Shangri-La of respectability and standing in the community, as well as dividends, so intrigued the Columbia officers that they went to unprecedented, determined and often ridiculous lengths to "purify" burlesque on the Columbia Wheel proper. The elusively tantalizing prospect of almost doubling patronage with women in the audience was always an absorbing and exciting concern. The keynote was sounded, a little too optimistically, by J. Herbert Mack in 1913: "In the early days it was supposed that the burlesque show was exclusively for men, but the Columbia Amusement Company has proven otherwise, and we are now playing to as many lady as men audiences."

The involvement of the United States in World War I lent further impetus to the hope for women audiences, in the unfounded fear that there might not be enough males left at home to patronize the shows. Drew and Campbell, Cleveland impresarios, followed up the Wheel ban on "hell" and "damn" by gratuitously advocating ankle-length skirts instead of tights. Even Fred McCloy was moved to protest mildly:

> . . . the directors of the Columbia Amusement Company in their zeal to overcome prejudice against the shows controlled by them, have gone to the extreme of excluding infinitely less offensive dialogue, "business" and costume arrangement than have been utilized without scruple by producers of shows of accepted quality.

As he pointed out, the Shubert and Ziegfeld productions were actually presenting girls in bare legs, and, in the Winter Garden, on a runway to boot. Vaudeville was coming out with feminine personalities like Texas Guinan, who was self-proclaimed as "God's Masterpiece and the Most Fascinating Actress in America." Rendering her genius more emphatic, she distributed gratis her illustrated booklet on weight reduction. All burlesque could come up with as a counter attraction was Zenoia, "The Girl with the Diamond Teeth," whose upper front teeth, she claimed, were studded with diamonds.

At this time, the simple smells of "Krausemeyer's Alley" were repugnant to the Columbia "establishment." Billy Watson's 1914 version disdained the alleys and the alley cats for "a superb throne-room in an Irish palace, a salon in a 'toney' East Side residence, and a brilliantly lighted roof-garden where a christening party is holding forth."

So strict was Columbia that Rose Sydell's London Belles, typically representative of "Approved Burlesque," drew this unbelievably drastic condemnation from McCloy: "A show such as this could only interest bestial, prurient and dead-to-shame minds." Nevertheless, W. S. Campbell continued in this show with his bathhouse scene culminating in the "Sandy-beach, Poppa" dialogue and the invariable retort, "Are you calling me names?"

Burlesque, having discovered homosexuality, hastened to exploit its possibilities with "nance" characters. When some benighted managers displayed a lamentable tendency to tolerate such scenes as a substitute for the prohibited shimmy-shakers, the Wheel immediately clamped down: "The exclusion of the odious effeminate male character or 'fairy,' as it is called in the vernacular, is infinitely more desirable than the elimination of dancers (Oriental) of the type referred to."

Columbia, following the lead of the Watch and Ward Society, which abolished all runways in Boston, adamantly continued to prohibit runways in the theatres of the Columbia Wheel. "A knee is a joint and not an entertainment," they agreed with the censors.

As a further concession to female patronage, the masculine prerogative of smoking in the orchestra was abolished on the Columbia Circuit. In 1918, *The Billboard* seriously suggested that burlesque should now aim for the patronage of children as well as women.

In 1917, Herk, now running the American Wheel, as Scribner ran Columbia, decided that his circuit could also use women patronage, since the United States was at war. His circuit, which had always been conveniently vague on the banning of coochers, now specifically outlawed them with special emphasis on those with a notorious and dishonorable past. With great fanfare, it was announced that some poltroon of a comic had been fined $100 for daring to tell an off-color story on the stage.

In the new era of elegance, the Wheel executives still looked askance at Billy Watson. In later years, extolled as a prototype of good, clean, old-fashioned burlesque, he was now considered too crude. He was ordered to limit the poundage of his hefty chorines to 160 pounds. Finally, he and his "Krausemeyer's Alley" were unceremoniously dumped off the Wheel altogether. Billy Watson then took his show on a musical comedy tour and flopped.

Sime Silverman again succinctly summarized it: "Really," he said in 1920, "Columbia is too strict." He advised the producers to claim not only that their shows were clean but that they were the cleanest of all entertainment.

The next step was the elimination of the name "burlesque," which was seriously contemplated but never consummated. The Columbia Theatre in New York City which had vaudeville only on Sundays put on its marquee the slogan "Devoted to Burlesque and Vaudeville."

In 1920, the last of the fat years for Columbia, the zenith of respectability was attained at a banquet held at the Ritz-Carleton Hotel in honor of Fred McCloy, the genial and versatile Pooh Bah of the Wheel. Honored guests who paid tribute included General John J. Pershing and Honorable Fiorello H. LaGuardia. Honorable Aaron J. Levy, Supreme Court Justice of New York, and star patron of the Columbia Theatre, contrasted, in a fervid speech, the low esteem in which the world held the five "revolutionary" Socialists, recently dismissed from the New York State Assembly, with the character of "Freddie McCloy, who stands as the highest type of American citizenship."

From such dignity and honor it was but a step to art. "We have paved the way for the younger fellows to take up the 'art for art's sake' idea and apply it to burlesque," wrote Samuel A. Scribner at this time. Purity was a settled question. The word finis had been written to indecent shows, he added. "And today there is not a more punctiliously conducted form of amusement in America," said McCloy in the annual Christmas outburst of enthusiasm.

The censors themselves echoed the benignities of Scribner and McCloy. So insistent a reformer as John M. Casey, Chief of the Municipal Licensing Division of Boston, conceded graciously in January 1921: "The entertainment furnished now in the average burlesque house is fit for any man or woman to see."

This was more than he would have admitted, no doubt, for the average nightclub or Broadway revue. Art, in truth, was just around the corner. But before that corner could be turned, the postwar era of the shimmy intervened; stock burlesque and the movies crept up practically unnoticed until, suddenly, like giants emerging from a shadow, they overwhelmed their surprised, frantic victim to whom all aid and succor could by then only prove unavailing.

Such unforeseen disaster finally overtook the Columbia Amusement Company; and when it did, the burlesque industry, without so much as a "by your leave," stolidly receded into its usual rut of smut.

THE GOLDEN AGE—SLIGHTLY TARNISHED

POWERFUL as it might be, the Columbia Amusement Company could not abolish sex, though it seems to have made the most valiant attempt ever to do so since Adam and Eve were ejected from the Garden of Eden.

There was some element of "sex" in all shows, with occasional overtones of "dirt" in many Columbia shows and most American Wheel shows. Since, in the final analysis, Columbia's insistence on purity was not a crusade but a financial strategem and, often enough, a publicity gimmick, there was enough flexibility to dirty a normally clean show if business warranted it. As *The Billboard* complained, there were always managers who "have held their own opinions of what a burlesque show should be."

Even as Sidney Wire hurrahed—"The Columbia Circuit after several years of ceaseless work and untiring effort, has lifted the burlesque show from the old slap-stick stage to its present, almost perfect standard"—Mickie O'Brien, a literate chorine who wrote feelingly of life in the "merry-merry," let the cat out of the bag:

> Fannie Anderson distinguished herself recently when the Stars of Burlesque hit the one-nighters and Fannie was billed as Fanita, the famous dancer from the Orient. They tell me that Fannie twisted and wiggled to beat the band and they also say that the show played to big business in consequence.

A typical American Wheel show such as *Girls From Joyland,* featured such interesting numbers as "Come Up Tonight," by Fatima and Girls, "The Night-Gown Dance," by Bedall and Girls and "The Twelve Months of the Year," by the "Living Picture Girls."

Not only were the old Eastern Wheel wigglers like Millie De Leon and Chooceeta still in demand, but a new addition, Zallah, was prosperous enough to form her own show, Zallah's Own Company. Almost as popular was Azetta, featured in Blutch Cooper's *Beauty, Youth and Folly* on the Columbia No. 2 Wheel.

Audience participation numbers still abounded. A chorus girl quit because she was burned by the cigarette of her impromptu dancing partner in a scene called "In the Garden of Girls." It was revealed that the male customer had been importuned to dance with the chorus girls who were coyly warbling "Waltz Me Around Again, Dear." In another show, soubrette Dolly Sweet came out with four chorus girls in different-colored costumes and invited the men to kiss the color of their choice. Sam Howe's *Lovemakers* at Miner's Bronx featured a "Dancing Around" scene, with the chorus girls walking up and down the aisles and dancing with the men, as the star, Dolly Dupre, sang "Kiss Me, I've Never Been Kissed Before." This was so popular it called for two dozen encores. And the *Gay New Yorkers,* presented at the New York Columbia Theatre in 1916, evoked this condemnation from *Variety*: ". . . and it's dirty, plainly and intentionally dirty."

One of the more pretentious shows on the American Wheel was the *Tango Queens,* starring Lena Daley, subsequently a star Columbia soubrette. In addition to Toikeeta, a frank cooch dancer, Lena Daley herself "produced a number of gyrations and touch of the 'cooch' during her singing acts, and the other principals indulged in actions and dialogue which were offensive and classed as vulgar," according to one critic who saw the show in Philadelphia.

In *The Dainty Maids,* not only did Princess Olga entertain with an "Oriental dance of her own creation," but in the golden age of clean Columbia, the chorus girls of this show walked down to the footlights one at a time, turned their backs and wiggled. This engaging scene did not even have the refreshing novelty of young chorines. According to Sime Silverman, a member of the audience asked his companion: "Is that your mother in the chorus?"

A top Columbia Wheel show, such as James E. Cooper's *Best Show in Town,* book by Billy K. Wells, playing the New York Columbia Theatre in 1918, presented the following numbers in the general outline of a plot wherein the leading lady had to marry a man or lose

The chorus, always a problem in burlesque. "Those dames kept many a guy from going wrong." *Culver Pictures, Inc.*

a legacy: "Woman somnambulist, lingerie parade, Eva Tanguay impersonation, five female principals singing 'Sleep Baby Sleep' to comics in bed, a bladder duel and a drunken girl bit."

In the highly touted *Behman Show,* also playing at the New York Columbia Theatre in 1919, the "biggest laughs . . . were obtained through double entendre, never nasty, some quite spicy."

Comedians in Columbia shows were always trying to crash a ladies' Turkish bath with little exposure but plenty of insinuation. Or else, they were engaged in adventurous amours while the wife was away. And in lieu of the cooch dancer at the finale, the closing scene was frequently a harem interior or an Egyptian climax, with a gaudily bedecked, if otherwise mild, Cleopatra.

As in the case of the old Eastern Wheel, there were a few leading shows which received lavish praise and practically achieved the eminence of musical comedy.

Max Spiegel's Watson Sisters Company, in 1913, was acclaimed as the biggest thing in burlesque since *Wine, Woman and Song.* This production boasted a continuous plot throughout with the Watson Sisters, who soon outgrew burlesque, "assisting in the creation of the general tone of refinement."

Another outstanding show was *Follies of the Day,* produced by Barney Gerard, who also was credited with writing the book, the lyrics and the music. Stars of the show included Gertrude Hayes, Barney Gerard's wife, Sam Sidman, and later George P. Murphy. The 1915 edition of *Follies of the Day* was based on a "New Idea Satirizing Events of the Day—Entitled What Does the Public Want?" The characters and program included:

Abner Pollywogg, a rube
Dick Smart, a slick article
Officer Grabbem, a cop
Sheza Badger, a Light on the Gay White Way
Hammerstein, Belasco, Reeves, Geo. M. Cohan
Virginia Blossom, a Southern Rose, played by Ann Propp
Polly Prude, a Demure Young Girl
August Furst, a hot dog man, played by Sam Sidman
Peg O' My Heart, a Daughter of Erin played by Gertrude Hayes

Musical Nos.

Yankee Doodle Boy—George M. Cohan
Give Me Credit—Al Reeves
Virginia Rose

I Wonder Why They Stare At Me (etc.)

Act II

Gertrude Hayes and her Dancing Bricktops
Presenting a Miniature Musical Comedy

Tangoland

Travesty on Three Weeks
Excerpts from Operas and "I've Got No Use for Opera When There's Ragtime Around."

The established shows of previous years were produced with more pretentiousness than had ever before been seen in burlesque. Dave Marion's Dreamlanders Company, starring Agnes Behler, the wife of Dave Marion, and Inez De Verdier was staged in 1916 by Leon Errol, with settings by Joseph Urban. It was proclaimed as the most decorative and opulent burlesque production ever to play Broadway. Jack Singer's *Behman Show* of 1916 cost $20,000 to produce—an unprecedented amount—and was given the honor of being the regular summer show for the New York Columbia Theatre that year.

Jean Bedini's plotless revues were top moneymakers for many years. His 1921 show, starring Clark and McCullough, grossed $350,000. Another clever and popular production was *Girls De Looks,* starring Joseph K. Watson and William H. Cohan as Slotkin and Slitkin, lawyers. Here, Watson also projected his popular Abe Kabibble characterization.

Unfortunately, as in previous periods, these superior shows were lost in the triteness and, at best, mediocrity of the great majority of the productions. Again, burlesque, even in this most affluent era, could not afford the talent, year after year to produce first-class continuous humor. The best of its comedians kept deserting the field just as Weber and Fields had done in the 1890s.

In the midst of Columbia's heyday, the generally friendly and favorable *The Billboard* had to admit in 1917:

> The weakest spot in present-day burlesque is the average book, and producers have no excuse for foisting upon the public the deleterious, unfunny, "hashed up" conglomeration of burlesque which is altogether too common in the shows of today.

In 1918 *The Billboard* again deplored the basic weakness of burlesque: "Most of the trouble lies in the absolute inanity of the book," which it declared to be about as exciting as a *Congressional Record.*

The *Broadway Frolics* of 1917, produced by Columbia's most successful showman in elaborate presentations, Jack Singer, and starring the outstanding talents of the Wheel, Loney Hascall, Vic Casmore and Harry Lang, was to be a burlesque landmark. But the reviews were highly negative: "There is hardly a flash of originality, hardly a spontaneous glint of comedy," Sime Silverman roared. "Rotten!"

As Herk himself complained at the end of the same year: "But outside of moral progress where are the mighty improvements we hear about? Where are they?"

Nevertheless, Columbia's fortunes rose. The seven years from 1913 to 1920 saw corresponding increases in the price of a Columbia franchise, even over the highly vaunted figure of $4,000 to $5,000. By 1916 a weekly gross of $7,000 was reached by several shows. Twenty years before a weekly gross of $1,800 was considered excellent. Columbia and American Wheel shows flooded the cities. In New York, for example, the Olympic, Garrick, Yorkville, Miner's Bronx, Hurtig & Seamon's and the Columbia Theatres augmented the Star, Gayety, Casino and Empire in Brooklyn.

In the customary Wheel arrangement the Columbia Amusement Company received 50 percent of a theatre's gate receipts. "Unprecedented is the present prosperity of burlesque," said *The Billboard* in December 1916. *Variety* agreed: "This year has been a memorable one for burlesque . . . 1916 seems to have been the apex."

By 1918 old-time franchise holders such as the Miner estate and Louis Robie were the possessors of highly profitable vested interests yielding a steady and substantial income. Columbia franchises, leased for five-year periods, were eagerly sought but not as easily obtained.

The New York Columbia Theatre led all the theatres. It charged as high as $1.50 for a front seat in 1919, and these were not available to the general public at that. Only "Politicians" could get these highly desirable locations. The theatre boasted of unbelievable weekly maximums of $15,000. Costs were low, profits high. Once a show was fully equipped and ready for the road, it did not cost more than $500 to $750 weekly to operate, and a fairly good production might net $175,000 over the year.

So prosperous were the operators, and so acute the perennial shortage of chorus girls, that the Wheel increased their wages to twenty and twenty-five dollars weekly with occasional bonuses. "No more sixteen- to eighteen-dollar chorus girls," it was boasted. It was too bad in a way. "Those dames kept many a guy from going wrong," said Sime Silverman.

Some of the old crowd failed to cash in. Ed Rush, of the old Bon Tons shows, somehow got lost in the shuffle. He was reported ill and desolate. Fred Irwin, disenfranchised by the Wheel, was in the throes of litigation with the Columbia Amusement Company.

But those who stayed with the Wheel found it highly profitable. Herk, now president of the American Burlesque Association, had an interest in the successful Bedini *Puss Puss* show. Hurtig and Seamon were the owners of six franchises, Jacobs and Jermon five, James E. Cooper, Scribner's brother-in-law, also five. At the height of this prosperity, the titans of Columbia—Scribner, Mack, Hynicka and Herk—bought the coal mine in Scribner's home town. But inevitably even their talents were to prove unequal to the inherent disabilities of burlesque.

From 1921 on, the fortunes of the Columbia Amusement Company were to decline, at first slowly, then alarmingly, then precipitately, and at the sad climax not even dirty shows could stop its demise.

THE FALL OF HOLY COLUMBIA

IN 1921, for the first time in its existence, the upward financial climb of the Columbia Amusement Company came to a halt. Receipts fell to a prewar level. "Depression!" screamed the Wheel, and immediately proceeded to cut salaries. The next year was even worse. Columbia's Brain Trust experimented with the addition of vaudeville and movies, advertising "three shows in one for the same price." This bargain failed to help. A further 25 percent cut in administrative costs was immediately instituted. To add to its problems at this troublesome hour, the federal government initiated an investigation of the Columbia Amusemen Company as a monopolistic trust.

The vaunted purity of the Wheel now backfired. Even the ladies, whose patronage Columbia had so assidiously courted, were not quite as effete as the Wheel executives had imagined. It seemed they liked a dirty joke as well as the next man. Flocking to the vulgar Broadway revues by the thousands, they evidently considered Columbia burlesque a bit too anemic and wishy-washy for their robust tastes.

Sardonic and illustrative was the article, "Burlesque and the Pure in Mind," written for *The New York Times* (January 15, 1922) by Bessie Rowland James. Anticipating wickedness at least on a par with Ziegfeld, Anderson and Dillingham, the lady had expectantly attended a Columbia performance of a show enticingly entitled *Bathhouse*

Beauties. But there was no bathhouse in the entire production, nor a beach, nor a wave, not even water. Scene one was a party in a summer home, wherein the chorines, in modest garb, sang demurely, and then scampered off. Following, a comedian imitating a Hebrew, joked and sang rather innocuously. Then there was a song about Kentucky, then some more feeble jokes, and so on. This was "Burlesque—well-behaved and bearing a standard with a clean, moral tone when all the rest strive to outdo themselves with supposedly shocking ideas." She concluded that disappointingly enough:

> This play is deliberately, painstakingly and for the purpose of gain, flatly decent, flagrantly and suggestively moral, pure in motive, word and action, lacking in profanity, exceptionally humorous and in every respect offensively legal under the statutes governing such matters.

The American Wheel also was in trouble. Columbia had Broadway revues and musical comedy for competition. The American Wheel had to compete with the ruthless, dirty tide of stock burlesque now in full flow. The Olympic by this time had found it more profitable to play stock burlesque. It discarded the Wheel shows. The Olympic and Irving Place Theatres on 14th Street and the National Winter Garden on the lower East Side were all cutting into the patronage of the American Circuit. The same pattern was evident outside New York City.

Herk had been at odds with Scribner since the downtrend began. His position had never been an enviable one even in good times. His circuit absorbed the attacks of civic groups and censorship, while the senior Wheel remained smug and prestigious under its halo, taking the cash from the subsidiary wheel, letting Herk keep the discredit.

Herk broke openly with Scribner in 1921, daring to disagree with the strategy of Scribner and his associates in their negotiations with the Stagehands and Musicians Unions. Herk was primarily a conciliator, but the more the American Wheel floundered, the more he stood up against Scribner. The struggle between the two henceforth subsided and flared up again periodically as each tried to impose his will upon the other. When it was all over, Scribner had his way but Herk had burlesque.

Now, in 1922, Herk made a definite break away from the supervision of Columbia by emphasizing in his shows one-piece bathing suits, union suits and lady wrestlers. At length Herk, in disgust, unable to get anywhere with Scribner, abandoned burlesque with a few other malcontents for a temporary and disastrous venture in vaudeville.

Simultaneous with his departure, the American Wheel severed all connections with the Columbia Amusement Company. Its death was almost instantaneous.

In May 1922, the secret that the American Burlesque Association was bankrupt was let out to the theatrical world. At once, the intricate tie-ups between the American and Columbia Wheels exploded into legal suits and countersuits, and while the two were snarling, the Mutual Burlesque Association was quietly incorporated, in July, as a substitute wheel.

The Mutual Wheel was not considered as a rival, at first. John G. Jermon, possessor of an interest in each circuit, was the acknowledged liaison agent between them, so that the Mutual Wheel also was considered a subsidiary circuit to mighty Columbia. But whereas the American Wheel had stagnated, as a result of its limitation by the policies of Columbia, the Mutual Wheel, from the outset, pursued its own opportunistic methods. Hence for the first time since the dissolution of the Empire shows, the Columbia Amusement Company was beset with effective wheel competition.

The first reaction of the older wheel was to inject a little salaciousness into its shows. Now that bare bosoms were emerging, Columbia permitted bare legs. It continued to allow a little more latitude, and still a little more, until in December 1922 *Variety* spanked the Columbia *Social Maids* show as a circuit show had never before been admonished: "For unadulterated filth, crass blatant vulgarity and offensiveness, the *Social Maids* of Columbia wins the brown derby."

The headliners of this production were the star duo George Stone and Etta Pillard. The items objected to are now routine in even a moderately clean burlesque show. George Stone sang a ditty about fishing for bass in water up to his—ankles, and there was a scene where a girl, refused permission to leave the room, crossed her legs, causing the comedian to remark, "Somebody has to leave."

So, Columbia had really not become as degenerate as had been indicated, and when it saw that it could not compete with the excesses of the Mutual Wheel and stock, it went in for more novelties, vaudeville and animal acts, revivals of old Broadway melodramas, anything and everything that would keep the wolf out and the customers in.

Nothing availed. Yesterdays surefire hits were today's flops. The *Chuckles* show of top moneymaker Jean Bedini lasted just three weeks as the summer show at the New York Columbia Theatre.

The properties of the Columbia Amusement Company were so substantial that it could not just go out of existence as had the American Wheel and the Progressive Wheel before it. In 1923 there were thirty-eight shows in the Wheel for a season of forty weeks, and every show had from thirty-five to forty performers and stagehands. The property value of the Wheel was estimated to be about $20,000,000. The pay envelope at the end of a season for all thirty-five hundred employees of the Columbia Amusement Company amounted to $5,000,000.

With the recent collapse of the American Wheel haunting the industry, Walter K. Hill, Columbia's newly acquired press agent, implored:

> Columbia Burlesque is the weekly money order for the folks at home, the loosening of the mortgage plastered on the farm that is being purchased for a later day. Columbia Burlesque is money in the First National Bank. It is bonds in the Safe Deposit Box.

He did not add that most of the money and bonds were concentrated among the officers and directors. In 1923, these included Scribner, Hynicka, J. Herbert Mack, Charles Waldron, Jules Hurtig, John G. Jermon and Gus Hill. About half of the theatres playing Columbia productions were owned directly or indirectly by the Wheel. A franchise on the Columbia Circuit was still a mark of distinction. Clark and McCullough, though out of burlesque as performers, still remained in it as franchise holders. The New York Columbia Theatre Building still stood resplendent with one of the most magnificent electric signs on Broadway. Just to polish up all the theatres during the summer slack, in preparation for the next season, cost $100,000. For two weeks before the fall opening, 500 cleaners, on their hands and knees, said Scribner, scrubbed the theatres of Columbia from the pit to the gallery.

It really was a pity that with such cleanliness, both on and off the stage, burlesque audiences preferred the creaking, unwashed runways of the Mutual theatres, tottering under the weight of such feverish shimmying and shaking as had never before been envisioned. By 1923, Mutual and Columbia had come to the parting of the ways. Herk, just back from vaudeville, was assuming charge of the destinies of the new wheel. John G. Jermon, the unofficial counsellor to Mutual, now gave his entire allegiance to Columbia. All Columbia managers were ordered to dispose at once of all their interests in the new circuit. In November 1923, the last link between the two, Jermon's associate, Al Singer, was forced to resign from Herk's circuit at the behest of Scribner. Henceforth, with Mutual chorines and soubrettes cooching and undressing, Columbia would wash its hands clean of such obscenities. Columbia decided to make a last-ditch, all-out effort for clean burlesque.

Barney Gerard was engaged to produce, in memory of the old days, a revival of his *Follies of the Day,* with scenery by Joseph Urban and dances by Semour Felix. Barney Gerard's niece, Gertrude Hayes, Jr., was starred. This was Scribner's retort to Herk. Buck and Bubbles, famous Negro dancing team, were added as a specialty attraction to bolster up one show, while another featured Mme. Vallenta and Her Trained Leopards.

The *Follies of the Day* revival was a flop. Gertrude Hayes, Jr., for all her publicized talents, eventually displayed them as a runway leader heading a chorus line at the New York Columbia Theatre. The vaudeville novelties, as well as all the other frantic innovations obviously conceived in panic, proved equally ineffectual. And more and more performers abandoned Columbia for the Mutual bandwagon. As tried and true comics like Billy Gilbert, George P. Murphy, Pat White and Sam Howe lined up with the new Wheel, Billy (Beef Trust) Watson was taken back hurriedly into the fold and rewarded with a franchise.

Perhaps, the brain-trusters decided, the fault was with the chorus girls, who were as ugly as ever. The girls in Mutual, getting twenty-five dollars weekly, five dollars less than their sisters on the more pretentious wheel, were even worse. But at least they provided other compensations for their patrons. So Columbia evolved the idea of a dancing school for chorines under the direction of its veteran ensemble producer, "Dancing" Dan Dody. The great experiment was begun with much publicity and little hope. The budding chorus girls were charged an instruction fee in the Columbia School of Dancing and Instruction. Simultaneously, bare legs for chorines were again banned, though permitted for soubrettes, in the hope of thereby eliminating any hint of nudity for the youngsters who might be wary of entering burlesque.

In December, Walter K. Hill could still label Columbia as the "garland of thirty-six family entertainments." There was no profanity, no suggestiveness, no nudity, it was claimed. Even the soubrettes, as the only women permitted to bare their legs in a Columbia show, could do so only if their legs were pretty. "There's no undressing of legs in burlesque simply to cater to the taste which likes undressed legs, beautiful or not beautiful."

These were the final utterances, however, of a yielding order. Just as 1920 was the last big financial year for Columbia, so was 1924 the last in which the fetish of clean burlesque was upheld. In the same month of December during which these pleasant sentiments were being echoed, a runway, that board of sin, appeared unbelievably at the chaste New York Columbia Theatre. "Burlesque As U Like It" was the ambiguous slogan, designed to entice audiences of every bent to the current attraction, *Step On It,* starring the well-known team of George

Niblo and Helen Spencer, the latter a graduate of the chorus of an American Wheel show, *The World Beaters.* Of this epochal event, *The Billboard* rather cryptically commented December 27, 1924:

> Suffice it to say that there was far greater exhibition of pep and personality in the show there than when we reviewed it at the Columbia Theatre several weeks ago . . . girls appeared on the runway shimmy shaking as they have never shook before in Columbia Circuit shows . . .

That other Columbia bulwark in Manhattan, Hurtig & Seamon's Harlem Music Hall, had already succumbed to a runway in the earlier part of the same year, engaging two runway soubrettes, one of whom was Isabelle Van leading her own chorus of eight, the Dancing Dolls.

Practically all other Columbia theatres were now provided with runways. As a final capitulation, the Columbia School of Dancing and Instruction, dedicated to pure and talented chorus girls for burlesque, was permanently discontinued. Talent for the runways required no formal instruction.

The end of clean burlesque was inaugurated by Scribner's declaration in 1925 that Columbia burlesque was *NOT* musical comedy, and as proof thereof even the chorus girls were actually permitted to bare their legs.

With its last energies, the Wheel braced for the gala fifteenth anniversary celebration that same year, held at the New York Columbia Theatre. Famous well-wishers at the midnight show—the Red Pepper Revue, produced by Billy K. Wells—were Fanny Brice, Clark and McCullough, Harry Von Tilzer, Gallagher and Shean, Will Rogers and Belle Baker. Miner's Bronx simultaneously proceeded to celebrate what it called its sixty-first year in burlesque, and Hurtig & Seamon's its thirtieth anniversary.

After the receptions were over, it was tacitly admitted and understood that Columbia producers and managers were to be granted wider latitude than ever before in the history of the Wheel. At the New York Columbia Theatre, in the fall, soubrette Jean Bodine, in the standard Golden Crook show with tramp comic, Billy Arlington, stripped down to a one-piece union suit, and after toying with buttons and clasps disappeared in a blackout. Columbia tableaux further permitted the posing of girls, in a group, with bare breasts.

Columbia was fast becoming like any other burlesque, only less successful. Reviewing the publicized premiere of the Wheel's sixteenth annual summer production, Harry Steppe's *O.K., The New York Times* remarked May 4, 1925: "There was an adequate amount of the stock material of burlesque, lest the regular votaries be displeased by unwelcome novelties." The chief comic effects by Harry Steppe, it was noted, consisted in hitting other characters across the face with celery stalks.

Variety gloomily surveyed the situation in December 1925:

> The current year in burlesque has witnessed a distinct setback for "clean burlesque" and a proportionate increase in the grosses of the Mutual Burlesque Circuit, operated upon the opposite theory.

Shortly thereafter, Columbia house managers were instructed to "go as far as any other kind of attraction in the matter of showing scantily clad choruses and principals."

At Hurtig & Seamon's Music Hall, shimmy-shaking "Queen of the Runway," Erin Jackson, was starred, in an attempt to get some of the college-boy trade from the more notorious and boisterous Apollo, run by Billy Minsky on 125th Street. At the Columbia Theatre, Lena Daley, now the leading soubrette on the Wheel, performed a "sensational hula dance in the near nude." At the Yorkville Theatre, midway between these two houses, the chorines on the runway playfully snapped the rubber bands on the backs of each others' brassieres.

Where once the Columbia Wheel had prided itself on the elaborate cost of its productions, it now resorted to tabloid dramatic presentations which required no chorus lines, production numbers, etc.—just six or seven actors. Rehashed versions of *White Cargo, The Bat, The Gorilla, Red Kisses,* were thrown at the customers. Gus Hill tried to come to the rescue with comic-strip tabloid shows, *Mutt and Jeff, Bringing Up Father,* etc.

Cartoon comedies, melodrama, clean burlesque, dirty burlesque, Negro aggregations, mixed black and white troupes, vaudeville—Columbia tried them all in the last dying years. To no avail. The Wheel even tried to get, as a feature attraction, Joyce Hawley, the girl who had bathed nude in champagne at a notorious Earl Carroll party.

The policy, hitherto so remunerative, of getting 50 percent of the receipts now boomeranged, since the shows were doing so badly. In November 1926, the Columbia production of *Not Tonight, Josephine* failed to meet expenses, and its cast was stranded without salaries—an experience hitherto reserved only for "turkey" troupes and shoestring one-nighters.

Fred McCloy, after sixteen years with Columbia as its most expert literary exponent of clean shows, left the Wheel for Mutual. Top-flight producers, Barney Gerard and Jack Singer, among others, also withdrew.

In April 1927, the Mutual Burlesque Association, in a startling and unprecedented action, sued the Columbia Amusement Company for $1,000,000 on the ground that the older circuit was soliciting clergymen, women's clubs and other reform groups to interfere with shows on the Mutual Circuit. The accusation may have been unfounded, but, at any rate, it certainly was a tempting strategy for Columbia in view of all the circumstances. The case never came to court. Legal action with Herk nearly always ended in compromise.

Before the year was over, the erstwhile affluent Columbia Amusement Company gratefully accepted a merger with that rowdy newcomer, the Mutual Burlesque Association. As a result, there was formed the United Burlesque Association, with forty-five shows. Herk was president of the new group, and Scribner officially given the face-saving title of Chairman of the Board of Directors.

The melodramas were at once eliminated. The New York Columbia Theatre submitted to another "first-time" humiliation and played a Mutual show, which grossed $8,000 in one week. The shows themselves were still called Mutual or Columbia productions, but the number of the latter were reduced to eighteen, a 50 percent reduction. As a concession to their greater expense and maintenance, Columbia shows received a guarantee of $2,000 weekly from the Wheel, as against $1,740 for Mutual productions, under Herk's system of guaranteeing theatre owners a certain minimum intake.

Those few theatres which had managed, somehow, to exist without runways, had them installed pronto. The New York Columbia Theatre sported on its streamlined, illuminated runway Isabelle Van and Her Dancing Dolls, cavorting in one-piece bathing suits for the delectation of an audience described by *The Billboard* as "sex-seekers."

Many of the old-line Columbia producers were gone. Charles Barton died in 1917, James E. Cooper in 1923, Rud Hynicka in 1927. Grandiose schemes of a new burlesque empire were regularly formulated by such survivors as John G. Jermon, Fred McCloy, Max Spiegel and Barney Gerard. None materialized. Barney Gerard finally went to Hollywood, where he collaborated with Arthur Caesar on the screen treatment of *King of Burlesque,* a movie which had practically no connection with real burlesque.

In 1934, Dave Marion died. A year later Fred Irwin. Whatever was left of the Columbia Amusement Company—its vast properties, producers, actors, theatres and audiences—was now absorbed into the Mutual Burlesque Association.

A flood of magazine and newspaper analyses now appeared, rather optimistically entitled, "The Last Days of Burlesque," "The Last Legs of Burlesque," etc. With what bitterness did Scribner read of their conclusions: "And having lost its spice, burlesque has also lost its reason for being." It was recalled that Burns Mantle had complained on his first visit to a Columbia show in 1915: "Is it better than the more common grades of musical comedy? Does it differ from them enough to give it the distinction we had hoped to find? . . . Burlesque should stand for something different." Another theatrical writer, F. M. McNelly, had warned Columbia at the time to keep aloof "from the damaging consequences of appealing to the public with second rate musical comedy."

Columbia prosperity had silenced these prophets. But after two decades destiny had at last caught up with the Wheel. Columbia burlesque had fooled most audiences with smart publicity and an occasional gem among the usual mediocrities. It had lived a long life because it was powerful enough to stifle effective competition in its field. When stock "Burlesk As U Want It" finally became strong enough to arouse interest and attention, when the Mutual Circuit proceeded and profited on the same principle, what chance did Columbia have with its smug pretentiousness, its essentially empty entertainment, based on an exploited reputation and the memory of stars who had long since abandoned it for other fields?

In 1929, the Empire and Casino Theatres in Brooklyn folded, yielding to the Star and Gayety Theatres, raucous Mutual stables in the same borough. At the Casino, Billy (Beef Trust) Watson officiated at the last rites, now appearing, appropriately enough for these anemic days, with his "Chicken Trust."

On March 29, 1930, the New York Columbia Theatre closed its doors. Its last show starred the other Billy Watson, Sliding Billy Watson. Walter Reade announced the immediate demolition of the theatre to make way for a movie house. In February 1931, the proud name of Columbia was unceremoniously removed. It was now the Mayfair Theatre. Sic transit . . .

STARS OF COLUMBIA

THE permanent heritage of the Columbia Wheel to the amusement industry was its stars. The more talented and more fortunate, as always, left burlesque for vaudeville, musical comedy and the Broadway revue. Many, not quite as gifted, but still possessing a fair measure of talent, remained in burlesque through the Mutual Wheel and even into the stock burlesque era.

Columbia's number-one soubrette, Rose Sydell, was not active as a performer after 1915, though her show, *London Belles,* starring her husband, W. S. Campbell, was a Wheel standby. Retired in 1919, she was reported living "in elegant style." She then became a suffragette and emerged from obscurity in 1931 to announce that "burlesque shows today are disgusting."

Her successor, Mollie Williams, also highly respected, was much saucier. She sported a French accent, indulged in occasional double entendre, and milked all the publicity she could get out of her supposed admiration for letter carriers. She was known for her "tra la" number delivered with flirty roving eyes. This number was followed inevitably by a parade up the aisles by the chorus girls passing out autographed photos of the star. Intimate in a snappy, wisecracking manner, ragging the chorines in pepper-pot rhythm to the perpetual delight of her audiences, Mollie Williams and her Mollie Williams Show grossed box office receipts exceeded only by Jean Bedini.

Jean Bedini remained the most consistently successful single male

Mollie Williams, Columbia's sauciest soubrette.
Culver Pictures, Inc.

attraction on the Wheel. He was rewarded with his own franchise, and when he prevailed upon some young unknown vaudevillians named Clark and McCullough to appear in his *Puss Puss* show, later renamed *Peek-A-Boo,* his career was at its zenith. Featured as a soubrette in his show was Pam Lawrence, the daughter of Millie De Leon. When the Columbia Wheel broke down, Jean Bedini practically did likewise. Shuttling back and forth between Mutual and stock burlesque shows, then vaudeville, and back to burlesque, the reigning star and producer of Columbia, the associate or discoverer of such talents as Eddie Cantor, Joe Cook, Ted Healey, George White, Clark and McCullough, rounded out his theatrical life as a bit player in the shabbiest of burlesque houses, a curious, anomalous interlude among the strippers and the coochers.

In a class by himself was the Irish comic Frank Finney, author of the book and star of the *Trocadero Burlesquers* and of his *Bostonians,* which co-featured Florence Mills. At his death in 1937, it was disclosed that this old-time trouper had one main ambition—to be a hotel clerk so that for once he could have a whole room to himself without having to pay for it.

Lena Daley, succeeding Mollie Williams, was the last of the Columbia soubrettes. She and her husband-manager, Ed E. Daley, made the transition from small-time vaudeville to the American Wheel, Columbia Wheel and finally Mutual. Not averse to cooching, and some stripping as well, Lena Daley and Her Candy Kids, Lena Daley as *Miss Tabasco,* Lena Daley in *Bare Facts*—all were familiar to two generations of burlesque fans. Her *Miss Tabasco* show of 1926 co-featured three stars of modern burlesque, Steve Mills, Billy (Bumps) Mack and straight man Lou Denny. Her last Columbia show, *Bare Facts,* starring comic Joe Yule, father of Mickey Rooney, was transferred intact to the Mutual Circuit with herself and her husband as franchise holders. Here she was not nearly as successful. Her belabored gyrations and self-conscious maneuvers could not compete with the uninhibited torso twisting of the brasher Mutual wenches.

Babe La Tour, the most versatile of the "I Don't Care" impersonators of Eva Tanguay, and a star of the *Bon Tons* show, typified popular soubrettes who flitted across the boards of every Columbia theatre from year to year—Leona Earl, Lydia Joszpy, Margie Catlin, Blanche Baird, Gladys Sears. With the passing of time, the buxom figure was replaced by marcel-waved, blonde, Dresden-doll silhouettes, exemplified by Mabel Reflow of the *Sporting Widows* and Laura Houston of *Frank Finney's Revue.*

Gertrude Hayes, the star of her husband Barney Gerard's *Follies of the Day,* was one of the few outstanding Columbia ingenues. The co-featured Dutch comic in that show, Sam Sidman, left burlesque in 1919 and later accused Bert Lahr of stealing his stuff.

Of the numerous racial, particularly "Hebe" comics, Charles J. Burkhardt, the Yankel Lashinsky of *Miss New York Junior,* and the Issy Cohen of *The Travelers,* also was the originator of a gliding gait across the stage, or a "slide." This became the stock in trade of other comics, the most prominent of whom was "Sliding" Billy Watson, rival of Billy "Beef Trust" Watson. There was even a lady "Hebe" comic, Sadie Banks. The most prominent of the later "Hebe" comics was Harry Steppe, who, ill and destitute in 1935, was the beneficiary of the Harry Steppe Fund, to which many famous stage personalities contributed. Practically all the racial comics transferred en masse from the Columbia Wheel to the Mutual Wheel.

A prominent husband and wife team that also transferred to Mutual was that of comedian Henry P. Dixon and Claire Devine. Henry P. Dixon, aggressive and talkative, a former director of the American Burlesque Association, was a better manager than comedian. He tried repeatedly to get out of burlesque with little success. Claire Devine, however, appeared as a burlesque queen in 1930 in the Broadway comedy *Stepping Sisters.* Their *Big Review Show* played both the Columbia and Mutual Wheels, and when they were too old to continue, they contributed their daughter to burlesque, Lillian Dixon, in her own "Big Review" show.

The ubiquitous Al Reeves headed a list of Columbia luminaries who became standard comics on the Mutual Wheel—Tommy "Bozo" Snyder, Sam Rice of "Sam Rice's Daffydills," Al K. Hall (Alcohol), Gus Fay, Billy Arlington, Clyde Bates, Manny King, Harry Seymour, among many others.

Almost as long as the list of the many standard performers who remained in buresque is that of those famous names in vaudeville and musical comedy who first appeared on the Columbia Wheel if only for one or two seasons.

The Watson Sisters, starring in musical comedy after appearing in Max Spiegel's Watson Sisters Company, were not related to any of the burlesque Watsons. Their father, William Watson, was the uncle of Mary Pickford. Primrose Seaman was co-featured in 1919 with George P. Murphy in Harry Hastings' *Wonder Show.* A year later she was in a Shubert musical. Blossom Seeley and Ethel Shutta repeated the same pattern, also set earlier by Fanny Brice and Sophie Tucker, of burlesque for a season or two and then musical comedy.

Lester Allen, a veteran of minstrel shows and of Joe Oppenheimer's *Fay Foster Show,* was a burlesque favorite for many years in the *Bon Tons* show before attaining Broadway stardom. Joe Cook, on the other hand, was in burlesque for but one season—the 1919 edition of Bedini's *Peek-A-Boo.* The trio of Bickle, Watson and Rothe popularized their skit "Me, Him and I" on the Columbia Wheel. This skit was later expanded into a musical comedy, and Bickle and Watson joined the *Ziegfeld Follies.*

Jay C. Flippen, of Lena Daley's show, and Willie Howard were in burlesque for two seasons before graduation. Bert Lahr attracted practically no attention in the 1922 production of *The Roseland Girls.* His triumph in a later show, James E. Cooper's *Keep Smiling,* brought him to Broadway. Hal Skelly started in burlesque appearing in the *Prize Winners* of 1914. Vic Casmore and Loney Hascall were other burlesque headliners before vaudeville claimed them. Herk's *Beauty Trust* show, which played the Columbia Wheel from 1918 to 1921, starred Jack Pearl and Harold Whalen. Jack Pearl deserted burlesque in 1921 for the Shuberts. He was immediately sued by Herk, who claimed breach of a four-year contract. Harold Whalen subsequently became a member of the well-known vaudeville team, Jans and Whalen.

Other numerous vaudeville and musical comedy teams associated at an early period in their careers with Columbia burlesque included Montgomery and Stone, Lewis and Dody, Gallagher and Shean, Val and Ernie Stanton, Lou Hilton and Dave Mallon and, of course, Clark and McCullough. Of these, Sam Lewis as Isador Kerensky and Sam Dody as Antonio Marconi in the *Hello America* show were the most conspicuous in burlesque.

There were also many male-female teams who achieved status outside of burlesque after their Columbia apprenticeship, including Midgie Miller and Bill Morrisey, George Niblo and Helen Spencer, George Stone and Etta Pillard, Russell and Morton (with Zella Morton playing the piano), etc. Even in the last fading years of Columbia, the Wheel came up with such talents as Ted Healey of *Cuddle Up,* Charles "Slim" Tiblin of *Talk of the Town,* James Barton and Gus Edwards.

The postwar shimmy exponents and sexpots, Gilda Grey, "Bee" Palmer and Ann Pennington, were never in burlesque. But eminent cooch artistes of a later day, Carrie Finnell, Hattie Beall, Lola Pierce, Nora Ford, La Villa Maye and similar others, all had their start under the chaste auspices of the Columbia Amusement Company.

The Columbia Wheel gave the world stellar performers even as it emasculated burlesque. But pruned and bowdlerized, the rough raw core of burlesque, encased by Columbia in a deceptive tinsel of pretentiousness and exploitation, finally was permitted to emerge, and waiting for it eagerly was Isidor H. Herk and his Mutual Wheel.

"I" (NAPOLEON) HERK

THE decline of Scribner meant the rise of Herk. In a field of generally mediocre talents and unimaginative operators, Isidor H. Herk was obviously superior to most.

A comparatively young man among the hierarchy of Columbia, Herk started in burlesque about 1906, when Scribner, Weber and Mack, with years of worldly experience behind them, were already shaping the nucleus of the Columbia Amusement Company. Just over twenty-one, Herk, whose theatrical experience had consisted almost entirely of a job as treasurer of the Valentine Theatre in Toledo, his home town, became the "Personal Representative" of Herman Fehr, a Chicago producer. This meant that he was the general man of all work, troubleshooter and "yes" man. His rise thereafter was rapid. He was soon recognized as one of the most promising young managers on the Empire Circuit with such shows as the *Jolly Grass Widows, Miss New York Junior* and the *Pacemakers*.

Herk was an unhappy combination of Scribner and Minsky. Even as he aped Scribner with edicts on "clean" burlesque, his *Pacemakers* show, for example, featured a strip poker session that was as daring as any on the Western Wheel. Unlike the other operators on that Wheel, however, who often ran their theatres like saloons, Herk, operating the Empire Theatre in Chicago, outfitted his ushers with fancy-dress uniforms.

A strict "Napoleon" to underlings, he possessed a talent for compromise and conciliation when beset by the usual rambunctious hostilities of circuit intrigue. Somehow, the compromises he effected were never to his disadvantage. Assiduously pulling strings on both sides, Herk was a motivating force in the merger of the Eastern and Western Wheels.

As a reward, he was admitted into the councils of Columbia—but, for all his ambition, he could never quite make the "inner circle" of the early Columbia oligarchy. As president of the American Burlesque Association, he did his work well. But he still represented the cheaper circuit, a reminder of the old Western Wheel to the Columbia executives, lounging in their exclusive palatial offices in the Columbia Theatre Building. All Herk yearned for, at the beginning, was admission to the intimate clique of Columbia confreres by an appointment as "Personal Representative" to Samuel Scribner. The moguls decreed, however, that he stay downstairs with the American Circuit.

He was perceptive enough to realize that burlesque, even as it prospered financially, was not getting anywhere as an important theatrical enterprise. He saw his judgment further vindicated when Columbia's string ran out, and it started to lose money.

At Columbia, he was always balked by Scribner. But, as top man of the Mutual Wheel, he was responsible mainly to himself, and he reveled in reorganizing the entire financial structure of leases and franchises, eliminating frills, and fancy production costs, finally succeeding in establishing a solid financial basis for the new circuit.

He geared his shows after the rough stock burlesque houses, but he had also learned his lesson well at Columbia. As his shows got dirtier, his slogans got cleaner. "Burlesque without a Blush," "The Working-Man's Musical Comedy," "Cleaner and Cleverer Shows," were some of his fantasies. And though he did not pay nearly as much attention to them as did Scribner, his publicized edicts were fully as sonorous and unequivocal:

> This is the last and final warning. If you cannot give an absolute burlesque show, full of low comedy and hokum, with pep, ginger and speed in your numbers, you don't belong on this wheel and I will tolerate you no further. . . . I will not permit for one day longer any filth in any show on this circuit.

In time, Herk, too, had his own sumptuous offices and subservient retinue, just as Scribner before him. He, too, had his own "General Representative" in the person of an enterprising youngster—just as Herk had been in 1906—Emmett R. Callahan, and his own Personal Press Representative, Charles Salisbury. He was elected a treasurer of the Friars. "How sweet it is!"

When he, too, was dethroned with the collapse of the Mutual Burlesque Association, he continued as a leading spokesman for the industry, heading the National Burlesque Association in 1933, in NRA Code negotiations, and generally popping up whenever an authoritative experienced negotiator was needed.

Why did a man of his talents remain in burlesque? The answer is that Herk did make two herculean efforts to get out of it. The first time ruined him financially. The second killed him.

In 1922, Herk, in company with other ambitious and dissatisfied burlesque operators, who felt frustrated at Columbia—namely, Max Spiegel, Barney Gerard, Jack Singer and Henry P. Dixon—organized a vaudeville unit to set the theatrical world afire and replenish their personal fortunes in a respectable field. Unfortunately, the complicated financial mechanism of this venture was connected with, and subject to, the machinations of the Shubert dynasty. The burlesque lambs soon discovered they were not dealing with a comparatively straightforward Scribner. They were now in a new world, with no quarter given. Plucked clean, Herk and all the others scurried back, penitent and much poorer, to the safe familiar portals of burlesque. It was just in time for Herk, as he applied himself to the new Mutual Wheel with a bitter and resourceful vengeance.

Then, in 1942, Herk again stepped out of his class as the producer of a lavish Broadway revue, *Wine, Women and Song,* presented at the Shubert's Ambassador Theatre. He fell afoul of a drastic censorship drive which was too much even for him, veteran of so many others. The show was closed down by the police. I. H. Herk, head of the second most powerful burlesque wheel in history, now almost sixty, a patriarch of the entertainment world, was arraigned before the court just like a third-string comic before a Wheel censorship board. He heard himself castigated, his whole life deplored as a moral menace and, finally, compared by the court to a procurer for a house of prostitution. Mae West had been given ten days imprisonment for a similar transgression. Herk was given a jail sentence of six months—the severest ever meted out for an offense of this nature. His lawyer pleaded that this elderly man had a heart condition, that imprisonment might kill him. He served three months. Three years later he died of heart failure, maybe of a little shame also.

But burlesque to Herk never was a symbol of sin or wickedness as such. He saw in it neither the adolescent glamour of fancy women, nor the riotous revelry of distended nude strumpets, but rather a cool, prosaic debit and credit ledger—and then conformed it to his own pattern.

JAZZ, SHIMMY AND MUTUAL

IN 1922, when the Mutual Burlesque Association was conceived, the Broadway musical arena had already attuned its productions to the pace of a giddy, jazzy, postwar binge. Its shows were all rapid in tempo, hot and nude, frivolous and irreverent. The legitimate stage was flooded with sex farces and so-called serious discussion pieces. The movies were preparing to glorify the flapper and the "It" of Clara Bow.

Only Columbia Burlesque remained aloof, methodically measuring the tights of the girls for their dutiful length, blue-penciling scripts and inhibiting the soubrettes.

A new wheel, with less pretentiousness and more vulgarity, could yield a greater profit with a small investment. The time was ripe, the combination irresistible. All it needed was an experienced show-wise promoter like Herk.

The original incorporators of the Mutual Burlesque Association were David Krause of the New York Olympic Theatre, Dr. George E. Lothrop, a physician who operated the Boston Howard Theatre playing American Wheel shows, and Al Singer of the Jacobs and Jermon offices representing Columbia. They capitalized the new circuit at $100,000.

None of these founders lasted. A year later Singer was replaced by Herk, as all Columbia connections were severed. Dr. Lothrop died shortly thereafter and was replaced by another physician, Dr. R. G. Tunison. A few years later Krause left the Wheel and burlesque when his Olympic Theatre was sold with the Tammany Hall Building, of which it was a part. Herk, as top executive, meanwhile surrounded himself with a group of hitherto obscure theatre owners and operators who had done little in the theatrical world except make money—Sam Raymond of the Star and Gayety Theatres in Brooklyn, Joe Catalano, Fred Black, S. W. Manheim, Charles Franklin.

Herk, with his talents for economy and administrative efficiency, wasted no time. At the outset, Mutual abandoned the Columbia system of leasing franchises to independent producers. Instead, the shows were sold outright to the theatres in which they played. The Wheel provided minimum production effects, scant scenery and a weekly payroll that did not exceed $1,200 for the entire cast. Chorus girls got $25 a week for their arduous and indecorous labors. Scenery and costumes were geared to a maximum outlay of $100 weekly. If the individual theatre owner preferred a more lavish production, or a higher salaried performer, he paid the difference himself. A few years later, these bare minimums were adjusted upward, and bonuses given in special instances, but as *Variety* commented in 1929:

> In the very nature of a Mutual Wheel burlesque show, a good performance is precluded. No Mutual manager or producer receives a sufficient income from his Mutual Wheel route to produce even a good burlesque show.

Though they did not produce "good burlesque shows," Mutual operators often grossed $7,000 to $8,000 weekly for twelve shows. This left a highly profitable balance, and producers flocked to the new Gold Coast. Herk was much more flexible than Scribner had been, and with a modicum of capital, let alone talent, a new show could be launched on the new circuit with comparative ease. The Mutual Burlesque Association developed into a highly successful enterprise. In 1925, its executive offices were moved to a lavishly appointed suite, just a block or so away from the Columbia Wheel offices, with all the accoutrements of the latter.

By 1929, the number of theatres playing Mutual productions was increased from an original low of twenty-one with sixteen shows to a high of fifty houses. By then, Mutual's roster of Columbia producers included Hurtig and Seamon, Al Reeves, Ed Rush, Ed Daley, John G. Jermon and Billy (Beef Trust) Watson.

With progress, there were even four censoring "doctors," headed by Jean Bedini. Their functions were described by one of them, James Morrison, as follows:

> I inserted 22 musical songs, scenes and suites, injected 47 scenes, reconstructed 8 shows, and made innumerable slighting corrections in dialog, wardrobe, stage business and several cast changes, all of which were backed unreservedly by Mr. Herk.

Once the Mutual Wheel was stabilized with a sound financial setup, the rest was easy. Talent and originality were not only costly but completely unimportant. The keynote to all Mutual shows was being sung and danced everywhere. It was the popular refrain of a jazz hungry public: "Everybody Shimmies Now." And Mutual operators saw to it that everybody who wore tights in their shows shimmied like the coochers of the old "turkey" shows, but in unison and on a runway.

Charles Salisbury, Mutual's Fred McCloy, expressed it with tongue in cheek: "The policy of the MBA is to study what the public wants and then give it," and "Mutual Burlesque is the jazz of American amusement. So keep the shows full of rhythm and joy, but keep them clean and wholesome."

The result was a frenzy of congregate cooching such as had never before been presented on a public stage. The chorus girls on the runway, yelling, shimmying directly at and over the men, the music blatant, jangling and dissonant, the audience alternately hooting or derisively encouraging—it was a demoniacal, orgiastic spectacle. Hands upraised to a merciful heaven, the girls would sprawl out on the runway, twist, writhe, squirm and shake, each to her own inventive, obscene devices. They were led by a soubrette, not nearly as ugly, but usually fatter and nuder, who after exhorting her charges to better their efforts, proceeded to exceed them all in her own bodily convulsions, paying particular attention, as befitted her superior rank, to the toughs in the boxes, whom she beguiled with postures of unmistakable meaning. They shimmied off the runway into the wings, but kept coming back for encores, as long as the applause lasted.

"Some of the shows on the first time round were unspeakably filthy," said *The Billboard* in 1924.

In the postwar prosperity, it was next to impossible to corral even passable pretty chorines for this kind of work at Mutual salaries. At one point, even a female impersonator was hired to fill out the chorus line—often enough, a misshapen mass of odd and assorted sizes.

Fat, lean, scrawny, pockmarked, haggard and aged, fleshy thighs bulging from skin tights splashed with runway dirt, they lived on "Varicose Alley," the runway on which they dispassionately jiggled their breasts and compressed their buttocks. It was a fetid sight, harrowing and debasing, yet at times possessed of a haunting frenzy.

Jerri McCauley, star shimmy-shaker of the Mutual Wheel. *Culver Pictures, Inc.*

Variety called it "glorifying the shovel and the American cow."

The skits, now called bits, were there, too, with the comedians. Instead of the labored, if feeble, attempts at comedy which had characterized burlesque from the beginning, there was now, as a rule, the simplest, most elementary dialogue, liberally sprinkled with lavatory scribblings:

> "What's the difference between mashed potatoes and pea soup?"
>
> "I don't know the difference between mashed potatoes and pea soup. What is the difference between mashed potatoes and pea soup?"
>
> "The difference between mashed potatoes and pea soup is that you can mash potatoes but you can't . . ."

When this, after it was passed around the Wheel several times, failed to produce any more guffaws, the comic would turn an accusing finger at the straight man and yell, "You big stinkotch you!" This always brought down the house.

Such was the Mutual Wheel.

But Mutual's receipts kept going up, while those of Columbia kept going down.

So the Mutual Burlesque Association, like the Columbia Amusement Company, also had about seven good years, but when the ride was over, Mutual did not suffer and linger on, as had Columbia. It merely pocketed the profits and folded.

Mutual producers were no more imaginative than the old-line operators on the Western Wheel. The formula had been given them for immediate success, and performance after performance, season after season, the same routine was preserved. It was difficult for them to evolve even new designs for obscenity. In this they were easily surpassed by the stock burlesque promoters. After the first few wild sessions, the orgies would deteriorate to listless, formalized grinds. This became more pronounced, as the traveling troupes, under contract for a full season anyway, tired and underpaid, refused to go all out. Borrowing a leaf from stock, the more enterprising theatres had their own chorus lines and a house soubrette who worked as long as they met audience approval, livening up a lackadaisical wheel unit.

At the end of 1929, for the first time in the history of the Mutual Burlesque Association, there was a decline in gross receipts over the previous year. In 1930, there were only thirty-seven full-week stands for the Circuit. A general wage cut was immediately instituted, and

Herk proceeded to maneuver again with the economics of franchises and leases. All to no avail.

Columbia, with a clean reputation, had gone in for dirty shows when in extremis. Now Mutual, with a dirty reputation, went in for clean burlesque. This killed the Wheel completely. The operators, recognizing the greater popularity of their supplemental stock units, abandoned the Wheel entirely, and put all stock burlesque troupes into their theatres. The following year marked the end of any large Wheel in burlesque. "Burlesque today, if it is anything at all, is burlesque stock," said Elias Sugarman, editor of *The Billboard,* in March 1931. By then, the Wheel was right back where it started in 1922—with just sixteen shows.

The Mutual Wheel had come to the end of the runway. And there were no encores. In 1931, the Mutual Burlesque Association quietly folded. The performers, producers, manager and Herk himself eventually transferred to stock burlesque, just as Columbia's entourage had surrendered to Mutual.

The Mutual Circuit, in its ten years of existence, had for practical purposes obliterated all traces of the Columbia Wheel. Stock burlesque was merely a continuation, along independent and more sensational lines, of the policy laid down by Mutual—the policy of shake, augmented in time by the strip act.

MUTUAL'S HEADLINERS

THE comedians on the Mutual Wheel were not, as was so often the case in the Columbia Circuit, apprentices on the way to stardom. They were, in the main, hardy and experienced performers, competent and proficient at best, but devoid of any superior capabilities.

There were all types of comics. Mike Sachs and Fred Binder represented the low, leering group; Charles McNally, Mickey Markwood and his sandpaper voice, and Irving Selig, the janitor with the Lou Holtz broomstick, were tramp characters. There were still more "Hebe" and Dutch comics than any other—Harry (Hello Jake) Fields, Max Fields, Jack LaMont, Harry Stratton, Harry Bentley, Harry Levine, Billy Tanner, Gene Schuler—the list is endless. Since many Mutual theatres were located in Italian neighborhoods, there were a few Italian racial comics, the most enduring of whom was Bennie (Wop) Moore, who was Jewish. There were comedians with some additional talent, as Billy (Bumps) Mack, who was a dancer of sorts, and Charles "Red" Marshall, a ventriloquist. And there were the innumerable "eccentric" clowns—Steve Mills, Joe Forte, Bert Marks, Frank X. Silk. Many of these had been on the Columbia Wheel. Then, Mutual developed its own talent, who worked side by side with former Columbia names like Johnny Weber, Jack Reid, Billy Inman, Brad Sutton, etc.

There were not many who achieved stardom outside burlesque.

Abbott and Costello are the most prominent, but they were still in burlesque when Mutual gave way to stock, and did not attain outside recognition for many years thereafter. Joe Penner and his "Wanna Buy a Duck?" routine came to Mutual in 1923, and three years later, his show, the *Band Box Revue,* was singled out for a police raid. Joe Penner survived both the raid and the Mutual Wheel to become a national figure for a time on the radio and in other entertainment fields. Though never on the Columbia Wheel, he was, in his characterization, the prototype of the small, droll, chief comic of the *Mollie Williams Show,* Harry Evanson, who never struck it rich.

The average Mutual cast consisted of three comics, a straight man, and three principal women who were still called soubrettes. Occasionally, a male singer or a prima donna with a well-known name might be included.

The soubrettes of Mutual were far removed from the overdressed divas of Columbia. They were, as a rule, uninhibited viragos, expert in all the tricks of carnal provocation. When a Columbia soubrette wanted to be daring, as Ina Haywood, she appeared in spider-web tights, topped off with a feathered headdress.

Mutual's headliners were more blunt. Their costumes, such as they were, usually consisted of a semitransparent brassiere and short skin tights, open at the hip. The slit at the hips, permitting a view of bare thighs, was the added measure of nudity permitted a soubrette's costume, over that of the choriries. There was no stripping, as a rule. Generally, they left the stage as they came on it. Nudity was subordinated to the shimmy and all its variations.

Mildred Cozierre, a plump and lusty redhead, was billed as "The Blue Streak of Burlesque with a Million Dollar Personality." This meant that she was adept in practically shaking her voluminous breasts out of her sparse brassiere. Margie Pennetti, sired in the rough revelries of stock, was a frequent "Added Attraction" who roughed up a lacklustre show by sidling up to the men in the boxes, grinding hips and thighs directly in front of them. Some theatres, in fact, had three runways, one for the general audience, and two side ones for the boxes.

Carrie Finnell was "The Girl with the $100,000 Legs," in one of the top shows of the Circuit, *Laffin Thru.* A versatile cooch, she perfected her specialty of popping up her breasts, to the tune of "Pop Goes the Weasel," singly and in unison, by purely muscular action, with no strings attached. As she grew older and even fatter, this specialty was tolerated as a "comic" interlude in respectable theatres, long after Mutual was gone.

Carrie Finnell in typical garb of a Mutual Wheel soubrette.
Culver Pictures, Inc.

Peaches Strange, the "Sheba of Shimmy," tall, willowy and shivery, was one of the many "shimmy-shaking specialists." Peaches' act was frenetic and ceaseless, without any camouflage or chatter. Jerri McCauley, of Henry P. Dixon's *Big Review,* on the other hand, would converse with the boys while in the throes. Her specialty consisted of swinging her hips way out of line, suddenly stopping, and screaming "Get me out of this position, boys!" She concluded her performance by handing out photographs of herself, autographed by Nancy Carroll, the Hollywood star, to whom she professed a certain resemblance. Both she and another "jazz specialist," Chubby Drisdale of the *Red Hots* show, were particularly susceptible to police raids. Their usual defense was that they were simply engaging in "athletic exhibitions."

Gladys Clark would appear with the chorus line, in male clothing, resplendent in a waistcoat, cutaway, top hat and cane. She would start by applying the cane to the girls, as they turned their backs and wiggled. Then, she removed the trousers by ferociously tearing open the front buttons. Also affecting male attire, and dynamic in her own manner, was Kitty Warren who ran the entire gamut of burlesque from minstrel shows to the American, Columbia and Mutual Wheels.

Also shimmying across to Mutual from Columbia was Viola Elliott, formerly of Jack Reid's *Record Breakers,* now the "Little Venus" of the *French Models* show, in a very tight one-piece union suit. Isabelle Van and Sally Van came to Mutual from the Columbia runways. Dixie Mason, now co-starred with her husband, Harry (Hello Jake) Fields, in *Chick Chick,* was an understudy to Lena Daley. Sadie Banks also was on the Mutual Circuit. She claimed to have received her training from Thomashefsky, even before she was with Columbia. Vi Buckley, who had attracted some attention by her rendition of "How'd You Like to Be My Daddy?" in the American Wheel show *Village Belles,* was a star Mutual soubrette, as were Frances Farr, Lola Pierce and numerous others who had started on the Columbia Wheel.

Under Herk, star performers, who normally commanded higher salaries than the Wheel doled out, were sometimes given their own franchises and operated their own shows. These ranged from prima-donna Stella Morrissey to soubrette Kitty Madison, and at one time or another included such comics as Harry (Hello Jake) Fields, Max Fields, Mike Sachs, Joe Leavitt and Harry Steppe.

Kitty Madison and her own *Jazztime Revue* was one of the more lasting and popular of the shows. A racy New Yorker from the lower East Side, she advanced from the chorus ranks of a Dave Marion show to a soubrette's role in Columbia's *Hip, Hip, Hurray.* On the Mutual Wheel, she sang with appropriate wink, wiggle and gesture such classics as "I Ain't Giving Nothing Away" and "How Can I Get It?" In common with all Mutual heroines, she was a facile coocher, directing brisk "personality" bumps at the balcony denizens.

The Mutual Wheel, like Columbia, had very many husband and wife teams in the same show, as comedian and soubrette. One of the best was the Anna Toebe, Billy Hagan pair. Anna Toebe achieved fame, almost immortal, by combining her meaningful shake routines with the equivalent of a modern strip. She had served her apprenticeship with Joe Oppenheimer's *Broadway Belles* on the Columbia Circuit. Billy Hagan could claim to be the modern successor to Al B. Reeves as Mr. Burlesque. After a start in musical comedy as one of the Hagan Brothers, he was in burlesque all his life thereafter, continuing as a star comic in the twilight zone that followed the collapse of most of burlesque after 1937. A past master of timing, a veteran of veterans, he knew every vulgarism in the books, engagingly delivered with his "Cheese 'n Crackers" expletives.

Nite Life in Paris, another moneymaker, starred Charles (Tramp) McNally and his wife, the redheaded La Villa Maye, whose specialty was a tortuous slow-motion grind. Vinnie Phillips, a former Columbia soubrette, and now a grandmother, contributed two bombastic daughters to Mutual and stock, Buster and Ritzie Phillips. Buster's specialty consisted in running furiously from one end of the stage to the other without rhyme or reason. She then explained to the audience that she had to go to extremes to get attention because she had very small breasts, as all could see: "Peanuts," she would explain, pointing to them disparagingly. She eventually wound up in scratch burlesque at the Bowery. More fortunate was Nora Ford, who became a star by bumping and grinding vigorously while her dress was lifted over her head.

The hottest coochers were proud of their vaudeville and musical accomplishments. As often as not, their songs were typically Mutual. Fay Norman would shriek:

> My name is Fay and I got class
> I shake my shoulders and I shake my—Yeah!

In 1924, Fay Norman's husband committed suicide, reportedly because his wife refused to leave burlesque. Margie Pennetti, in quieter moments, vocalized in Italian, with songs both ribald and sentimental. Her favorites were "O Sole Mio" and "Where You Worka, John?" Gladys Clark did a jig with the ancient comic, Pat White, and also played the clarinet. Lola Pierce, who learned to play the violin while with Columbia, played it on Mutual runways. At the conclusion of a soft lullaby, she would turn round, slap her buttocks resoundingly and shake them vigorously.

Since they were still soubrettes, not strippers, they considered themselves actresses and took their roles in the occasional dramatic bits quite seriously. As mothers pleading for their son who faced the electric chair, as penitent prostitutes with hearts of gold, etc., they hugged their prop shawls closely and held forth at great length to the total sublimation of their sexual selves.

In the last few years of the Mutual Wheel, younger and more shapely leading women became known, presaging the beginning of the strip era. Among the better known strippers of a later day who started in Mutual were Georgia Sothern, Evelyn Meyers, Zonya and Betty Duval, Frances Parks, Peggy Reynolds, the Foreman Sisters and Lillian Murray, to mention but a few.

At the same time, two ambitious young men, flanking Herk on either side, supplanted older operators in Mutual's Brain Trust. These two were Emmett R. Callahan and Rube Bernstein. Emmett Callahan had started as a performer in vaudeville and burlesque in an act that included his brother and Midgie Miller. He soon discovered that his forte was really behind the scenes, not doing them. After managing the Gingham Girls for Mutual, he advanced to the full rank of Special Representative of the Mutual Burlesque Association.

Rube Bernstein, a former baseball official, was the producer of the *Bathing Beauties* show on both the American and Columbia Wheels. In 1922, he created a minor sensation by presenting at a Harlem theatre one of the first burlesque shows ever presented to an all-Negro audience. He could never see eye to eye with Scribner, but on the Mutual Wheel, he got along so well with Herk that he was advanced to "Pesonal Representative" of the Mutual Burlesque Association.

In addition to these administrative functions, Callahan and Bernstein united to produce their own show on the Wheel, the profitable *Follies of Pleasure*. Their prestige was such that Callahan and Bernstein were elected president and vice president, respectively, of the Burlesque Club, Callahan remaining president for over ten years.

Two unusually young and pretty girls were brought to their attention. They stood out from the rest of the fat and fading soubrettes, just as Callahan and Bernstein were superior to the average unimaginative burlesque operator. One was Ann Corio, then known or unknown variously as Anna Coria and Ann Coreo, a second-string principal in *Girls of the U.S.A.*, starring Margie Bartel, the "Shimmy Sensation." The other was Hinda Wassau, playing second fiddle to Kitty Madison in her *Jazztime Revue*.

These girls were too attractive for Mutual. Ann Corio, in fact, was already about to join Earl Carroll's *Sketch Book* revue. Callahan and Bernstein also toyed with the possibility of producing their own musical comedy, but they stuck to burlesque, first taking the precaution of binding the girls to burlesque with long contracts.

Thereupon, they concocted two of the most successful and well-balanced shows on the Wheel, offsetting the young soubrette star in each with a gruff, tough, tramp comic. Thus were evolved Ann Corio and her *Girls in Blue,* featuring Clyde Bates, and Hinda Wassau and her *Hindu Belles,* featuring Hap Freyer.

Under the expert exploitation of their two sponsors, these slim and supple belles appeared as guests of honor at innumerable banquets, conventions and clambakes, and evoked so many newspaper and magazine essays about their really ethereal yearnings that the two girls jumped into print almost as often as they leaped upon the runway. Disdaining the unseemly cooch antics of their competitors, they were the forerunners of the new breed of strippers who were now about to envelop all of burlesque.

With the end of the Mutual Wheel, Callahan and Bernstein were in and out of burlesque, occasionally working as company managers for legitimate productions on Broadway and the road. Ann Corio and Hinda Wassau joined the stock burlesque parade of striptease and then strip-please, duly taking their places among the foremost exponents of that art, no matter how nude it later became. But it is only just to report and somewhat to emphasize, that as a respectable aftermath to a rowdy and smutty circuit, Emmett R. Callahan duly married Ann Corio and Rube Bernstein similarly obliged for Hinda Wassau.

STOCK "BURLESK"

"THIS is stock burlesque, strippers and tossers, hip weavers and breast bouncers—this is stock burlesque." Thus cried out Sime Silverman in 1931 when stock burlesque engulfed the Wheel shows. Sime Silverman saw in stock burlesque with its smaller investments and irresponsible producers the most formidable threat to any possibility of clean entertainment.

With the rise of the Circuits, the smaller owners, who were excluded from the combines, could hope to compete with the Wheel shows only by making their own exhibits rowdier and rougher. The stock promoter was in a perpetual dilemma. Unless his show was smutty enough, he could not survive. On the other hand, vigorous police action, as often as not, helpfully thrust upon him by the influential Wheel politicos, could also put him out of business. As a result, those stock burlesque theatres that were able to gain a foothold and gradually develop into substantial enterprises were usually those who had powerful connections of their own.

Of the few early reputable stock promoters, Joe Oppenheimer was acclaimed in 1914 as the "recognized king of stock burlesque producers." Many of these stock shows were played in Wheel houses during the regular summer layoff. When Frank Gersten introduced stock burlesque at the Prospect Theatre in the Bronx in 1914, *The Billboard* announced that he had "established a record as the first man to show stock burlesque in the regular season."

Rough and ready stock burlesque was introduced in New York City at Daly's Theatre in 1915 by Jerome Rosenberg and Benjamin A. Lavine. The theatre was raided at once. But the door was opened, and sporadic stock ventures were begun at the Folly Theatre in Brooklyn, near the Gayety Theatre, and at Kessler's Roof Garden.

But the center of burlesque sin in New York City was in the Union Square area, in the vicinity of Tammany Hall, where Jerome Rosenberg's later venture, the 14th Street Theatre, and Ben F. Kahn's Union Square Theatre competed with the Olympic presenting American Wheel shows. And a short distance away, the Minskys were experimenting with stock burlesque at the National Winter Garden.

The 14th Street Theatre and Jerome Rosenberg did not last, but Ben F. Kahn and his Union Square Theatre flourished with shows that were frankly salacious for the times—without apology and without pretense. Reviewing a performance at the Union Square Theatre in 1918, Sime Silverman wrote:

> To those who recall the Western Wheel Shows, the worst of them, and they were so bad when they were in the worst class, it may be said that the poorest of the Western Wheelers, as a performance, never held as little as the present Union Square stock show does or did in that first part.

He did not remain to see the second part.

The same theatre provoked this stentorian blast from reporter Jack Lait in 1920:

> Out in Chicago in the old days of Whiskey Row, the Haymarket District and Hinky Dee's levee, smoky burle-ques ballyhooted their live bait for the dimes of sailors on a spree and castle rustlers smelling of fertilizer. But never in the glad days when the West stood for murder and grinned at jackrolling, did the bleary eyes of the soggy suckers in the submerged sections see such free and easy sights as this week's carnival of censorless ginger at the hallowed old hall of New York's grandest theatrical tradition. . . .
>
> It made a purist sigh for the hootchy-kootchy of a generation back as Quakerish prudery.

Notwithstanding, or perhaps because of, such "censorless ginger," stock burlesque theatres, once they were established, prospered and thrived on a par with the wheels. The Kahn and the nearby Minsky houses, located in lowly immigrant slums, were tolerated with an easy rationalization. "After all—look at the neighborhood!" Lait pierced this supercilious condescension with one querulous complaint: "Why should the East Side get so much more than any other side?"

Ben F. Kahn died in 1922, leaving as the wages of sin an estate estimated at $70,000. He had no heirs, and the Union Square Theatre gave up burlesque, leaving the field to the Minskys.

Outside New York City, the most consistently successful stock promotors were Warren B. Irons and Arthur Clamage, operating the Haymarket Theatre in Chicago and the Avenue Theatre in Detroit. Originally circus showmen, they were conspicuous on the American and Columbia Circuits as directors and franchise holders. Rather than join Mutual, they concentrated on stock productions, and have continued to remain in the forefront of Midwest burlesque producers long after the end of stock burlesque in the East. In 1940, Arthur Clamage graciously gave Herbert K. Minsky a job in his organization as a general supervisor of production. Other enduring stock producers included Hon Nichols at the Baltimore Gayety Theatre and Issy Hirst who began humbly as the owner of two decrepit houses in Philadelphia, the Bijou and the Troc, and expanded his operations, eventually to head his own burlesque circuit in recent years. On the West Coast, the Dalton Brothers, former concessionaires in a Texas Fair, dominated stock burlesque with their Follies Theatre in Los Angeles.

It was comparatively simple to open up a stock burlesque troupe, and with the decline of the Wheels they mushroomed everywhere, in the manner of the old "turkey" shows. Most of them were just as temporary. One of the most notorious and typical, and enduring longer than most, was the Chelsea Theatre in New York City which opened for business in 1926 with a brash flourish. It featured four women principals, three comics, a straight man, character man and seventeen chorines. Two of the comics were Columbia veterans, Billy (Grogan) Spencer and Harry Seymour. The third was a graduate of tabloid shows, Lew Rose, who went by the name of Izzy Pickle. Breathing defiance with its very first performance, the Chelsea company boldly presented without any frills four posed models, stripped to the waist. The Chelsea Theatre was one house where a buzzer tipped off the cast that a censor was in the audience—an ancient device that in this case did not seem to diminish the regularity of the raids.

By 1927, standard Wheel theatres, including the Hurtig & Seamon Theatre on 125th Street, joined the stock parade headed by the Minsky houses, the National Winter Garden and the 125th Street Apollo.

The most ambitious of the stock undertakings was the opening in

1929 of the American Theatre on 42nd Street in the heart of New York's theatrical district.

This venture in the glare of Times Square was begun by Joe Hurtig and continued to its unsuccessful close by Herk. It featured Irving Selig, a comic good and dirty, Ann Corio for a time, and later, another favorite of the burlesque cognoscenti, Lillian Murray, a young lady of massive buttocks and udder-like breasts, who stripped with a serene and thoroughly emotionless placidity. No less than Jean Bedini was stage director. But there was none of the bizarre showmanship that marked the opening of Billy Minsky's Republic Theatre on the same street a few years later. Apparently, the central location of the theatre awed the producers. The shows were timid and routine, despite their obvious attractions, and in a short time 42nd Street found itself again without a burlesque house.

With the depression in 1930, stock burlesque approached its zenith. Up to that time, many stock theatres just managed to survive as shoestring or scratch troupes, and if they did last, they did so only by exceeding their nearest competitor in salaciousness. Chicago particularly abounded in such houses. Respectable women hardly ever ventured into the State-Congress Theatre on the underworld side of State Street. Its formula was simple: "Shake It Up!" The National Theatre on the same street was known as a "lodging house for bums." It gave its dazed customers two feature movies, a two-reel comedy, and a burlesque show with a cast of nine—all for fifteen cents. Detroit had six fiercely competitive stock houses, each dirtier than the other.

With the coming together of stock burlesque and the depression, the theatres veered away from the traditional two-a-day policy in favor of grind burlesque. After the Empire Theatre in Brooklyn had paved the way with a three-a-day show policy, the City Theatre, open for a short time on 14th Street, inaugurated what turned out to be the normal grind routine in most of the houses. This alternated four burlesque shows a day with movies. The theatre was open from noon to almost midnight, presenting continuous performances without letup except for intermissions. In effect, the theatres were not too far removed in pattern from the wretched National scratch house in Chicago. Not only could homeless vagrants park in the theatre interminably, but the performers also spent practically the entire day in the theatre, seven days a week, with an additional midnight show on Saturday.

Typical of stock burlesque were comedians Joe (Souse) Rose and Lew Rose. Joe Rose was an aggressive talker who topped his leering efforts with a white wig. Producer as well as comic, he could usually be discovered opening a new scratch burlesque venture whenever he

Early Mae Dix, "a ringletted red-haired, flirty-eyed gingery soubret."
Culver Pictures, Inc.

was out of an engagement. Lew Rose dispensed "Izzy Pickle" humor. However, oddly enough, he possessed some authentic talent. He did not shout for effect, like so many others, nor did he belabor a point too strenuously. His slight voice had a crackling whining irony that in its own small way was pure comedy. He was a favorite on the tabloid burlesque circuit which devastated local neighborhoods for a time. He teamed up in tabloid shows with a three-hundred-pound comic, Tiny Fuller, and Chick Hunter, a straight man who had been on the Columbia Wheel. Tiny Fuller and Chick Hunter advanced to regular burlesque. Izzy Pickle vanished into the anonymous indecencies of the scratch houses.

Three uninhibited beldames of stock, to burlesque born, were Hattie Beall, Margie Pennetti and Mae Dix. With Joe (Souse) Rose, they were all novitiates at Kahn's Union Square Theatre. The shimmying of the blond Hattie Beall as she took an electric treatment that supposedly revitalized her—a routine bit—had evoked Jack Lait's vigorous comments on the proceedings at that theatre. As they all grew older and more experienced, they took their places with the accomplished coochers of the Mutual Wheel.

Mae Dix, shapely, and voluptuously rounded, excited the interest of Jack Lait when he saw her at the Union Square Theatre in 1920: "This Dix bimbo is a dangerous woman . . . a sassy girl with red hair and a tippy nose and a figure—more than a figure—a physique." And *The Billboard* commented:

> . . . a ringleted, red-haired, flirty-eyed, gingery soubret with a pleasing plump form shimmied continuously and what she could and probably would have done with an Oriental number can be easily imagined.

After some stints on the Columbia Wheel (*Broadway Flappers*) and Mutual (*Mae Dix and Her Dancing Fools*), she struck out in 1925 for the libidinous pastures of Chicago stock. Before long, she found an agreeable haven at the State-Congress Theatre. Here, her costume consisted of papier mâché cherries between her legs. She plucked the cherries one by one, tossing them with appropriate vocal and cooch accompaniment to an appreciative audience.

Thus, stock burlesque with such as Mae Dix and Izzy Pickle pursued its sinful course, until it overtook the big Wheels.

"Stock burlesque is a racket," complained Elias Sugarman of *The Billboard*.

"Stock burlesque is the killer of all burlesque in the United States," snarled Sime Silverman.

But, if so, it was a prophecy scarcely heeded by the prosperous stock promoters headed by some lower East Side upstarts who brought the industry to a new level wherein the word "burlesque" was synonymous with the name "Minsky."

THE MINSKYS, THE NATIONAL WINTER GARDEN, THE APOLLO

THERE were four brothers Minsky, but only one Billy Minsky—the showman. Abe, the eldest, with the conservatism of the firstborn, presented on his own, after Billy's death, a pragmatic succession of completely nude women in surefire inexpensive productions that, somehow, miraculously, he managed to make tedious rather than exciting. The younger brothers, Herbert K. and Morton, could never reconcile the dill pickle rowdyism of burlesque with their highflown college degrees. As a result, when they were on their own, they usually made a mess of things.

Their father, Louis, was a member of the Board of Aldermen of New York City. And he started the boys off by acquiring the National Winter Garden Theatre on East Houston Street, in conjunction with his lawyer, a rising young attorney, Max D. Steuer. Louis Minsky had apparently bought a lemon, because he found himself unable to rent the theatre. As a last resort, he turned it over to his two elder sons to do with as will. And they did plenty.

At first, the National Winter Garden, located in a literal 1913 ghetto, tried movies, vaudeville, movies and vaudeville together, stock burlesque, Wheel burlesque, and finally stock burlesque before the correct formula was discovered. Billy, who had been, strange as it may seem, a society reporter, trifled briefly with Jerome Rosenberg and his 14th Street stock troupe. But he returned almost immediately to the ancestral castle on East Houston Street and 2nd Avenue and, as the guiding genius of the tribe, eventually set the pace for all stock burlesque in the country.

At first, even burlesque circles turned their noses down at the "greasers" and worse who reputedly frequented the National Winter Garden in its early days. The soft seductive lights in the theatre and its oriental color schemes attracted, it was claimed, "would-be sporty boys and girls . . . ever yawning smokers of hop and the dreadful degenerates."

When Abe and Billy Minsky made the mistake in 1918 of leaving stock for the milder American Wheel shows, there was an immediate drop in attendance. Alfred Nelson, commentator for *The Billboard,* friend and adviser of the Minskys, consoled them:

> Business would have been better . . . had the managers ignored rules and regulations (which we are glad to say they did not do) and given the National Winter Garden songs and dances well seasoned with ginger, the kind that appeals to the animalism in people who have not as yet been educated to appreciate clean burlesque.

However, the Minskys were not out to give education. They immediately reverted to raucous stock and, with financial success, attained some prestige just the same. Several years later, Nelson acclaimed: "There was a noticeable change in the clientele since the days the American Circuit played down there to dopes and degenerates."

Regardless of what they thought uptown, Billy Minsky emphasized neighborhood camaraderie and good fellowship. "Our patrons know each and every performer by their first names," he boasted.

These early performers were known, evidently, only to their customers. Most of them started here as apprentices, but in a very short time could be called hardened apprentices. The *All-American Beauties* show presented as its contribution to the American theatre the following cast of characters in 1918:

Issy Hockalovitch	Jack Shargel
Miss Staken	Lillian Franklin
Miss Dearly Love	Ethel De Veaux
Miss Justa Flirt	Sedal Bennett

Ethel De Veaux and Lillian Franklin became standard burlesque performers. Jack Shargel and Sedal Bennett were considered "eccentrics." Sedal Bennett left the National Winter Garden as the self-styled "Jewish Vampire" in vaudeville. Then she had herself ordained as the "Champion Wrestler of the World." She returned to burlesque briefly, this time as "The Princess of Pep." In 1936 she climaxed her theatrical hoboism by blossoming forth as Sedal Bennett Mills, carnival lecturer, and author of a dissertation entitled, "I Wasn't Born Yesterday," which nobody could deny.

These principals were surrounded by a large chorus of as many as thirty girls singing "in a manner that could be heard all over the house" and representing "many varied types of femininity." They had other attributes as well. In 1919, fully twelve of the girls were arrested for "cooching."

With affluence, hastened by such raids, and coinciding with the return to the clan of Herbert K., just back from the AEF after the World War I armistice, the National Winter Garden was renovated to the publicized amount of $10,000. Billy Minsky served notice that he was just as good as any other burlesque operator, and had Alfred Nelson get him elected to membership in the Burlesque Club. Billy Minsky then sent in to *The Billboard* a weekly letter of supposed criticism signed by the "Komedy Kid Kutie," which was never known to be derogatory of anything in a National Winter Garden performance.

The Minskys met the challenge of scarce chorines by offering salaries as high as thirty dollars weekly. The more brazen, and therefore the shakers most in demand, were featured—Carrie Finnell, Hattie Beall, Margie Pennetti, Mildred Cozierre, Mae Dix. Of course, the National Winter Garden had a runway, and as tough as the Mutual shows got, the National Winter Garden, which had shown the way, could always go them one better.

Emboldened by his continuing good fortune, Billy Minsky, in 1922, made the first costly mistake of his career. It was the only one of its kind. He opened up a clean burlesque theatre.

Possibly that "ole dabbil," respectability, that inevitably assails every successful burlesque producer had by this time penetrated the Minsky hide. Or perhaps the Minskys themselves were victims of the conceit that only on the lower East Side would audiences flock to see dirty shows. At any rate, they opened the Park, also known as the Cosmopolitan, Theatre on Columbus Circle.

Everything was attempted in this grandiose venture—except East Side burlesque. There was vaudeville, musical comedy and the kind of burlesque that is called "superior burlesque." And it was a flop from beginning to end. Within a few months, prices, which had been optimistically scaled down from a $1.65 top, were reduced to a $1.00 maximum. There was so much pure vaudeville that even the billing "burlesque" was dropped in a frantic effort to save face. But that just about doomed the project entirely. Not even the presence of comedian Tom Howard, the best that stock could offer, was of any avail. In February 1923, the Park Theatre closed at an estimated loss of $50,000.

The only one to gain was Tom Howard, who was signed in the fall of the same year for a leading part in the *Greenwich Village Follies,* for which treasonable abandonment he was sued by the Minskys.

Billy returned to dirty shows and the National Winter Garden, and as insurance signed up Hattie Beall, for one, for the coming season. Hattie was married to Billy Curtis, a stagehand, and was not only a wife but a mother as well. Nevertheless, when it came to bumping with energy and abandon directly at the boys in the balcony and in the boxes, there were few more adept. Also featured was a Mme. Cleo, one of many Mme. Cleos and Fifis who were engaged as super added attractions in stock theatres. They appeared in brief and carnal specialties that outmaneuvered the normal shimmy contortions of the regular soubrettes, just as the stock house soubrettes in a Wheel house exceeded the ribaldries of the regular Wheel principals.

Mme. Cleo was arrested in September 1923, because of both the nature of her dance and the scantiness of her costume. Arraigned with her was Walter (Schultz the Butcher) Brown, the small and excitable comic who fell into a fit of wolfish delirium tremens every time a soubrette accosted his vision during a scene. The manager of the theatre, Nick Elliott, alleged spite work, claiming, as usual, that conditions were as bad and worse in the uptown revues. Magistrate Louis D. Brodsky dismissed the charges, observing, "The standard of morals is no higher on the East Side than at Broadway and 42nd Street." This indeed was progress. A judicial declaration had been obtained to the effect that the ethics of the lower East Side were not distinguishable from those of Times Square.

By 1925, there was practically no limit to the size of a Minsky cast, with well-placed emphasis on the feminine contingent. Comedians Joe (Souse) Rose, Billy (Scratch) Wallace, gravel-voiced tramp clown, and Harry Seymour shared honors with no less than nine leading women—a preview of the days of the strip parade.

Such triumph deserved expansion and duplication. The end of 1924 saw an even rowdier counterpart of the National Winter Garden in Harlem with the opening of the Apollo Theatre. Billy Minsky personally took charge. Without any Park Theatre high jinks, but with undiluted National Winter Garden tactics, the Apollo exceeded the lower East Side house with phallic prop symbols and Cleos and Fifis who provoked a police raid with the very first performance.

Since Billy Minsky was occupied at the Apollo, the routine details at the National Winter Garden were handled by Tom Bundy, who was straight man, character actor and stage director, with Rose Gordon organizing the dance ensembles, and Mother Elm, the publicized wardrobe mistress, purportedly drawing an imaginary line between the male and female dressing rooms. Not only did Tom Bundy prepare the scenes and act all over the place, but his wife was a star soubrette, and one of the first strippers at the theatre.

A pert and refreshing young redhead, she was first known as Edna De Lillis. She then left for the West, and returned as Edna Dee, the "Redheaded Sunshine Girl." As the Sunshine Girl, she sang demurely and prancd about rather innocuously until the very end of her number, when she turned around, lifting her dress up, as she bent over, to reveal a narrow strip of colored ribbon setting off her bare buttocks, which she compressed to musical rhythm—an innovation that may have been producer hubby's idea.

In 1927, a particularly nasty raid at the National Winter Garden saw the house manager and eleven of the cast taken into custody. Those arrested included Chubby Drisdale, Mary Walton, a blonde doll-like runway leader, Billy (Scratch) Wallace, Joe Devlin, a plump, glib straight man, and Ray Paine, character actor. The publicity was so bad that Billy Minsky himself and in person had to take charge. Not that he could be easily spared from the Apollo. Just then, it was engaged in a three-cornered dogfight with Hurtig & Seamon's Music Hall and the Alhambra, which had recently intruded on 125th Street with Mutual shows. The competition was fierce, and all the theatres smuggled hundreds of cut-rate passes into the nearby colleges.

However, an indictment had just been secured against Mae West and her play *Sex,* and reform was in the air. Some immediate action was necessary. Billy Minsky returned to the National Winter Garden which, of course, he announced, might have gone beyond bounds only because he was not there. He waited out the storm and, when nobody was looking, emerged from the Court of Special Sessions with a verdict of "Not Guilty," and then placidly returned to the Apollo.

In 1928, the ancient Hurtig & Seamon Music Hall was taken over by Billy Minsky and the Apollo. The Alhambra had already given up with its Wheel shows. Commemorating his supremacy, Billy Minsky put tuxedos on his box-office men and raised prices to $1.65 top. The shows were quite lavish, with as many as eighteen principals, ten of whom were women. The house also permitted itself the luxury of a prima donna, Katharine Irwin, who neither stripped nor shook, and a clean Negro comedian, Eddie "Coffee" Green. Alternating their principals in their two houses, the Minskys could guarantee them long engagements, a very important advantage for stock burlesque performers.

The Apollo, in contrast to practically all Wheel and stock houses, including the National Winter Garden, went in for a great deal of audience mixing. Before the show even started, the chorus girls were often directed to stand in the rear of the orchestra floor, in their scant costumes, for more intensive and unhurried ogling by the early customers. During the performance, they frequently jumped off the runway, circulating among the aisles, and then jumped back on, shimmying most of the time. The soubrettes, arrayed in costumes of miscellaneous erotic interest from skin tights to loosely drawn men's BVD's, ran around from one side of the orchestra floor to the other, and then to the boxes, while for the benefit of those who could not be reached by the circulating girls, another group of chorines performed on the stage in pajamas and nightgowns.

Minnie Fitzgerald, a youthful appearing "cutie pie" from the Star and Garter in Chicago, was imported to the Apollo for a very long engagement. She was a specialist in baby costumes, and dressed, or rather undressed, as an infant, sat on the laps of customers, crooning hoarsely, mussing up their hair and imprinting the inevitable scarlet kiss on shiny bald heads.

The National Winter Garden and the Apollo combined long engagements with a wage scale that would reach a high of $175 for a top performer. Walter Brown, who had been on the Columbia Wheel, was now "Schultz the Butcher" with the "longest salami in town." He was an Apollo fixture. Mae Dix starred regularly at both theatres. Though actual nudity was not widespread as yet, she would come out in a bit with comic Shorty McAllister devoid of all clothing except for a handkerchief wrapped around her middle, which, in "bits of business" with the comic, would disappear and reappear in a feast of sexual legerdemain. She was often given the chore of announcing the next week's luscious attractions, after which she invited all and sundry to see her after the show with any suggestions they might have. "I'll do anything at all for you," she winked, adding after the guffaws, "within reason."

Favorite long-term comics were Steve Mills, who sported outlandish costumes and props and still does to this day, and the two Bobbys, Bobby Nugent and Bobby Wilson. Bobby Nugent, heavy-set tramp type, was entitled to some distinction by virtue of his experience on the Columbia Wheel, in the *Golden Crook* with Eve Sully. Bobby Wilson was strictly stock. Pint-sized, his chief stock in trade was a cheerless, toothless, leering grin that seemed as big as he was.

By 1930, as Billy Minsky concentrated on grandiose schemes of burlesque on Broadway, the National Winter Garden and the Apollo started their decline. At the National Winter Garden, where there had always been a certain beguiling primitive, elementary rawness, Herbert K. and the youngest brother, Morton, as directing geniuses, were now prone to interpose fancy ballet numbers among the cooch specialties, and moral tracts like "The Straight and Narrow" among the dirty bits and the pickles dipped in sauerkraut. In the old days there had been rowdy special nights, Chorus Girls Nite, Oriental Nite, Shimmy Nite, and the like. At the Apollo there had been a Dance Nite with the patrons dancing onstage with the chorus girls. Now, there was instead Country Store Nite or a fake amateur program.

To make matters worse for the National Winter Garden, the once despised lower East Side had by now outgrown burlesque. The older generation was too religious. The middle generation had become important and affluent and had moved away. The new youngsters were too smart and knowing to find much pleasure in the barren inadequacies of a burlesque show. Most of the patronage now came from other localities, often from other cities, curiosity and sensation seekers, to whom the National Winter Garden still represented a bawdy shrine. There were also a few uninitiated adolescents to whom the prospect of riding up in an elevator to reach the orchestra floor—another distinguishing mark of this theatre—heightened their illusion and hopes that they were sneaking into some kind of disorderly house. But these aspiring groups felt let down with the counterfeit atmosphere of art that was the bane of the lesser Minskys.

There were still in attendance a few cuddly shakers. Steve Mills occasionally brightened the proceedings with his running description, from the runway, of an artist's studio complete with model and couch, but the special Billy Minsky touch of startling and unvarnished vulgarity was conspicuously missing. Finally, the Irving Place Theatre, practically within walking distance, was attracting the more worldly. The arena of burlesque had shifted from the shake, which was the forte of Mutual and the National Winter Garden, to the strip, which was the specialty of the Irving Place Theatre.

In the same year, 1931, that Billy Minsky opened the Republic Theatre on 42nd Street, Billy, Herbert Kay, and Morton relinquished the National Winter Garden. Abe Minsky, who for some time had severed himself from the hectic activities of his juniors, then tried to operate the theatre on his own. When he failed, Mike Sachs assumed the burden, only to find an injunction facing him, forbidding his use of the hallowed National Winter Garden name. Sachs, always the comedian, then asserted that he had merely rented the theatre and was not producing its shows. There were still other attempts to keep the ancient landmark going. It did not matter one way or another. Less than a year after the opening of the Republic, and two months after the last of the Minskys had walked out, the National Winter Garden closed its doors—in January 1932.

At the Apollo, too, there had been a noticeable slackening, a lapse in the customary meticulousness of vulgar detail. Katharine Irwin, the prima donna, sang and sang and sang, finally to be followed not by a Mme. Fifi, but by a pretentious ballet, "Madame Butterfly," employing a full stage of "Oriental Splendor." Or else, there was a "futuristic" sequence, "The Story of Love," which unbelievably featured ponderous male commentators in tuxedos.

The Harlem house was given a temporary transfusion by rotating its shows with those of the lusty Republic. But Billy Minsky (age 41) and the National Winter Garden and the Apollo all died in 1932. The National Winter Garden became a Yiddish theatre and a fraternal lodge hall. The Apollo was converted into a Negro vaudeville theatre. Nobody knows about Billy Minsky.

The Minsky name became the property of outsider Joseph Weinstock, a shrewd, aggressive building and theatre contractor, who had been Billy Minsky's financial "angel" and partner in the opening of the Apollo and the Republic. Weinstock had once been retained by Herk, futilely, as it turned out, as an "efficiency expert" for the declining Mutual Wheel. He was much more successful in the operation of the Apollo, which had been a bonanza for himself and Billy Minsky.

Their collaboration on the bombastic Republic operation was equally lucrative. It was begun on Lincoln's Birthday in 1931, with the customary Minsky ballyhoo. Unlike the Park Theatre fiasco, there were no apologies for burlesque and little vaudeville. There was, instead, with the opening performance, a chorus indignantly described by shocked observers as "nude coochers." Skillfully managed and publicized, the Republic brought the customers in daily and nightly to a packed house, started the burlesque gold rush on Broadway and changed the entire perspective of the entertainment, hitherto content to remain hidden in remote secluded haunts.

The depression that afflicted the burlesque industry before 1932 was lifted by the depression that overcame the rest of the country. Pretty girls were now available to burlesque wages. Their names, in a profitable publicity barrage, were presented before the public no less relentlessly than their bodies. A dying profession was transformed into a household topic. Burlesque became big business again. And it did business now, not in alleyways, but on Broadway.

Eventually, burlesque got so much publicity that it was ruined by it. And it all traced back to the day when Michael William Minsky took over his father's National Winter Garden and, going the Columbia Wheel 100 percent better, made even dirty burlesque respectable.

STRIPTEASE TO STRIP-PLEASE

THE strip act is as old as burlesque itself, and it is just about all that is left of burlesque today.

Its appeal lies not only in the piquant suggestiveness of a female undressing knowingly while men are watching, but in the gestures, winks and cooch movements—the modus operandi—that are essentially a part of it. In this, all shades of opinion converge to agreement. *Variety* expressed it thusly: "Any dame can walk around a stage taking off a piece at a time. That's no tease, that's merely going-to-bed exercises." The academic thesis of probation officer David Dressler, "Burlesque as a Social Phenomenon," pointed out: "The burlesque-goer is titillated not by nudity alone, but by the salaciousness accompanying it." The police, in a formal complaint against the Star and Oxford Theatres in Brooklyn, put it this way:

> The defendants . . . "while dancing also made alluring and seducing motions to the spectators of the theatre, tending to the corruption of the morals of the spectators." Also, they . . . "sang songs and walked up and down the stage and danced in the course of which they did remove their clothing until they were completely nude with the exception of a narrow strip of gauze and while so nude did contort their bodies in such ways as would tend to corrupt the morals of youths and others."

Burlesque has always featured soubrettes and chorines who uncovered themselves to the limit the law would permit, whether in tights, union suits or fleshings. When stock burlesque followed the lead of the Broadway revues, nudity came into being.

The lady minstrels disrobed as they swung over the heads of the male oglers. The "turkey" shows and barnstorming troupes continued the trend, but even in the classier shows of the 1880s and 1890s stripping was not uncommon. Truly Shattuck, who somehow managed to be both plump and shapely in that hefty era, advertised in the *New York Clipper* that she was "prepared to accept engagements for an entirely distinctive specialty in which is introduced an instantaneous change from full costume to tights, making one of the most beautiful specialties now before the public."

In the Eastern and Western Circuits, stripping persisted not only in the Salome versions of the Dance of the Seven Veils, but in the prize exhibits of both wheels. The 1911 edition of *London Belles* with Rose Sydell, W. S. Campbell and Johnny Weber had three girls stripping in unison in a bathhouse, behind a transparent curtain. T. W. Dinkin's *High School Girls* show was written and staged by Leon Errol. Sandwiched between two acts called "The Dude Pig" and "Get Trimmed Quick Rube," as presented at Miner's Eighth Avenue Theatre in 1912, Dainty Marie popularized the idea of presenting her cast-off clothing to a presumably panting audience:

> Appearing first in a charming lingerie dress, Miss Marie sings and dances. During the last chorus, she commences to undress and as each last article of clothing is taken off, it is distributed among the audience. Everything goes except the outside dress. Stripping down to champagne-colored tights, the back of the waist cut extremely low to show an exceptionally well developed back, the act goes into full stage, showing rings and a handsome velvet drop. . . . Working in a spot all the time the curves and development are the more easily seen and appreciated by the audience.

There was plenty of striptease. In the *Yankee Doodle Girls,* the star, Etta Victoria

> . . . with a slow undressing process interests the audience with a few contortions until she strips to tights when the interest wanes. . . . At one time it seemed as though Miss Victoria would make a sensational exposure and the excitement was high.

Sime Silverman plaintively observed that in the *Dreamland Burlesquers*

Truly Shattuck, called "the handsomest woman possessing the best voice and most perfect figure" in burlesque in 1898. *Culver Pictures, Inc.*

Virgie Royden "is always suggesting a great deal but showing very little."

The cheaper shows and finale dancers were more provocative. And there were always the compulsive strippers, like Millie De Leon, as described by the *St. Louis Globe-Democrat* in 1915:

> First Miss De Leon comes on wearing a much beruffled gown and carrying a parasol. As the spotlight strikes her, away goes the parasol and off come the ruffles, a row at a time, until she stands before the audience clothed in drapery.

She then jumped into the aisles and kissed various males until "she has left the imprint of her vermillion lips on the forehead of a dozen or more. Then oblivion."

Stock burlesque was always more receptive to the strip act. The early Prospect Theatre, featuring a vaudeville headliner, Simone De Beryl, in its stock burlesque show, the *Froliques of 1915,* was admonished by an irate reviewer that "burlesque is not in need of the uncovering stunt that Simone De Beryl introduces as the piece de resistance . . ."

The strippers' song in modern burlesque was "Clap Your Hands and I'll Take Off a Little Bit More," a strategem which restored applause to burlesque houses. But the Columbia Wheel came up with its own version in 1919, in Max Spiegel's *Cheer Up America,* billed as a "patriotic revue." Here, according to *The Billboard*:

> Edna Maze who is Divine Form, the model, sang an apparently original song "I Take Off a Little Bit," and, while doing so, discarded her outer garments until finally she stood revealed in black lace trunks, covering silken tights that gave a pleasing view of her symmetrical form.

The same song reappeared in the American Wheel show, *Round the Town.* Following Marie Elmer's ditty, "My Father Is My Dad, but My Daddy Is Not My Father," Vinnie Phillips, described as "a refined ingenue," scored a hit "leading the girls in 'Clap Your Hands' which the Olympics did until the entire ensemble stood revealed in union suits that displayed their slender symmetrical forms surmounted by pretty faces."

The Mutual Wheel shied away from actual nudity, but shimmying was occasionally accompanied by sleight-of-hand fingering of brassieres, and the customary tights slit open at the hips were sometimes replaced by large newspapers they would teasingly tear to shreds, ostrich plumes, Mexican hats, fans and barrels. The authorities tolerated cooching, but nudity was likely to bring the police. Joe Penner's

Band Box Revue was raided in 1926 because its soubrette, Eve Bradford, "took from her person her dress, garters, hose and chemise, leaving parts of her body exposed to public view."

In the last years of Mutual, the younger and shapelier soubrettes, led by Ann Corio and Hinda Wassau, abandoned the riotous cooching of the shimmy-shakers for "sophisticated" squirming to the strains of sweet, languorous music, all the time unfastening hooks and buttons. Ann Corio, in the *Kuddling Kuties* show, was dubbed by *Variety* as "Mutual's champ stripper and brassiere manipulator." Hinda Wassau, coyly inquiring if her audience would like "seeing a little more of me," was not yet called a stripteaser. Instead, she was still a soubrette with "sex-teasing seductiveness." The others followed suit with their own improvisations and refinements. Zonya Duval, for example, in *Girls from the Follies,* wore "a transparent veil covering her entire body and gets applause by the subtle expedient of opening it, one clasp at a time, stopping each time to ask the boys for their approval."

From Ann Corio and Hinda Wassau, it was but a step to nudity above the waist for principal women while in motion, and when Mutual folded, stock burlesque carried on. Striptease became strip-please.

In imitation of Broadway revues, burlesque shows had, from 1925 on, presented girls, nude from the waist up, in a tableau setting, stationary and supposedly in an aura of "art." In burlesque houses, this artistic atmosphere was not easy to obtain. When the Chelsea Theatre opened with four "art models" stripped to the waist, *The Billboard* candidly called the scene "an ordinarily realistic description of nondescript flabby flesh." There was also a specialty strip act, as befitted stock burlesque: "Emily Clark, after singing a popular number in a blue dress, stopped traffic by removing her shoulder straps and indicating she might go the route if the applause warranted. It did but she called it a day." This was in 1926, when it was still "striptease." To make up for the lack, however, Emily Clark joined the chorus girls in the aisles and urged the boys to "get acquainted."

The next step in the furtherance of the art was achieved by the pioneering strip house, the Irving Place Theatre. Here, the chorus girls were permitted to parade while exposed, holding transparent slips of chiffon where a brassiere usually rested. When lightning did not strike the theatre down at this breach of the decencies, the Irving Place trailblazers proceeded to the next phase. They had each chorine leave the line for a solo spotlight, slowly and portentiously lift the flimsy strip of silk covering her bare breasts, stand thus for a few seconds, and then solemnly retreat to her place in line as the next girl repeated the rite. Still no heavenly recriminations. In a short time, the Irving Place

Hinda Wassau, a soubrette with "sex-teasing seductiveness."
Culver Pictures, Inc.

Theatre had the girls prancing up and down the runway with nothing on above or below, except for a G-string. The other houses quickly followed, and soon it was standard to have two chorus lines—one for dancing, and another for stripping.

While the New York theatres were setting the pace for the rest of the country with nudity for chorus girls, the West Coast, led by Dalton's Follies and Burbank Theatres in Los Angeles, was doing the same with its women principals. They were no longer soubrettes, they were strippers. They exhibited nudity in action.

Evelyn Meyers, ace houri of the West, showed the Eastern sisterhood how it was done, where she came from. Making her debut at the Harlem Apollo, she concealed her bare bosom behind a backdrop. Then, after jangling her brassiere defiantly in midair, slowly parted the curtain, until, finally and with measured casual effect, she thumb-flipped a rouged nipple to the audience side of the footlights.

By 1932, practically all leading women in burlesque, except for an occasional singing or "talking" principal, bared their breasts as they cooched. As it all had evolved gradually, step by step, the final denouement did not seem too startling.

The police were lenient and accommodating. The professional censors complained that the managers had been given a leg, and now took the entire body. But public opinion, at this stage, was not with them. *The Billboard's* Nelson stated the case for burlesque: "With the advent of short skirts on the street, leg shows lost their sex appeal, and, in self-defense, the operators of burlesque shows introduced the strutting strips, spotlighted parades of slender, symmetrical personalities, as far as the police permitted."

As the depression deepened, more and more girls turned to burlesque for a living, and the more competitive it got, the more they stripped. They found spiritual kinship with the new customers, who, unemployed, whiled away the long hours in the grind burlesque houses. Experience was not needed. And the industry was swamped with new pretty girls who, in turn, kept attracting new audiences. Burlesque thrived while the rest of the country, and particularly all other entertainment fields, was at its lowest ebb. According to *Variety,* in 1936: ". . . burlesque remains unique in that, among the various branches of show business, it has the lowest rate of unemployment at the present time. No competent burlesque actors are out of jobs, and the demand for even 2nd rate talent is considerably in excess of the supply." The strip act had enriched the industry.

By 1932, there were at least 150 strip principals in burlesque, of whom about 75 percent were new to the industry. And of this 75 percent, practically all were without any experience in show business.

The censors made it worse for themselves by prescribing explicit rules and regulations of undress and behavior. This resulted merely in sanctioning what was not expressly prohibited. By defining the length of time a girl could undress on a public stage, the reformers condoned, by inference, the actual stripping itself. If the limitations were disregarded, the theatres were, at worst, subject to a police raid, which was something the operators had patiently borne for more than fifty years.

In 1934, there was a publicized raid on the Irving Place Theatre. The ensuing storm was finally cleared to everybody's satisfaction by the abolition of the runways in New York City, and eventually in most other theartes.

The producers themselves had grown weary of the runway. It had more than served its purpose in the raucous days of "Varicose Alley." Now it was a nuisance. It did not lend itself to the dim lights, sentimental music and illusory flourishes that were the background of the strip act. The stock in trade of many headliners was the pretense of just, just revealing all—and the familiarity of the runway rendered such deception much more difficult, and actual revealment too daring. It was, in fact, a choice between the "shake" of Mutual and the "strip" of stock, and the operators, prodded by the censors, chose the latter. Herk stated discreetly, for public consumption: ". . . they had outlasted their usefulness as entertainment features. They had their day and they're done; that's why they came out."

And out they came. In their stead, it was expressed, with the usual ludicrous hopes and promises, there would evolve "a higher form of the burlesque art."

With the elimination of the runway, there was nothing left for female principals to do but to strip, and this they proceeded to do with unanimous diligence and conscientiousness. A tenor sang offstage of Mother Machree, and a luscious lady undulated on the stage proper, bare from the waist up, and wriggling from the waist down. Each show had a minimum of five or six strippers and, as a rule, but two comics and a straight man for the shortened bits.

At this point, some strippers felt that life was grossly unfair to their talents. These were girls who were more fully endowed below than above. As matters stood, they might never achieve the status symbol of successful a stripper—feature stories about her "art" of the striptease, her sensitive inner aspirations, her excellence as a cook. Indeed, they were fortunate if they could just hold on to their jobs.

One day one of them, Anna Smith, a minimum wage stripper, with a strapping derriere, but minute breasts, lowered her elastic tights and rolled them down below her hips as she withdrew to the oblivion of the stage exit. This drew tremendous applause and more encores than had been considered possible. The appreciation for this additional vouchsafement was heartfelt. As if moved by a common humanitarian impulse, all the strippers in the same theatre, then in the same city, and soon throughout all the burlesque houses, started to do the same thing.

A striptease would, after the first encore, slither back on the stage sans brassiere. But this was now routine. All eyes were concentrated below. And soon, trunks, tights and panties were lowered and then completely discarded in favor of a narrow ribbon or band, crystal beads, rhinestone strings or G-string. To this, too, there were many individual cute variations. Mae Brown, the "Dresden Doll," for instance, would roll down her tights and have the orchestra leader poke his baton just where the back ended, and the top inch of where the tights should have been began to descend into two plump areas of provocation.

So popular was the strip act that it caught on not only in all of burlesque, but in nightclubs, Broadway shows, cabarets, carnivals and what was left of vaudeville. In 1935, thirty-five out of thirty-eight vaudeville units in operation in the East had one such dancer. As for burlesque, Joe Bigelow of *Variety* claimed in 1936, "The routine remained 99 percent strip with the other one percent just there to pad out the running time."

Much as many in and out of burlesque deplored the new "art," the burlesque operators could not stop even if they wanted to. There was no answer to the fact that without stripping there were no audiences, and hence no money for the venerable comics who looked askance at the new trend which chose to all but ignore them. As *Variety* plainly stated:

> With stripping still the basis of all burlesque layouts, business was best when conditions and the attitude of the authorities permitted more stripping. When there was no stripping, there was no business, and usually no burlesque. A few stouthearted gents attempted to buck the dry spots anyway with "clean" shows, but they didn't last.

Inevitably, the humble strip became futuristic, baroque, pretentious and trashy. When, in July 1936, Leon and Eddie's nightclub held a striptease contest, *Variety* commented with appropriate satire on the trend in the "danse moderne" wherein the "deadpan" and languid walk act gave way to "tormentedly-young, stark white-faced, red gash-of-a-mouth style."

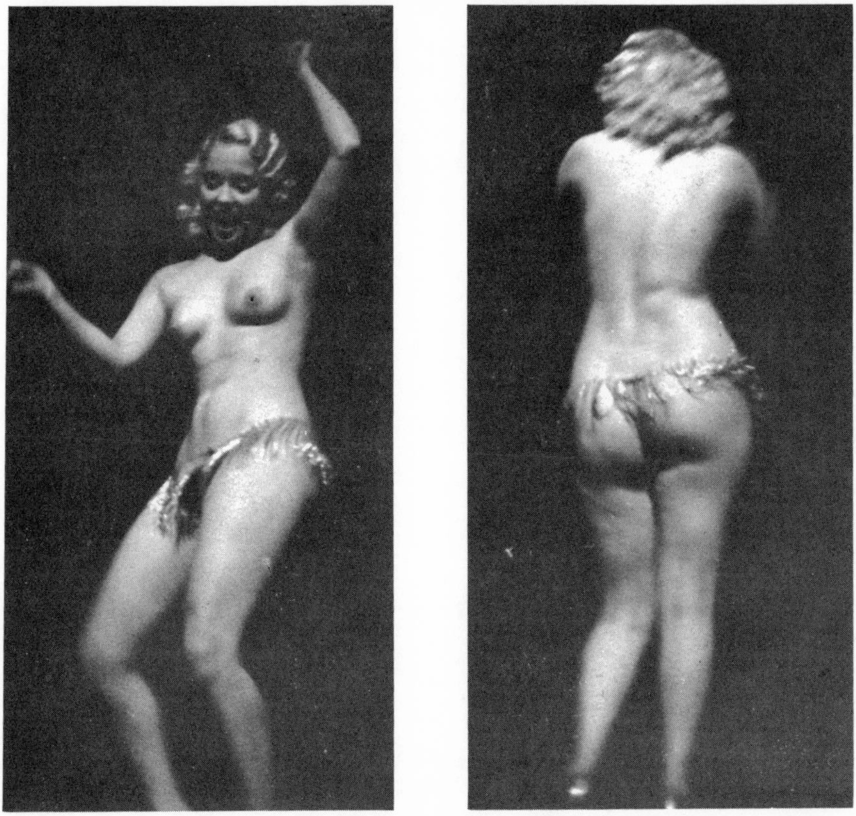

Striptease becomes strip-please. *Culver Pictures, Inc.*

Inevitably, too, in some benighted regions the ultimate of the strip act was attained. The G-string also came off! In most theatres in New York City, this decisive affront to the decencies and License Commissioner Paul Moss did not occur. But in one or two houses, here and there in every large city, there would be nothing between the lady and the tiger audience but a dainty well-manicured set of hands, and when the damsel, coyly, in the spotlight waved her hands to nobody in particular and darted for the wings, she resembled during this final and most gratifying phase of the strip era nothing so much as, in Tennyson's phrase, "a bearded meteor trailing light."

THE STRIPPERS

To become a star, a stripper had to possess certain attributes in addition to the obvious minimal qualifications. She might be graced with an exceptionally pretty face and fine figure, as with Ann Corio, or be particularly adept in startling extremes of undress, as per Margie Hart, or be gifted with a knack for purring innuendo and singsong double entendre, as in the case of Gypsy Rose Lee. But there were, undoubtedly, scores of other girls in the business, unknown and unheralded—minimum wage strippers—who were as ravishing as Ann Corio, could divest themselves of every last particle of raiment as artfully as Margie Hart and could be as wistfully provocative as Gypsy Rose Lee. The difference was largely due to exploitation and publicity.

Ann Corio

Ann Corio was dreamy-eyed, languorous, inspiring. Unfortunately, it is one of the ironies of life that such ethereal personalities can be runway exhibitionists. Still, when this delightful young creature was thrown in, unceremoniously, among the embattled viragos of the Mutual Wheel, neither Ann Corio nor anybody else thought much about it, at first.

She led a typical soubrette's life, a training in stock burlesque, a hunt for engagements as the second or third female lead in a Wheel show, a struggle to make both ends meet at the conclusion of the Wheel season. She was just another soubrette in *Sugar Babies,* a show as simple as its title, and in another typical Mutual masterpiece, *Girls of the U.S.A*. Even after Emmett R. Callahan publicized her attractions and she was recognized as "probably the prettiest girl in burlesque," her big show, *Ann Corio and Her Girls in Blue,* was not outstanding. One critic snapped: "In *Girls in Blue,* the girls are blue in dress and the comics bluer in talk."

It was unseemly for one so precious to shake on the runway. Still, this was burlesque, and Mutual burlesque at that. Ann Corio could not remain in her gown, expensive as it was advertised to be, and keep the customers inside her theatres, pretty as she was known to be. So, a compromise was effected. Mutual's star did strip—from a skirt and a purple spangled top to abbreviated shorts and a mesh brassiere—but only as an integral accompaniment to Indian folk lore. Her act was not a strip, but a sorrowful saga depicting:

> An Indian maiden, watching by a waterfall, dreaming of her lover, hears him in the distance, as he sings along the trail. She follows the sound of his voice and sees him just as he is shot by a rival brave from ambush. In a wild frenzied dance of vengeance she hunts the woods for the escaped assassin, finally to return, sobbing, to the waterfall.

A year later, after she was featured as the runway leader at the New York Columbia Theatre, she progressed, in 1930, to nothing less than a heavenly body:

> . . . in which Ann Corio gave an artistic interpretation and portrayal of her own conception of an angel in gorgeous raiment, that discarded, revealed her slender symmetrical form a la natural as an optical feast of delight to her ever-increasing army of admirers.

This was all so dignified and high class, that she announced her three-year-old nephew would play the violin during her act.

Her earnings rose from $150 to $200 weekly (fifty-two weeks of the year) to $375 weekly at the Irving Place Theatre at the height of the depression. When she was prominent enough to demand a share of the box-office receipts, she enjoyed a weekly stipend of $1,500.

In common with all other strippers, once it became fashionable, Ann Corio had to disrobe, but otherwise she continued to be triumphantly circumspect. It was a miracle of successful ballyhoo that despite the excesses of her competitors, she was still considered the ace attraction in her field. No other stripper could show so little, and do so little, and even survive.

After censorship closed all the theatres in New York, Ann Corio's favorite number was "Mr. Strip Tease Is Dead—I Would If I Could, But I Can't." However, even when Ann Corio could, she never did.

Gypsy Rose Lee

Gypsy Rose Lee, teaser with a wink, instead of a leer, mellifluous crooner of scurrilous lyrics, sophisticate, author and television personality, was as obviously superior in intelligence to the rest of the flock as Ann Corio had been in looks to the Mutual wenches. As a result, she was a publicist's dream, surpassing even Ann Corio in that extracurricular activity. *Variety* remarked that "Miss Lee has received more free space in two months than the rest of the burlesque business, including everybody in it, usually gets in two years." Indeed, she could claim with some justice, as she did, that she made burlesque famous, rather than vice versa.

After a childhood of trouping in small-time vaudeville with her mother and sister, as fully narrated in the book and play *Gypsy,* she was driven by the depression to burlesque. For a short time she was under contract to Ed Ryan. Ryan's claim to fame hitherto had been a $1,000 bonus awarded him by Mutual for having the best show on the Wheel—*Girls from the Follies.* She advanced quickly enough in the business to be spared most of the indignities endured for many years by less distinguished strippers. No comedian spouted forth the contents of a seltzer bottle onto her waiting and outstretched buttocks; she never sat on any stage toilet seat during a bit and gurgled lines about going to Flushing and having stock in Consolidated Gas and American Can.

As a star of the class burlesque houses in the East, the Republic, the Irving Place and the 42nd Street Apollo, she did not even have to strip unnecessarily. She was a "teaser," a remarkable feat, considering that teasing was as outdated as the runway. As Burns Mantle put it: "Miss Lee was very careful not to take off more than she has on."

Her costumes were suggestive and seductive, rather than the flowery, pseudo-virginal frocks assumed by the less imaginative. Black silk stockings, lace panties, red garters, mesh nettings were her tools of the trade. Not nearly as innocent or as trashily arty as Ann Corio, she did manage to get arrested, on one occasion, with the entire cast of the Republic Theatre, though it seemed from the newspaper accounts that Gypsy Rose Lee, and nobody else, was affected. And to achieve precedence in publicity over Billy Minsky, she had to be good.

She could turn this unpleasantness, like others, to her own final ad-

"Gypsy." *Gary Wagner, Pictorial Parade, Inc.*

vantage. When her mother brought suit in 1941 against her two successful daughters, Louise Havoc (Gypsy Rose Lee) and June Havoc for nonsupport, Gypsy Rose Lee made it seem as jovial as one of her pseudo-strip numbers. According to the New York *Sunday News,* "Gypsy roars with laughter about the time her mother sued in New York for support from her daughter. It never got to court." The whole affair was a joke. "Every once in a while, she puts on a good act for us, especially when one of us is in the chips."

In like manner, new to burlesque, she transmuted her alien feeling to its tense, hot atmosphere into a mocking, spoofing jest. She discarded the pins on her trick costumes, one by one, each with the aplomb of a historic event. Where other principals were frightened to death at the thought of speaking in words of more than two syllables, she, in her expertise, loftily let her erudite, insinuating stanzas trail off into a purple nothingness. After four or five minutes, she condescended to disrobe more intimately. And from all the hocus-pocus and mumbo-jumbo of occult promise there emerged a flash of breast and a bare hipbone, as, chortling, she sidled off to the wings. She was a big hit. Her minimum price for her simpering tease, after success, was $1,000 a week.

She was featured in Ziegfeld shows, Billy Rose nightclub revues, Hollywood, and in fairs and carnivals all over the country. Of all the gigantic affairs for Bundles for Britain, few were remembered as vividly as the one in which Gypsy Rose Lee auctioned off her star-spangled costume, star by star. She emerged from the rut and smut of burlesque with sufficient distinction to rub bare shoulders with the most prominent and notable personages of the day. She divorced her husband, Robert Mizzy, a dental supply manufacturer, wrote a best-seller, *The G-String Murder,* and gives the impression that she is not averse to a turn on the boards even now, as celebrated and venerable as she is.

Not much worse could be said of the depression than that in it someone like Gypsy Rose Lee had to resort to burlesque for a livelihood.

Margie Hart

More orthodox, more in conformance with burlesque tradition, was the third-ranking stripteuse of burlesque, redheaded Margie Hart. Margie Hart was born in a small Missouri town, of a rather poor and overcrowded family. The year—on or about 1916. A runaway from home before she was sixteen, she found another home on the runway. A school dropout, she gave a highly liberal education of her own to innumerable male proselytes. From chorus girl in a Chicago burlesque house, she migrated to the Garrick Theatre in St. Louis, operated by Bill Pickins, and after balancing some books on her head to gain poise, was promoted to a solo stripper. Following some tolerable success here and there, she was brought to New York, where she first became widely known. Credit for this glorious discovery is attributed both to Nat Mortan, a burlesque booker who claims he spotted her at the Bijou, Philadelphia, and to Allen Gilbert, show producer at the Irving Place, her first port of call in New York.

At any rate, she was an ordinary run-of-the-mill principal during her early days at the Irving Place Theatre, in a routine act devoid of surprise or personality, embellished by a perpetual, vacuous, almost frightened smile. As this theatre, enjoying an immunity to outside interference not generally shared by other houses, became more emboldened, Margie Hart, outstripping any of the other prolific and accomplished peelers at the Irving Place Theatre, seemed to show the patrons more than they had ever expected to see on a public platform.

Margie Hart popularized the type of trick dress that eventually became standard with all the advanced practitioners of the art. This consisted, in its penultimate stages, of narrow strips of silk hung from the waist down the front and back, with the sides bare—in practical effect, a dress tied around the hips, with the sides cut out. This costume permitted exposure by merely and intermittently flicking the protective slips of chiffon fore and aft with a casual twist of the fingers. As it did not call for actual removal of the dress, though this might also come in time, this routine had its obvious advantages. For the staring men, it meant that they did not have to wait until the very last moment, the split-second flash, to be vouchsafed a glimpse of whatever was in store for them. Their interest was riveted throughout the entire act, as the play of fingers along the edges of the narrow strips of dress made every second of the routine meaningful. For the performer, it added a certain degree of subtlety, and since the dress could be worn throughout and still permit revealment, a censor could not detect and prove charges of indecency.

This manner of delivery was appreciably enhanced by the simple and gratifying fact that, as often as she could, Margie Hart obligingly performed without a discernible G-string beneath her dress. Hence, the experienced burlesque-goer—and this type constituted the brunt of Margie Hart's public, as contrasted to the tourist trade attracted by Ann Corio and Gypsy Rose Lee—followed with avid concentration every slight movement of the fingers toying with the folds of the trick gown, every sudden twist of the wrist, for, who knows—after all, as acclaimed by *Variety*, was she not the "most daring" of all the strippers?

The newcomer at the Irving Place might see Margie Hart parading around with bare bosom, as the accepted procedure, before coming down to the G-string. But he would be unable to understand, at first, the hush of expectancy that accompanied her seemingly ordinary routine. He probably would feel somewhat disappointed, for she did not, as a general rule, cooch or sing dirty songs or pretend to be arty or kiss baldheads. All she apparently did was slink from one side of the stage to the other. But then he might notice that all eyes were fixed not above the waistline at what was openly and commonly exposed, but several degrees south, where our coy heroine was indifferently, with sly and becoming insouciance, brushing away the slips of taffeta which remained between the audience and her inmost self.

Through the skillful manipulation of the labyrinthian recesses of her costume, she seemed to grant a glimpse every now and then of what her audiences were always yearning to see—or else a reasonable facsimile thereof.

Though her IQ could not compare to that of Gypsy Rose Lee, nor her publicity image to Ann Corio's, she was quite proficient in her own simple, direct way at getting her name and her picture in the newspapers. When the Irving Place Theatre was at long last raided with an alarming thoroughness, she was abashed not one whit. In the very courthouse itself, where she and the others were arraigned, in an anteroom adjoining the honorable judge's chambers, she stripped to the waist for the benefit of the photographers. She then returned to the bar of justice triumphant and self-satisfied, as she calmly adjusted her shoulder straps. Her picture would be in the papers. Regardless of the court's decision, she had already won the day.

After this coup, there was no stopping her. Press agents were hired and fired. Walter Winchell dubbed her "the poor man's Garbo," and she rapidly became known as a leading stripper in the East.

At the conclusion of an extremely prosperous season in 1934, climaxing two steady years at the Irving Place, Margie Hart had her nose, which had contained just a suggestion of a hook, straightened out, since with the spotlight of the press as well as the stage upon her, any slight imperfection was unduly magnified. As the newspaper notices multiplied, the small-town burlesque girl became acquainted with the literati, who also found solace in her company. She lost her half-frightened air, acquired a personality, talked to the boys in the front rows during her turn by way of showing her sophisticated unconcern, cooched a little and even sang, somewhat in the manner of Gypsy Rose Lee.

The two-year lucrative engagement at the Irving Place Theatre was

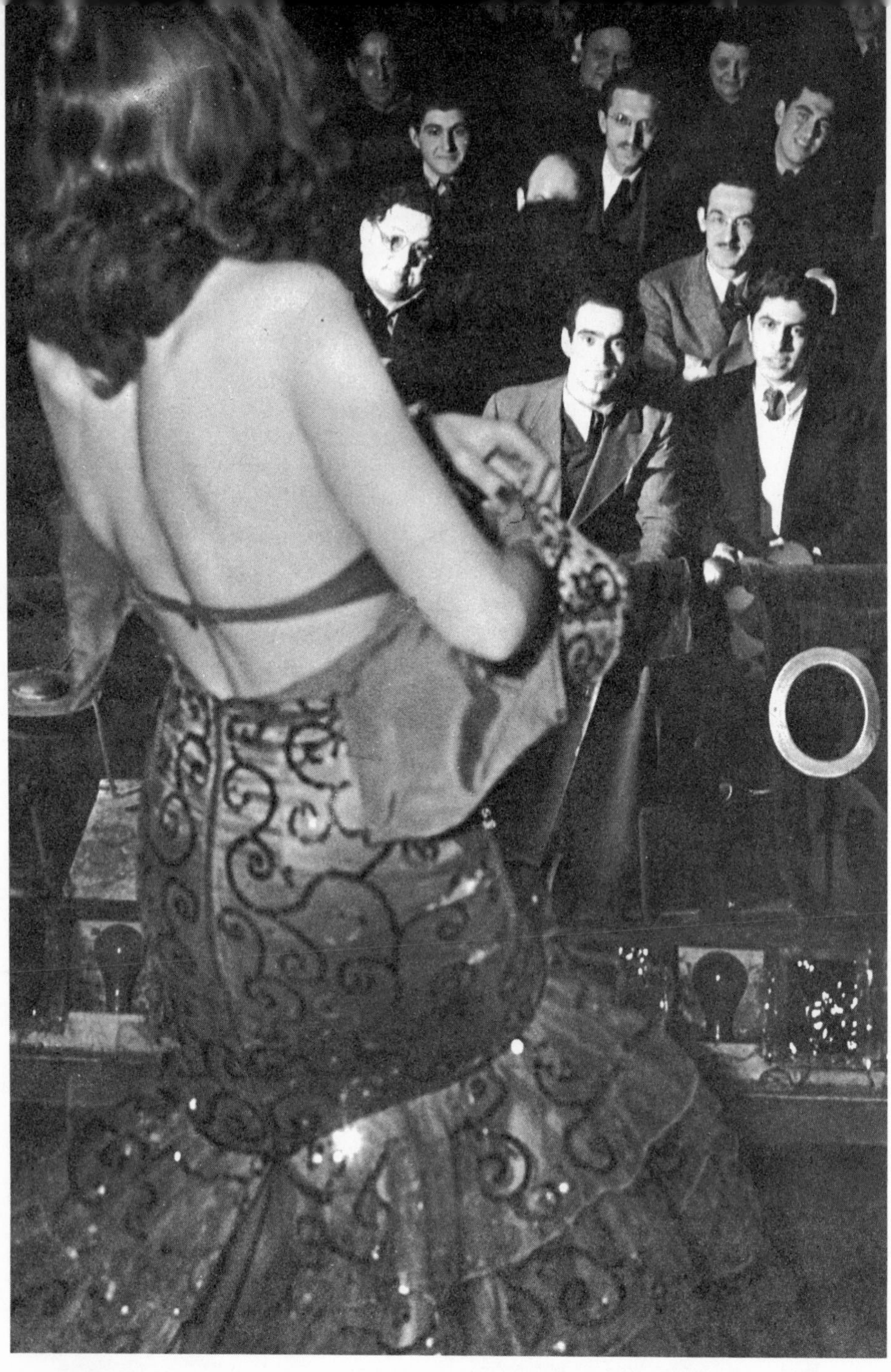

Margie Hart, "providing an education of her own." *Culver Pictures, Inc.*

followed by a two-year contract with the Minsky-Weinstock combination, after which she appeared as a star and super attraction in various houses throughout the country, and not even censorship managed to dim the lustre of her special appeal.

With Gypsy Rose Lee in and out of burlesque, Margie Hart was second in popularity only to the redoubtable Ann Corio, who was a soubrette when Margie Hart was still learning the 3 R's, evidently with some difficulty.

Though subsequently married and retired, she was single while in burlesque and could well sing the popular refrain, "If I Shake, It's for Mother's Sake," for as a matter of public and repeated record she supported, from her salary, her parents, brothers and a sister, Mildred Hart, also a stripper, but of lesser attainments. Also, according to her version, she refused Hollywood offers, because "I don't like to be kissed publicly."

The reason for her popularity is not difficult to determine. One had but to see a suitable performance. However, there might conceivably be some differences of opinion. It is just, therefore, to record Margie Hart's personal explanation for her phenomenal success. "Maybe," she suggested, as quoted in *Collier's Magazine* (July 1941), ". . . it's because I'm just a wholesome, clean American girl trying to get along."

Hinda Wassau

Though sidetracked by these other high-priestesses of the profession, Hinda Wassau was a rightful Queen of Burlesque on her own merits. Her career paralleled that of her sister-Mutual star, Ann Corio, both before and after recognition. In 1927, she was found guilty of indecency following a raid in a Milwaukee theatre. The same year, the Irving Place Theatre was raided, yielding as a victim one known as Anna Coria. Here the charges were dismissed.

Whereas Ann Corio became an angel and a lonely Indian maiden under the guidance of Emmett Callahan, Hinda Wassau, under the aegis of Rube Bernstein, was transformed into a "classic dancing specialist." As such, she camouflaged her hippy movements with a maze of head jerks, arm swinging and deep breathing spells.

She also left burlesque on many occasions for nightclubs, in one instance being engaged by Billy Rose on Fanny Brice's recommendation. And her own financial rewards encouraged two younger sisters to start as chorus girls in a tabloid show. In one respect, she was more important in burlesque than many others more prominent, because she anticipated the latest, most modern technique of the strip—that of running the hands over the body slowly and lingeringly, of self-caressing. One critic described her routine as follows: "She pants, darts spasmodically, lets her hand glide over her body; she exerts herself, full of sex movement." Not as high salaried as some of the other stars, she did not protract matters unduly. After the audience was let on to the appetizing probability that there was nothing beneath the dress except herself, she teased a little, dallied a little, fondled the curves of her dress, then a few "spasmodic sex movements," a tug at her dress which ripped off entirely in one master stroke of the arm—and she and the spotlight were gone.

Georgia Sothern

Georgia Sothern, redheaded and dynamic, deserves mention because she was the most consistently energetic of the top strippers. She bumped so vigorously and incessantly and speedily that her act transcended the boundaries of obscenity into the domain of unmannered eccentricity. Such tremendous exertion necessitated complete freedom from the impediments of clothing, a requirement usually complied with in full.

Her frenetic movements gained her a solid engagement of twenty-eight weeks at Issy Hirst's Gayety Theatre in Philadelphia. After that she stormed the burlesque houses all over the country as a top attraction, more or less accepted with melancholy resignation by the censoring authorities as a "necessary evil."

In June 1940, she fainted at a performance while in the midst of her energetic convolutions. It was discovered that she had a heart condition. Undaunted, she resumed, therefore, as if nothing had happened, and without any noticeable slackening of vigor.

She also benefitted by newspaper and magazine publicity, most of which consisted of inquiries as to what she was actually thinking about when in the heat of her bodily contortions. Her usual answer: "Nothing —it is just a form of exercise."

Carrie Finnell

Though middle-aged and corpulent in the strip era, Carrie Finnell was one of the most publicized, and the only representative of the strippers on the board of the BAA, the union of burlesque performers. When some of her contemporaries were not even born, she had already, in 1918, played the part of Mrs. Casey in Columbia's *Sam Rice and His Daffydills* show. A year later, she shared honors with Tom Howard in *Kewpie Dolls*. Then followed several years of stock, where she unlearned the refinements of the Columbia Wheel; and in 1926, under the guidance of her husband and manager, Charlie Grow, she appeared in her well-known pleaser, *Carrie Finnell and Her Red-Headed Blondes.*

A typical Mutual runway shaker, she was arrested in May 1928 and fined for indecent behavior. With these additional credentials, she took over the coveted spot as star of the *Bowery Burlesquers* on the Mutual Wheel after it was vacated by Hattie Beall. It seemed unlikely that this holdover from the Mutual generation would be so popular in the heyday of young, lissome strippers. But she knew what they wanted, and her bouncing vulgarism was just as popular then as in her younger days, when it meant something.

And Many, Many Others

There were innumerable other aphrodisiacs who emerged from their clothing and the minimum wage classification by introducing erotic features of their own. Countess Nadja's specialty consisted of a series of sweet poses and then sudden hot cooching. Diane Rowland came out in cap and gown, diploma in hand—a sweet young graduate. Then, she turned around slowly, to reveal a bare and quivering backside. Rose La Rose appeared in a long flowery dress, which covered her body completely, except for three strategic openings in front, two above and one below. The back of the dress had no midsection. Since she was exposed from the start, she could devote more time to such tidbits as her favorite song, "Who Will Kiss My Ooh-La-La." She became a top attraction of the later years. Mimi Lynne would expose her voluminous breasts, letting everybody know "I'm more scarlet than Scarlett O'Hara." Sally Keith and Ermaine Parker were tassel girls. Each claimed the honor of being the first in their specialty—attaching silk tassels to their bouncing breasts and revolving rears.

There were the more subdued strippers who got by on "class." Chicago yielded Mary Sunde, an educated blonde who knew seven languages, and the stately Maxine De Shon, ex-wife of comic Rags Ragland. Crystal Ames was a recruit from George White's *Scandals.* Sherry Britton looked like the high school girl she was, just before going into burlesque, and would have her former classmates on hand to applaud her full disrobing ritual. Marie Cord and Julie Bryan claimed to be exemplars of Gypsy Rose Lee. Roxanne inveigled the audiences inside with the intimacies of her body, and on the outside with the printed intimacies of her divorce from the ex-heavyweight prizefighter, Battling Kingfish Levinsky.

There were very many sisters who were strippers. Diane Rowland had two sisters in the business, Betty and Roselle. Betty, a hardworking petite twister and shaker, was married to an equally hardworking comic, Gus Schilling, who later went to Hollywood at the invitation of Orson Welles. Diane herself was married to Paddy Cliff, burlesque juvenile and singer. Roselle, however, known as the Golden Girl, hit the publicity jackpot with the announcement of her marriage to an English nobleman. Ruby (Tangara) Foreman and her younger sister Gertrude were, respectively, typical of the Mutual Wheel and the strip era. Ruby shook incessantly. Gertrude paraded sweetly. Hardly any of the sisters worked together as a team. An exception was the Mavis Sisters (Joan and Connie), who started in a Bowery scratch house, stripping in unison, Joan shaking her breasts while Connie did likewise with her rear—or vice versa.

There were Chinese strippers such as Amy Fong and Anna May Young. They had been preceded by Ada Lum, comedienne in the *Charming Widows* show.

There were the girls with the unusual "gimmicks"—Rosita Royce, with doves in lieu of a brassiere; Lois De Fee, six feet six inches of inert flesh; Tirza and her Wine Bath; Dorothy Henry and her Milk Bath; Leda and the Swan; Noel Carterthe "party" girl; Zorita and her snakes, etc., etc.

At the beginning of the strip phase there was a great deal of cooching in continuance of the Mutual practice. Later, the newer and younger girls made it fashionable to parade bouncingly. In the final stage, the headliners reverted to uninhibited body shaking, even as they stripped, and were stripped—Patricia Perry, Scarlette Kelly, Marion Miller, among others. As a final triumphant achievement this was further combined with the newest vogue of feeling their way around—on their own bodies, as exemplified by Valerie Parks, Vickie Welles, Jean Mode. In the most recent phase Lili St. Cyr, much-married sister-in-law of Harold Minsky, claims top honors, a distinction disputed by the "Treasure Chests"—Blaze Starr, Tempest Storm, Irma "The Body," Anne Howe—all claiming unique mammary talents. But as the joke goes, "When you've seen two, you've seen them all."

Regardless of techniques, looks, or ability the highest rewards, as a rule, have always gone to those who garnered the most publicity. A glowing, brackish wench doing eight shows a day before a sprinkling of degenerate drifters in a sideshow peephole could possibly be just as exciting as these exploited headliners.

Notwithstanding all their differences, the strippers could meet on one common ground—they were all, or nearly all, devoid of any authentic talent.

"A glowing, brackish wench doing eight shows a day." *Culver Pictures, Inc.*

THE IRVING PLACE THEATRE

WITH the end of the big wheels, the ascendance of stock and the prevalence of the strip, the subsequent history of burlesque is largely a history of the individual theatres that housed the new productions. The comic material, the comedians themselves, the framework of the shows, the music, the songs—all were stereotyped and antiquated, or secondhand at best. They were duplicated in every burlesque theatre in the country. Whatever interest a burlesque show induced depended upon the limits to which strippers could go in the respective theatres they played. Whatever success an owner enjoyed depended upon the leniency of the police or, when the heat was on, upon his skill in camouflaging the production with effective surefire specialties and novelties, or gaudy settings and scenery, until normal operations could be resumed.

There were many wheels and circuits attempted after Mutual, the most substantial of which was the Hirst Wheel. But it was the name of the particular theatre, not the reputation of the wheel, that attracted patronage. The very names of the new circuits were unknown to the general public.

Of all the theatres playing burlesque, those in New York City were the most typical of both the progress and retrogression of the industry throughout the entire country. From time to time, theatres in large and less evenly regulated cities, particularly Chicago, Detroit and Los Angeles, would transcend even the extremes which most of the New York houses could hazard. But, in general, the pace of all burlesque, the prevalence of the strip, the publicity craze exemplified by the Minskys and the leading strippers, primarily emanated from New York City. When the runways were abolished in New York, most of the theatres throughout the country likewise removed their runways. When burlesque was banned in New York City during 1937, the gigantic event affected every burlesque theatre in every other city, one way or another.

Probably no theatre in the country has been so directly a part of the strip era as the Irving Place Theatre, on 15th Street off Union Square in New York City. Embracing within its ancient halls the cast-off diehard audiences from the shuttered doors of the defunct Olympic, Union Square, 14th Street and National Winter Garden houses, it rose in popularity as the strip act developed, and was forced to close when censorship severely limited the number and extent of operation of the strippers it had always provided in generous profusion.

It took some time for the Irving Place enterprise to jell. It was first opened in 1922 by the roving comic Joe (Souse) Rose. Routine bits, such as "Kissing It Where It Hurts" and the one in which a henpecked husband and abused wife turn the tables on their spouses after a few drinks, bored the burlesque-wise audiences of Union Square. Neither Joe Rose's white wig nor Hattie Beall nor Margie Pennetti could keep the Irving Place Theatre from going into a blackout of its own. Another comic, Sol Fields, then took over with equally futile results.

In 1925, Charlie Burns assumed operation of the theatre. His experience as a producer had been gleaned from his duties as a caretaker of the Union Square Theatre and a bouncer at the Olympic. He was also superintendent of the adjoining Tammany Hall premises. He opened with the Charlie Burns Irving Place Stock Company, which included a full chorus of twenty girls. Present were Johnny Weber, of Columbia's *Sandy Beach* renown, and the team of McAllister and Shannon, who had been in the Columbia show *Step Lively Girls.*

Shortly thereafter Shannon left. "Richie" McAllister became "Shorty" McAllister and joined Johnny Weber for a new and sensational comic duo. Shorty McAllister was a diminutive Scotsman with a large head and rolling eyes, Weber the fumbling bewildered Dutchman. Though their material was basically slapstick, Shorty McAllister was always prone to roughen matters up a bit by conveniently resting his chin on a soubrette's bosom, for which accomplishment he was of the exact proper height. Both comics seemed unusually slow-witted, even for burlesque, but their use of comedy props—including derby hats, ragged coats, large checked trousers, dashing suspenders, oversized shoes, a battered horn, a brown jug, a cowbell, a bass drum, all in addition to the usual inflated bladders—elicited the admiration of Brooks Atkinson. "You are drenched in artless beauty and comic madness until eleven o'clock," he rhapsodized.

This must have sounded very impressive to Shorty McAllister, for immediately thereafter he took a flyer in Pantages vaudeville. But in the fall of that same season he was back again with Johnny Weber at the Olympic where they were greeted as the heroes of Union Square.

The Irving Place Theatre, meanwhile, had been struggling along, rotating through the weary cycle of unwanted theatres—Yiddish melodrama, Italian opera, sex pictures, stock burlesque, and "Closed for Alterations" signs. As *Variety* remarked, "When stock burlesque supplants Yiddish drama at the Irving Place, East Siders know that spring is here."

Through it all, Charlie Burns hung on grimly to his lease.

He was rewarded in 1928 when Tammany Hall was sold and the Olympic Theatre closed. The prime Olympic favorites McAllister and Weber rejoined the Irving Place as steady featured attractions. And Burns put an electric sign on 14th Street pointing the way to the sole remaining oasis in that vicinity. Henceforth, the Irving Place Theatre prospered.

Soon the theatre became a haven for the burlesque connoisseurs. Most of the other theatres were ruled by raucous adolescents, kept within some bounds by an ex-pug pacing the aisles belligerently. At the Irving Place, a sophisticated, knowing audience of middle-aged, seemingly well-to-do men duly tipped the pretty usherettes who led them to their reserved seats in the orchestra. The rougher elements were shunted to the balcony.

To these audiences the routine pyrotechnics of the Wheel were not nearly so refreshing as a modest strip by an immodest girl, barely out of her teens. Comedy was reduced to a satisfactory minimum. The girls here were younger, fresher, yet equally bawdy. Soubrette Rae Allen offered to pay for seats in the orchestra for the galleryites so "You can see what I got a lot better." Mary Walton, blonde vision in a schoolgirl frock that even covered the ankles, bandied small unchaste talk with the men as she undulated up and down the runway. "Didja hear about the schoolteacher who said to her visitor: 'Are you the father of my children?' " "Hey, mister, are you married? You are? Well, are you working at it much?"

Then she took off the long dress in the earliest manifestations of the striptease and, practically nude, rubbed her palms slowly, with deliberate deliciousness, over the powdered pink of her backsides.

The Irving Place audiences were far from appalled at such exhibitions. In fact they were delighted. They likened it, in completely illusory rationalization, to a situation where a bunch of frivolous schoolgirls had taken a burlesque theatre unto themselves and obsessed with a flair for lewd ingenuity were themselves having the time of their lives as, brazenly, in this intimate rendezvous, they exhibited their persons for the amusement of their own private admirers. As one observer stated: "It's the free-and-easy, everybody-in-on-the-party attitude of the house and the performers that makes their shows consistent smashes—plus the stripping array, which is of ace calibre."

The Irving Place experimented briefly with Mutual Wheel shows, making sure that it kept its own stock comedians McAllister and Weber, and its own precious stock strippers, adding a new feature, the rotund Peggy Reynolds and her trick G-strings. Management soon saw which side of the production was the most popular, and it went back to complete stock with Mildred Cozierre as the headliner.

As the Irving Place Theatre continued to enjoy increased patronage, rival theatre owners charged that the police were spending too much time at their places and too little at the Irving Place. It was common knowledge, as claimed by Frederic Coudert, running for District Attorney of New York County against the Tammany candidate, Supreme Court Justice T. H. Crain, in 1929, that the latter's family owned the property at the site of the theatre. And, of course, there was still Charlie Burns and his undisputed connections with Tammany Hall. At the same time, coincidentally or otherwise, Charlie Burns announced his resignation as a director of the Irving Place Theatre.

Burns was succeeded by Max Wilner, a theatre owner and operator for about forty years, though new to burlesque. He had no enthusiasm for the ancient bits so dear to the old-time comics. Shimmying and the cooch were likewise distasteful to him. Still, he admitted, burlesque must contain enough "spice" to please "the ordinary red-blooded human being." This, to him, meant stripping—for both the chorines and the female principals.

As a result, the chorus girls were stripped practically nude, and the principals, to justify their rank, always went them one better. At this theatre ". . . they want their burlesque rough, ready and raw," stated *The Billboard* in 1930.

Wilner's producer of ensemble and production numbers was the "Wonder Boy of Burlesque," Allen Gilbert. Gilbert had little patience with the boisterous clatter normally associated with burlesque chorus numbers. His dance routines were smooth, melodious—and sexless. Under his direction, and with the better-trained girls available at this house, some harmonious effects were achieved. Unfortunately, his methods were imitated by all the other dance directors, none of whom had any of his talent. They tried to make Rockettes or Tiller girls out of their bewildered charges. The results, particularly in the grind houses, were harrowing.

While the showgirls paraded up and down the runway, and from one side of the stage to the other, clad only in a G-string, the musicians played "refined" selections, such as "Kiss Me Again," or "Beautiful Lady," or "You Ought to Be in Pictures, You're Wonderful to See." Sometimes, for real class, a boyish singer, Mitch Todd, would engage in a softly tender tête-à-tête with a youngish girl singer. This was called "Glorified Burlesque."

When Gladys Clark played the Irving Place, she brought everything and everybody down to earth. She would preface her forthright strip routine with casual comments to the audience: "Anybody here wanna take a ship for themselves?" or "Hey, you, take your hands out of your pockets, you're a big boy now." She also played in the bits, teaming up with Jimmy Dugan. Jimmy Dugan, wearing the same glassless goggles he had affected in the Columbia show *Jack Reid's Record Breakers,* was the master of a brash, smutty, rapid-fire delivery that even "Glad-Ass" Clark, as he called her, could not match. In their favorite bit, Gladys Clark would insist on a "receipt" from her escort, Jimmy Dugan, for the money she spent on him—reversing the usual order and having the woman act as the aggressor. And Gladys Clark could certainly be aggressive, even if she had to hold her man by the front of his trousers.

The star attractions, Gypsy Rose Lee, Ann Corio, Georgia Sothern, all played at this burlesque showplace. But, as a rule, the steady, long-term strippers at this theater were of the Allen Gilbert "Glorified Burlesque" assortment—Margie Hart, Peggy Reynolds, the tall redhead, June St. Clair, the chubby blonde Honey Bee Keller—who slinkily teased the audiences for half of their act, and in the other half smoothly emerged from their trick costumes, coy and smiling and all but nude.

In February 1934, the Irving Place Theatre outstripped itself. Its female contingent, encouraged more than ever by recurrent applause, had remained in a somewhat denuded state for sustained periods of audience delight while, as luck would have it, policemen especially dispatched for the purpose of arrest were in attendance. They applauded for encores in the line of duty, and after sitting through what they considered a corking good show, proceeded to take into custody most of the cast and the house manager.

Mayor La Guardia, and his Fusion administration, were in power. One could bargain with Tammany. But with Fusion one could only

The Irving Place Theatre. *Culver Pictures, Inc.*

plead—usually guilty. It looked for a time that the defendants would get nothing less than, as a burlesque comic would put it, "life and then the electric chair." Finally, however, the compromise removing the runways was reached. No other penalties were imposed. Certain rules and regulations limiting nudity and dialogue were listed, and then quickly forgotten.

The Irving Place removed the orchestra pit and unceremoniously herded the musicians into a side box. A horizontal runway was installed in their place, just over the front row. A flight of stairs, leading down from the stage on either side, on which the girls could pose, was erected. The strip policy was "glorified" still further by augmenting the number of strippers to a new maximum of eight and nine, beyond which number it was impossible to go within a two and a half hour show, unless the comics were eliminated entirely. "The nudity goes the limit," wrote a reviewer in 1936.

Throughout, the Irving Place Theatre was one of the very few houses that was still two-a-day, with reserved seats. Though prices were comparatively high—$1.35 for orchestra seats—the theatre was packed nightly. Just as the Minskys, after the bonanzas of the National Winter Garden and the Harlem Apollo, transferred to Broadway with the Republic, so did Wilner, aided and abetted by Allen Gilbert, all but desert the Irving Place for his 42nd Street Apollo Theatre, the "Home of Glorified Burlesque." The Irving Place operation was entrusted to Tony Miccio, who had been running the lowly Peoples Theatre on the Bowery.

Meanwhile, the team of McAllister and Weber, which had started the upward rise of the Irving Place, broke up. Johnny Weber was sixty-eight years of age in 1935, and destitute. He had no savings. He could not work as a comic, since he could not talk loud enough to be heard. He made a living of sorts as a "mechanical man" in Coney Island. Max Wilner got him a job as stage doorman at the 42nd Street Apollo, and the profession contributed gifts of clothing from time to time. It was a sorry ending for one who, in 1912, had been lauded as "a paragon of regularity. In addition to total abstinence from strong drink and tobacco—excepting an occasional cigaret—John is an 'early to bed' advocate and it is seldom that one can find him around after midnight."

Shorty McAllister teamed up with a voluble and loud-voiced comic, Harry Katz Fields, and they have continued to function as one of modern burlesque's most popular comic duos, known as Stinky and Shorty.

McAllister and Weber were followed by Mike Sachs, a jovial red-faced tongue twister. A family man and a father, nevertheless Mike

Sachs' chief source of comedy consisted in pointing with great exaggeration as he talked; the point of the pointing was that he thereby felt the breasts and other anatomical portions of the women in the bits with him. With singular appropriateness, he therefore teamed up with his wife, Alice Kennedy, and thereupon left the rest of the girls alone. Mike Sachs added to his woman-baiting repertoire a tongue-tied eye-blinking routine that was funny the first few times it was seen and heard, and that helped in making him a headliner for a two and a half year run at the Irving Place Theatre. Mike Sachs subsequently was stricken with blindness. His eye-blinking had not been all comedy. Even blind, he still worked as a comedian. Alice Kennedy later appeared in bits with other comics who would occasionally take liberties with her, as Mike Sachs had done, though not called for in the script. "Stop padding your part," she would reprimand them.

The ban on strip shows by License Commissioner Moss in 1937 was a death blow. The house of strip had little else to offer. "House shows the effect of poor business," *Variety* stated simply at the end of that year. As luck would have it, Miccio had spent $20,000 to renovate the house just before Commissioner Moss' edict. In 1938 there was no money to meet the payroll. In 1939 there was no season. The first successful operator, Charlie Burns, who had been operating stock burlesque at the Park Theatre in Bridgeport, suddenly reappeared. He lasted less than a month.

And the Irving Place Theatre went back again to Yiddish melodrama and Italian opera, just as if nothing at all had happened during all those fifteen years.

BURLESQUE ON BROADWAY

BEFORE the opening of the Republic Theatre in 1931, all burlesque ventures in the Broadway area had been conceived and advertised as miniature musical comedies. Lacking the talent of musical comedies, and minus the dirt of burlesque, they had all been miserable failures.

Billy Minsky opened the Republic with reverse billing. Dirty as it was, it was advertised as being more so. The title of its first show, *Fanny Fortson from France,* and most of the succeeding titles each week were startling Yiddish vulgarisms. No sooner did the curtain rise at the premiere than the chorines started to grind and bump, the strippers, practically nude, shimmied and shook, the runway clattered with the sounds of female bodies, outstretched throughout its length, cooching horizontally, matching the rawest excesses of the rawest stock houses.

In this super effort, Billy Minsky had not been sparing in other departments. There were four top comics—Hap Hyatt, the fattest comedian in burlesque, who, when all else failed, bumped his massive tummy against the embonpoint of the nearest girl, and three veterans who were adept at milking laughs, no matter how, Harry Clexx, Bert Carr and Harry Seymour. Al Golden, distinguished-looking smoothie, was straight man. There was even a prima donna, Ina Hayward. Stripping honors were entrusted to imported strip and shake specialists from

Chicago, and a local product, Marie Voe, later the wife of Harry Clexx, who had impudently tweaked her breast nipples as the inspiration of the "Does She Vo De Do Do" shows at the Harlem Apollo.

There was also some pretentiousness. "Costumes and scenery are splendiferous," wrote Elias E. Sugarman of *The Billboard,* looking at the bright side. Brooks Atkinson declared that the dancing and comedy were "the bawdiest this neighborhood has seen for years." Sime Silverman, who by now had given up on burlesque, was vitriolic: "For this stock burlesque of Minsky at the Republic is just rotten, with parts of it lousy, comprising as it does, the cheapest dirt, the dirtiest coochers ever forced upon a stage or platform and with no talent."

The Republic opened as a two-a-day with prices of 75 cents to $1.50. And business was excellent. The notoriety given the opening of the theatre by the scandalized reviewers served in reverse effect. It became fashionable to attend burlesque on Broadway, instead of getting kicks in a moldy theater on a hidden side street. After its intemperate opening, the Republic had to tone down its shows considerably. However, the lasting impression of sin and wickedness prevailed through all the succeeding years, to the financial benefit not only of the Republic but of all burlesque in that area.

One month after the Republic opened, Max Rudnick, an operator of Brooklyn film houses, decided to get in while the pickings were good. He leased the Eltinge Theatre, a former legitimate playhouse, also on 42nd Street, from A. H. Woods, the theatrical producer, at a rental of $45,000 yearly, and he was in business. Without much fanfare, the Eltinge was launched with a grind policy of four shows a day, alternating with cheap talkies. The performers, headed by Bert Carr, who had just left the Republic, were not the handpicked stars of the Minsky stable, but they were reasonably competent in their field. The straight man was Allen Forth, whose main qualification for burlesque was that he looked dignified enough to be the President of Standard Oil. Romayne, a tall sinuous brunette, was the girl-of-all work at this theatre. She appeared and reappeared as stripper, talker, singer, ensemble dancer and specialty cooch. One of the first headliners was Billie Shaw, who undressed to the tune of "If You Want to See a Little More of Me, Clap Your Hands, Clap Clap." She was so good that she married the boss, Max Rudnick. A long-term standby at the Eltinge was Wilma Horner, who as a stripper and talker in the bits seemed possessed of a wistful innocence, despite the lewdness of her lines. At least, she so impressed the orchestra leader, Max Davis, who married her. Similarly, Irene Austin, a workmanlike stripper who had played in all the burlesque houses at one time or another, married another orchestra leader at the Eltinge, Murray Friedman.

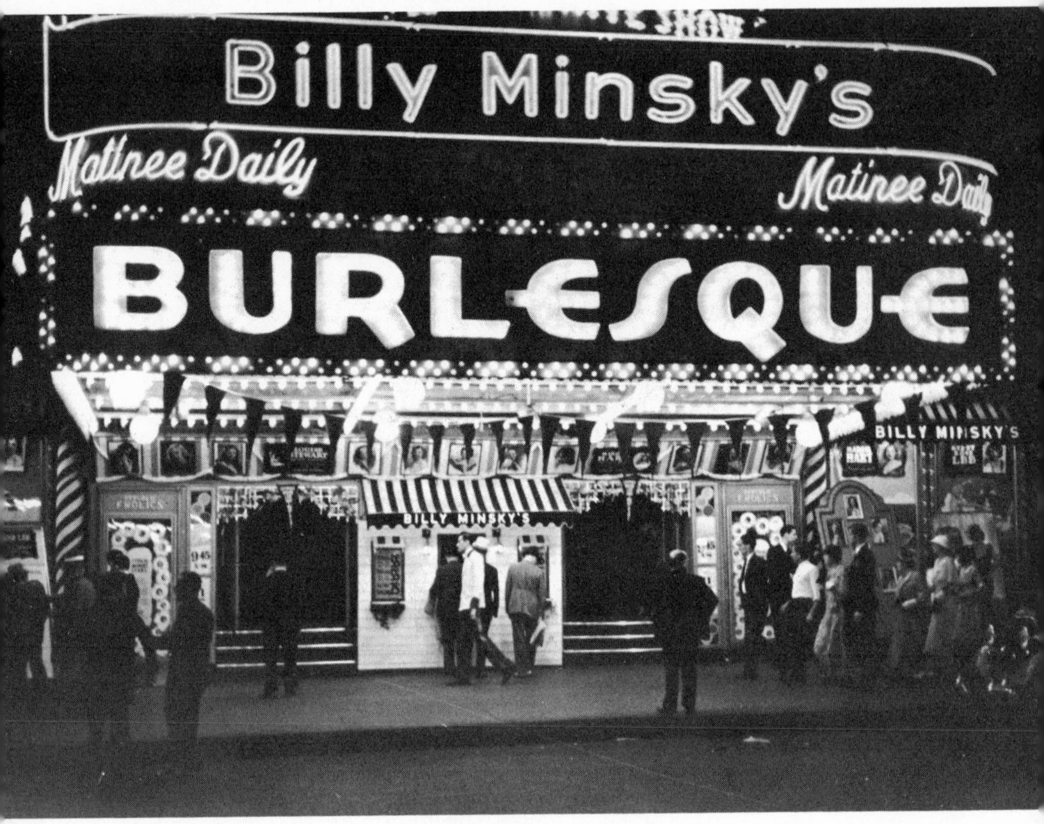

Billy Minsky's Republic Theatre on 42nd Street brought burlesque to Broadway.
Culver Pictures, Inc.

Romance may have flourished off the stage. But on it, the shows were as rough as those at the Republic—and much cheaper. If a customer came early enough, he could get in for fifteen cents. The competition forced the Minsky house to lower its minimum to fifty cents, and a few years later, the Republic also adopted a four-a-day grind policy.

In the meanwhile, Herk, observing all this hectic activity with considerable and understandable concern, if not envy, decided to join the parade. He reconciled whatever differences had existed between him and Billy Minsky, and under their combined mighty auspices, the Central Theatre on Broadway and 48th Street was leased from the Shuberts and opened as a grind burlesque house in the fall of 1931. Not to be outdone, Abe Minsky joined forces with Harold Raymond of the Star Theatre in Brooklyn, and they opened their own New York Gaiety Theatre operation, adjoining the Central.

Notwithstanding such excellent sponsors, none of these ventures fared as well as the Republic and the Eltinge. They intermittently opened and closed, changed ownership, and reorganized with new backers, some of whom had money but no theatrical experience and were, therefore, quite sensitive about it. One of them engaged in a fist fight with Billy Minsky's backer, Joe Weinstock, over a taunting sneer one had made to the other about "button-hole makers" who intrude upon the theatre. Throughout all the involved financial manipulations, one name, unknown to the public, but more important than practically any other, recurred again and again—Oscar Markowitch, candy concessionaire.

After Billy Minsky's death, his widow and Joseph Weinstock became the financial trustees of his empire, with Herbert Kay Minsky in charge of production, and general supervisor. Then, Herbert Kay and Weinstock organized an auspicious new circuit, the Supreme Circuit, to play all the established houses in the East with the Republic as the hub of the Wheel. The best talent burlesque had to offer was engaged—including Charles "Red" Marshall, Jack Diamond (later in the Broadway musical *Kiss Me Kate*) and Joey Faye (later in the Broadway farce *Room Service*). The Supreme Circuit was going to be another Columbia Wheel.

To their dismay, at this time, a legitimate actress sued the Park Theatre in Boston, playing Supreme Circuit attractions, for defamation of character. Her photograph had been exhibited in the lobby of that theatre without her permission. She was awarded $2,500 damages by the Massachusetts Supreme Court, which added insult to injury by characterizing burlesque as not art, not acting, but "among the lowest if not the lowest forms of production on the stage."

Undaunted, Minsky and Weinstock issued impressive statistics about the $2,500 weekly cost of each production, the 700 persons in the employ of the Wheel, etc. They even got themselves written up in *Fortune Magazine,* which summarized the efficient traveling techniques of the Supreme Circuit: "A Minsky show plays a week in Brooklyn and then sets out by bus (at 2:30 A.M. Sunday) for Boston and six weeks on the road, thence back to Broadway for a week. A trailer follows with costumes and scenery."

As for the shows, however, the Circuit was not nearly as proficient. Long-winded ensemble numbers and flamboyant scenic effects, aping Columbia, bored the audiences who had become accustomed to rawer stuff. The Supreme Circuit lasted about a year, after which most of the houses, including the Republic, signed up with the modest Independent Circuit of Issy Hirst for combination stock and wheel shows. Herbert Kay and Weinstock then pooled their collective talents for another pretentious project—*Life Begins at Minsky's* at the Hollywood Playhouse in Los Angeles. This collapsed as soon as it went on the road.

In the fall of 1934, Max Wilner, also yearning for the prestige of Broadway, decided to open his Apollo Theatre on 42nd Street, just a few doors away from the Republic and opposite the Eltinge. The city fathers were understandably reluctant to license another burlesque house on 42nd Street. But associated with Wilner was the respected Samuel Scribner. Wilner got his license and presented really "glorified" burlesque. Allen Gilbert was production manager and Emmett Callahan theatre manager. There were more strips per hour in this theatre than in any other in the country. The keenest comedians, notably Abbott and Costello, played there.

All burlesque was now prosperous. The operators continued to expand operations and open new theatres for burlesque. The now veteran chorus ranks regularly yielded their quotas of new principals who became the strip stars of the future. With all other live entertainment in the doldrums, burlesque people could crow for a change. Carrie Finnell, in her capacity as an executive board member of the Burlesque Artists Association, proclaimed unreservedly: "Burlesque producers should realize that they are the future of the American theatre." Allen Gilbert gave this fatherly advice in 1936: "Come into burlesque as either a stepping stone to better things or a chance to tide yourself over until the break, with the right attitude, in the right state of mind . . . you are not stepping down to burlesque, you are coming over to it."

All of which led to the logical absurdity of the Oriental Theatre on 52nd Street and Broadway.

The Oriental was opened in December 1936, with engraved invitations to the elite to attend in formal attire at a top tariff of $1.65. There was a special mezzanine section reserved for an even more select group. Herbert Kay Minsky and Morton Minsky, the producers, conceived of the production as some kind of swank soiree. There were cute decorations and intimate knickknacks reminiscent of a "little art" movie house. One could retire to the lounge for a cup of coffee, and smirk with superior nonchalance at a "Little Egypt" on exhibition there, or have one's fortune told by Adrienne the Psychic—all on the house. There was no Oriental Nite or Shimmy Nite, of course. Nor anything so coarse as Wrestling or Amateur Nite. Instead, there was Celebrity Nite.

Norman Bel Geddes did some of the sets and murals. Margie Hart was hired to give the show a good sendoff the first few weeks. The comics, comparatively new, were the best in burlesque, Phil Silvers and the "Slob" character, Hank Henry, both on their way to better things. There were witty, if less ribald, titles for the shows—*I'd Walk a Mile for a Camille, Mind Over Mattress, From Bed to Worse, Anatomy and Cleopatra.* Walter Winchell contributed *Three Smart Girdles.* More publicity was obtained when the producers of the Broadway musical *Red Hot and Blue* enjoined the Minskys from using the title *Red Hot and Nude.*

The only trouble was the burlesque show itself. After all, it was only burlesque, and the glare of all this exploitation attracted censors like flies to sugar. The tremendous stage, more appropriate for a Ben Hur spectacle than an intimate strip, handicapped the comics as well. On one occasion, stripper Queenie King walked off the stage in disgust. Hank Henry had to deliver his lines from a horizontal runway.

Notwithstanding the hoopla, the dress suits, the coffee in the lounge, *Variety's* verdict was: ". . . the show that they present at the Oriental is, despite a stab at 'class,' just another burlesque show only worse." A month later it added: "As a burlesque show, it's still an advertisement for a picture."

For better or worse, burlesque, in 1937, was threatening to engulf the entire Broadway area. Herk leased another Broadway house, the Fulton Theatre. Burlesque publicity and exploitation were becoming more daring and impudent. It was brazenly flaunted in the show capital of the world. A few months later, in May 1937, the License Commissioner of New York, Paul Moss, with one stroke of his pen, put a finis to burlesque on Broadway. The theatres fought and floundered for a while. The Oriental was the first to go. Eventually they all surrendered.

The only remnants of burlesque that persisted on Broadway were

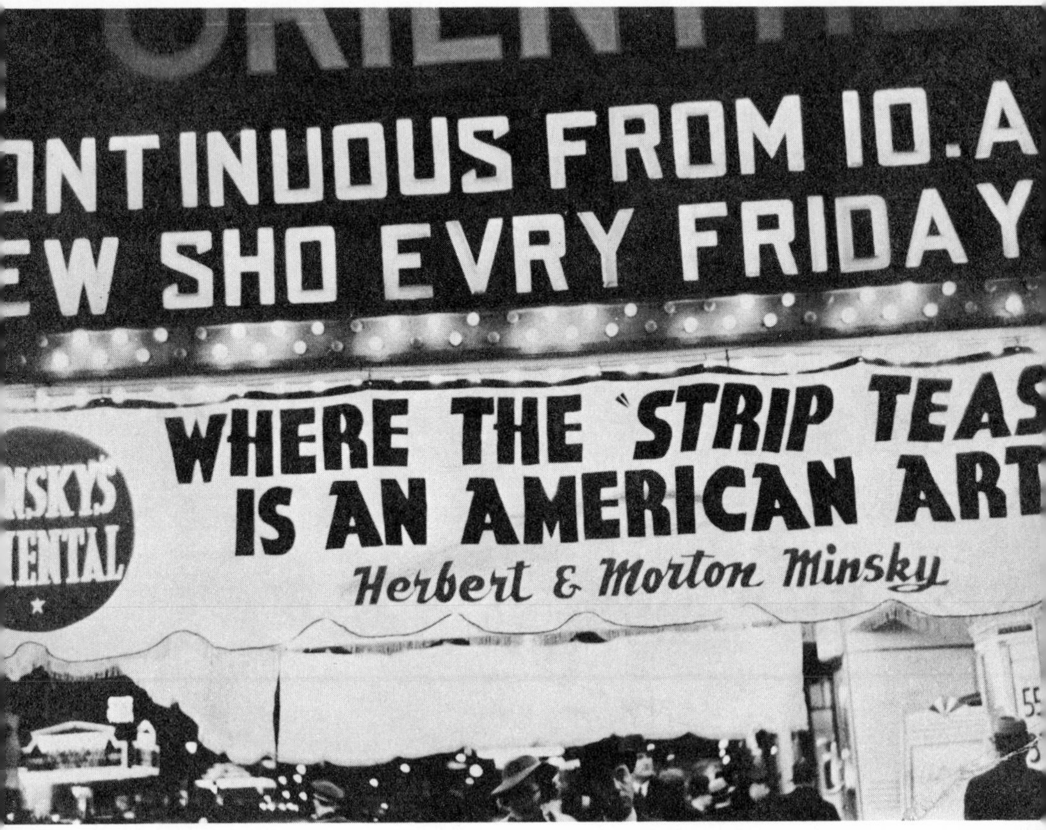

The logical absurdity of the younger Minskys (high-class division).
Culver Pictures, Inc.

the strip clip-joint nightclubs on 52nd Street which succeeded the burlesque houses. They survived for several years only because they were, in the main, unadvertised, unpublicized, and generally unknown—in exact antithesis of the exploitation that brought about the downfall of the burlesque houses. After a while, they became noticed and noticeable. They had moved from storefronts near Sixth Avenue to gaudy bagnios near Broadway. So they were closed down also. And all that remained were the belly dancers.

BURLESQUE IN BROOKLYN

BURLESQUE on Broadway was volatile and changeable. Its shows, subject to frequent visitations by unwelcome visitors, whether the police or social critics, had to be watered down with vaudeville novelties and high-flown flummery. This was the price of prestige.

Elsewhere, however, burlesque houses were pursuing with little interference a mutually satisfactory arrangement between themselves and their steady patrons. The operators gave the customers pretty much what they wanted, and the customers kept returning every week, often bringing a friend, who in turn would bring another.

Brooklyn, which had always abounded in burlesque theaters, did not at first share in the prosperity of the stock era. The Casino and the Empire, playing Columbia productions, and the Star and Gayety under the Mutual banner, had more or less gone the way of the Wheels. They were closed more often than they were open.

The flag-bedecked Star Theatre, in the Borough Hall section of Brooklyn, was the oldest burlesque house in New York City. As such it deserved a better fate. The Hyde and Behman theatrical interests had controlled the Star, the Gayety, and the Brooklyn Olympic. The Olympic was destroyed by fire in 1921. The Star and Gayety then came under the control of Sam Raymond, who had been a manager for Kahn's Union Square Theatre. Never "class" houses, the Star and

Gayety played American Wheel rather than Columbia shows. Sam Raymond ran his two theatres practically as a one-man operation. He was owner, producer, manager and director of his two inconspicuous but profitable houses. When the Mutual Wheel was organized, the theatres joined the new circuit, and Sam Raymond was taken into Herk's inner councils. Simultaneously he installed his son Harold as local manager of the Gayety.

Harold took to burlesque like a baldheaded man to an audience number and within a few years operated and produced his own shows on the Wheel. The Gayety, boasting three clattering runways, was always raucous and spirited, to say the least, though it did not keep pace with the strip acts, preferring occasional startling novelties such as an illuminated cat's head in lieu of a G-string for a soubrette's costume. In 1933 the Star Theatre was closed, partly because of the aggressively competitive Oxford Theater nearby, and the Gayety about to fold. When License Commissioner Geraghty singled out the Gayety Theatre for specific condemnation it shut its doors for good and never reopened.

Harold, now acting head of the clan, occupied himself for a while with the Central Theatre, and then was on the verge of giving it all up to become a licensed burlesque booking agent. In 1934, however, he and his younger brother, Leonard, backed by one Jerry Adler, reopened the Star Theatre on a grind four-a-day basis.

Audiences at first were very sparse. A nonunion set of musicians was employed, and the house was picketed day and night. But prices were very low, twenty-five cents for any orchestra seat, and the old Mutual soubrettes who were engaged at minimum salaries literally shook the customers out of their lethargy.

Gradually the audiences came back. When they did, it was a heckling, sarcastic, filthy mob that barely permitted the performances to proceed. Epithets so vile and obscene were thrust at the performers, particularly the women, that even the smutty bits seemed pure by contrast. On Amateur Night the unemployed small-time vaudevillians who appeared as "amateurs" were regularly shouted down as the house was torn with indecent expletives. But the choicest insults were reserved for the burlesque contingent. As the finale stripper prepared to introduce the other women principals for the final curtain, a ruffian's voice would rasp out: "Bring the rest of the whores out!" Kenza Vinton, the wife of a favorite comic there, "Peanuts" Bohn, had to interrupt her shimmying to implore, "Give me a break, boys!" Mildred Clark, a popular added attraction in many of the theatres because of her enormously curvaceous posterior, was so derisively ridiculed that, abashed, she took a leave of absence and subsequently reapppeared with so anemic a figure that she lost all her former effectiveness. When the newer and younger Mimi Lynne was hired, she would shout, "Look what the good Lord gave me," as she exposed and shook her ample breasts—whereupon the audience roared back as one, "You'll never go hungry, baby!"

The important thing, however, was that the customers kept coming back, and by 1935 the Star celebrated its twenty-fifth anniversary by adding another stripper to the show.

In this atmosphere some comics were developed who advanced to somewhat higher status, including Tommy (Moe) Raft, small and droll, who starred at the Oriental Theatre with the Minskys, and "Peanuts" Bohn, a diminutive mimic who was a London music hall performer. Red Buttons also did an arduous stint at the Star Theatre.

The Star also nurtured the talents of Gus Schilling, who had previously worked behind the scenes as an assistant stage director, and had marveled discreetly at all the riotous goings-on. At first he was a straight man for "Tiny" Fuller. Pasty-faced, deliberately awkward and hesitant in movement, he gave himself the classic name of "Jerk" upon his debut as a comedian. It was thrown back upon him roaringly by the crowd every time he made his appearance. Whereupon, Gus Schilling would acknowledge this salute with typical bits of business. Notwithstanding his newness as a performer, he had hung around burlesque theatres long enough to know all the situations from memory. He knew how to please the clientele he was facing without too much practice. His antics were rewarded with long engagements at the Star, the Republic and other top houses as a featured comic. Thence, he was graduated to Orson Welles' Company, playing a grim, almost sinister character in *Citizen Kane*. Gus Schilling was followed by Fred Binder and Jack Rosen, a new roughhouse team, who combined slapstick with the rawest routines and tried them all out at the Star Theatre.

In due time, the Star was again the leading Brooklyn burlesque house, and the management now decided it was time to clean out the undesirable elements. It was a little difficult, but it was done. One or two of the most brazen Amateur Night hecklers were taken into custody and turned over to the police. Word immediately passed around to the petty ruffians, who were cowered by this one forthright action. When applause for the strippers was too prolonged, or uncalled for comments persisted, a huge flashlight was spread over the entire theatre to detect the culprits. The female ushers were augmented by a couple of tough-looking bouncers. Thereafter, order, if not discipline, was maintained.

In December 1936, the theatre released its non-union orchestra. The leader, a sweating worthy who had labored through nervewracking years with a handkerchief tied round his neck, was exiled to the Peoples Theatre on the Bowery.

Ironically, by 1937, when the crash came, the Star had lost its original brashness. It had less stripping, in fact, than most of the other houses. The audiences were still large, but they now let out their hoodlum frustrations, not by heckling the performers, but by consuming innumerable hot dogs bought from the concessionaire strategically situated on the way to the men's room.

When Brooklyn District Attorney Geoghan, following the cue of Commissioner Moss, raided all the Brooklyn burlesque theatres, the Star alone survived the holocaust and managed to exist as a "Follies" theatre for several more years, starring the most popular comedians then obtainable—Tommy Raft, Tiny Fuller, Stinky and Shorty, and Bert Marks. The Raymonds, who had been left out of the burlesque scramble in the early 1930s, now were the only survivors in New York. They assumed the operation of the Peoples Theatre on the Bowery and invested in some Coney Island peephole sideshows. In time they too surrendered to progress and censorship. The Star Theatre was closed for good and taken over by a bank.

Without any background and, as it turned out, without much of a future, devoid of publicity and frills, the little Oxford Theatre, near Flatbush Avenue, managed to drive the memory-bound, traditional Star Theatre out of business after but a few years of ruthlessly frank stock operation. Its simple, straightforward policy of sheer and simple dirt resulted in the most consistently indulgent burlesque in the city.

Other, more pretentious Brooklyn enterprises, particularly the Werba's Theatre, with Minsky-Weinstock Supreme productions, could not withstand the competition of this small new theatre. Its continuing success delayed the reopening of the Star Theatre until 1934.

In March 1930, one Charles Schwartz, without any previous burlesque experience, started negotiations for a burlesque stock company in his Oxford Theatre, then an independent and rather unsuccessful movie house. The theatre was advantageously situated near the Long Island Railroad and all subways. It was an intimate house, just right for stock presentations. As a movie theatre it was lost amidst the cinema palaces nearby.

The new operator had no truck with tradition or pretense. He had the common idea shared by many laymen that burlesque was supposed to give as smutty a show as circumstances permitted, was not to be pretentious, and was not to be a developer of talent—not on his money anyway. It was simply to be burlesque. And everybody knew what

The Star Theatre in Brooklyn. *Culver Pictures, Inc.*

burlesque was—Hot Stuff. The Oxford started on this pleasant premise and ended on it—stopped only by Commissioner Moss in 1937.

Though a shoestring operation, and one of the very first houses to institute a grind four-a-day policy, the Oxford managed to steer clear of the sure-death comics who afflicted the scratch houses just a step below. It specialized, at the beginning, in principals long past their prime, who did not command high salaries. But they were experienced and knew all the tricks. There were no prima donnas, acrobatic dancers, talking women or other excess baggage among the female principals. They were all strippers and coochers, and they all took their turn in the bits as well. Scenery was practically nonexistent, and that which the theatre did possess came, it was alleged years later, from the comparatively swank Werba's Theatre, without the knowledge of its owners. The only luxury the Oxford permitted itself was a male singer who, supposedly, was paid off in liquor anyway, and who was very useful in staving off disturbances in the theatre by jumping out on the stage with a sodden rendition of "Mother Machree."

The first Oxford feature was Evelyn Ramsey, a fat and frumpy redhead who had been active in the twenties as a soubrette in Columbia's *Mollie Williams Show,* warbling, "I Don't Know How to Say It in English." Now in her last years as a trouper, she gave her all for the Oxford. In the better houses, especially on Broadway, the performers were particularly energetic in the hope of being discovered by a talent scout. Here, the performers were equally diligent, because if they failed, there was nothing left but scratch burlesque on the Bowery.

Evelyn Ramsey sang, stripped, shimmied and was the foil for the comics in most of the bits. On top of it all, she was number producer for the routines of the chorines. Eventually, despite her devotion and some connection with the Werba's Theatre through her husband, a stagehand there, Evelyn Ramsey descended to the Bowery scratch houses. Buster Phillips, the minimum wage Georgia Sothern, succeeded her and followed the same pattern from the Oxford to the Bowery, as did many others at the Oxford. Tom Bundy, who had been in charge of practically everything at the defunct National Winter Garden, now engaged in the same chores here, doubling as straight man and stage director, and bringing his wife, stripper Edna Dee.

Charles Schwartz was able to maintain a fairly good-looking chorus line by accepting applicants who could not dance a step. The Allen Gilbert routines, copied everywhere else, were completely ignored by him. A big production number at the Oxford consisted in the girls coming out in tight black dresses, shortened on one side, going through a cabalistic ritual of pushing their black-sleeved arms forward and back, then parading to the soulful lament of "Night and day, day and night . . . there is oh such a hungry yearning burning inside of me . . ." Sometimes, the girls would not parade, but merely turn around to show that the trick dresses had no back.

More important than their dancing skill was the availability of the chorus girls for such added features as "Garter Night." Here, the girls would stand behind a half-lowered curtain, revealing their legs up to the thighs. A red garter was perched high above the knee on a black stocking. The holder of the lucky number was privileged to step upon the stage and remove the garter. Charles Schwartz himself officiated to see that the legs were not smacked too lingeringly in the process.

Long-term featured attractions were Betty Duval and Bubbles Yvonne. They would be mauled by the comics in the bits, and as the star strippers of the shows, would exhibit their well-proportioned breasts in full view, then their well-developed buttocks in full view, all the time shaking whatever was exposed, and smilingly walk off after four or five encores—a hard day's work well done. After the Oxford folded, Bubbles Yvonne was one of Larry McPhail's extra attractions at his circus night games in Ebbets Field and, according to some reports, was considered as a possible radio announcer for the Brooklyn Dodgers.

The favorite comic was Art Gardner, who never minced his improprieties. He came directly to the smutty point of the bits without any tiresome detours and, disdaining embellishment, spouted them forth with a grinning facility. As the Oxford operation continued to be profitable, better, fresher and more standard principals were obtained, including Phil Silvers.

In 1936, Charles Schwartz, ever the individualist, had a brainstorm. The chorus line had always been a problem to him. The chorines did not strip, they did not cooch, they did not act. Sex appeal was provided by the featured strippers. Why, then, a chorus? There was but one obvious solution. Eliminate it. Accordingly, without any further apology than if he had discharged an usher, Schwartz abolished the one immutable feature of burlesque. Burlesque shows may have been clean or dirty, they might have been housed in a State Street dive or in a Minsky emporium with uniformed attendants, but some chorus girls they had to have. The Oxford proprietor did away with all tradition in one bold sweep.

All the Oxford could think of, however, to replace the chorus was a succession of stale vaudeville acts. They were as dull as the ensemble numbers, and there were no girls to ogle. The noble experiment died, and burlesque chorines the length and breadth of the land drew a collective sigh of relief.

The Oxford, with its small overhead and steady patronage, might have gone on forever. When the blow came in 1937, however, its demise was not drawn out as with the Star. Before the end of the year, Charles Schwartz got himself a job in Hollywood, and the Oxford Theatre is now a parking lot.

THE BOWERY

THE phrase "Burlesque on the Bowery" has an appropriate lilt to it, like "Paris in the Spring," "Reunion in Vienna," "Castles in Spain." One may have a fleeting thought of the "frankly profane" Miner's Bowery Theatre in the 1900s, of rough-and-tumble unvarnished gleeful boisterousness.

The modern Bowery has had its share of burlesque theatres. But they usually have housed some of the shabbiest and sorriest of all spectacles.

In 1913, Miner's Theatre in the Bowery was a theatrical showplace, playing Barney Gerard's *Follies of the Day*. That was the last reminder of its past glory. Thereafter, burlesque on the Bowery skidded downhill as fast as the Bowery itself.

In 1918 appeared the first of the numerous scratch stock troupes that regularly opened and closed in the area, this time at the Thalia Theatre. After it closed, one P. F. Shea reopened the house in 1920. Again it failed. At the same time, the once famous Miner's Theatre at 165 Bowery, where Maggie Cline, David Warfield, Pat Rooney, Weber and Fields and Harrigan and Hart had appeared, was playing Italian drama, when open, and was known as the Majori Royale Theatre, or the Royal Theatre.

A few years later, the Royal Theatre, encouraged by the success of the National Winter Garden, a few blocks away, reopened as a burlesque house. In lieu of its pristine, bawdy frolics, there were now a few gloomy, mechanical routines with half a dozen flabby, aged chorus girls, two or three soubrettes, two comics and a straight man. Where once gay gallants had disdainfully quaffed their beers, now dreary derelicts gnawed at sandwiches stored away in cavernous, torn pockets and belched away insolently at the equally seedy performances. Bob Nugent, the former National Winter Garden comic, was the stage manager in 1927, when a police raid brought on countercharges that the whole thing was a plot engineered by the rival Minsky house.

The resultant publicity stimulated the opening, in June 1928, of the Lipzin Theatre, also on the Bowery, once famous as the London Theatre. This was slightly more substantial, boasting five principals and eight chorines. There was a change of the show twice weekly. The head comic was Abe Gore, a diminutive unfunnyman, who had seen better days on both Columbia and Mutual Wheels. So, for that matter, had the star soubrette, "Pep" Bedford, formerly of a Columbia chorus line, and Lew Rose, the Izzy Pickle of the tabloid shows. The pattern was now set for the modern Bowery. It became the last stop on the downward toboggan slide of burlesque performers.

The pattern also was set for the scratch houses of the future. The physical theatre was much dirtier than the shows. A stench of beer, cheap whiskey and urine seemed ingrained into the premises. An overpowering, all-pervading miasma commingled with a presentiment of dismal futility. The seats alongside the runway would be occupied. Most of the other seats were vacant. Half of them were broken, anyway.

The performance would start about three quarters of an hour later than scheduled. The patient group of skid-row drifters, accustomed to being insulted or ignored, would wait silently for the musicians to appear and play the overture. After about a half hour, a few would applaud, thereby indicating their irritation at the delay. Then silence. Still nothing happened. Then a few more would applaud. Again silence. Again no musicians, no opening, nothing. Finally, all the men would stamp their feet for several minutes. At long last, the piano player came out. He stared for a few seconds at the nondescript audience with obvious disapproval and then pretended to study the notes at the piano for several minutes. The other two musicians followed the same drawn-out procedure. When they finally started to play, it was obvious they were playing for time. Innumerable and interminable choruses of the same song were repeated. Something had gone wrong backstage, no doubt. Possibly, the few props were missing, or the costumes had not been delivered, or the cast had not been paid off, or any one of a dozen mishaps so likely in a moneyless venture could have arisen.

When the curtain finally did go up, the real monotony began. The big skit, lasting about half an hour, might concern a deaf character with an ear trumpet who always said "Eh, Eh?" to everybody else. This was supposed to be very funny. For the benefit of the stage manager, the bit could be dragged out to take the time of two, with endless repetitions of "Eh, Eh?" or for variety, "Eh, What?"

The five chorines would lean over the runway, smirking pathetically in their hardened ugliness, croaking, "Now, how'd you like to have a baby like me to sit on your knee, huh?" As a rousing climax, "Pep" Bedford would appear from time to time, with her name spelled out on the back of her tights. She gave all and sundry ample time to read the letters, after which she shook the embroidery vigorously.

The average weekly gross for such enterprises was about $350, which had to cover the salaries of the performers, musicians, stagehands, production costs and all other miscellaneous expenses.

Shortly thereafter, the Royal Theatre, once the effervescent Miner's Bowery, unable to take it any longer, burned to the ground.

In 1931, burlesque on the Bowery was given some promise of permanence, if nothing more, with the opening of the Peoples Theatre by Rudy Kahn, another fugitive from the National Winter Garden. The aged Bob Nugent was the star comic. Appearing also were the Bowery perennials, who were not on the downgrade, because they had never amounted to much at best—Smokey Burns, a huge fellow in a tramp make-up, with a frightening steam-shovel voice, or Pinto and Della, an Italian dialect Mutt and Jeff team. And also, Abe Gore. Admission prices were ten cents, twenty cents and thirty cents.

The Peoples Theatre, despite all hardships, refused to bite the dust as had all other previous attempts. Given a breathing spell with the collapse of the Odeon Theatre, a competitive scratch house in the heart of the lower East Side, the cast went on a "cooperative" basis, which meant that they got paid only if and when. But they were working. They worked from 11:00 A.M. to 11:00 P.M., seven days a week, between shows rehearsed for the completely new exhibit due in a day or two (shows were changed twice weekly), did a midnight show on Saturday, and regularly faced the twin spectres of police arrest and unemployment every week. For this, the principals received twenty-three dollars a week, but only if there was anything left after the stagehand, musicians and chorus girls were paid off. However, they did manage to survive, because the girls stripped to the waist, which at ten cents might be considered a Bowery bargain.

The cast could not stand even this meager prosperity. Rudy Kahn deserted the troupe in pique. He was unable to fire one of the chorus girls, who happened to be Abe Gore's wife. Joe Rose bobbed up and joined the company as producer and chief comedian, assisted by Abe Gore and his missus. Joe Rose doffed his wig at intermission and implored the audience to keep patronizing the house, as the bread and butter of more than two dozen employees depended on their support. His pleas were as futile as his comedy.

In less than two months, the agony was over. But after a short spell with "The Best in Silent Motion Pictures at the Lowest Prices," the Peoples Theatre reopened for burlesque, and a new tactic was tried. At intermission time, the straight man would come out, pretend to look around for any menacing policemen, cup his hands over his lips, and in a hoarse whisper exhort the men to keep coming to the shows—"The lid's off, boys, if you know what I mean. A word to the wise is sufficient."

Unfortunately for this side-of-mouth promise, the then influential National Winter Garden saw to it that the lid was never off at this competitive house. Nevertheless, Abe Gore and wife did manage to get in sixteen solid weeks of labor, with occasional compensation.

In the fall of 1933, with the National Winter Garden out of the way, Max Wilner assumed the operation, presenting "Glorified" burlesque, though on a distinctly minor key. Standard performers, on their last legs, but still capable, now regularly made the descent from the Irving Place to the Oxford to the Bowery.

Allen Gilbert's assistant, Cleo Douglas, was imported to give the chorus girls some class. Their costumes were still hand-me-downs, the scenery consisted of Irving Place discards, but the girls were now taught involved gyrations comparable to those of the uptown ensembles. For their additional exertions, their wages were raised to fifteen dollars a week. Abe Held, assistant to Emmett R. Callahan at the 42nd Street Apollo, was installed as house manager. The still foul-smelling theatre literally stank with distinction.

Performers on the way up and on the way down now worked tirelessly at the Peoples Theatre, with twenty-eight weekly performances and rehearsals. Either they were anxious for recognition, or they were staving off unemployment in the depression. The faded Peggy O'Neil, a hardworking stripper and shaker, would play here with her husband, Artie Lloyd, a peppery, energetic little comic. Peggy O'Neil, down to her last burlesque engagements, would sprawl out on the runway, legs wide apart, and smirk ingratiatingly: "Didja see it fellas?" (Actually they didn't.) Eventually, Peggy O'Neil got herself an evening gown and a job as "sophisticated songstress" in a Brooklyn bar and grill. Artie Lloyd became a singing waiter for a while, but is functioning again as a comic. On the other hand, Bobby Faye and his brother, Herbie, of the Phil Silvers Sergeant Bilko television show, served time at the Peoples Theatre before their ascent. Straight men tripled in brass as occasional comics, singers and character actors, and were rewarded with little pay, but long engagements, and the promise of eventual escape to happier regions. Bob Alda served in this capacity for twenty weeks before being promoted uptown to the better houses and, ultimately, to stage and movie stardom.

Unlike the Star Theatre, decorum was usually preserved among the men in the audience by diligent ex-pugs who paraded up and down the aisles, even cutting off any applause they considered too prolonged.

On Tuesday night, however, Amateur Nite, these monitors relaxed their ceaseless vigil, and the theatre was a riot of hoots, jeers and hisses. The talent was, as a rule, nonprofessional and of an appalling ineptitude. A brazen-looking tough, decorated in torn trousers and an old Jersey sweater, moth-eaten and filthy, would appear on the stage for his debut. His manner and appearance betokened a truly vicious character. The rowdies in the audience were amazed at this spectacle of one of their own braving the footlights as an actor. Immediately, a fierce chorus of gibes was set in motion. "Aw, he's a pimp from Mott Street," "Whatsa matter, did they stop your relief check?" "Back to your shovel on WPA, you bum!" etc.

One wondered what this heathenish fellow would attempt on the stage. Some crude and violent posturings, no doubt. But, after the yells had subsided, he clasped his hands, rolled his eyes, and in a tremolo soprano cooed, "Now, I'm gonna sit right down and write myself a le-e-tter." It was such moments as this that set the Peoples Theatre on the Bowery apart from all other burlesque houses in the country.

In 1937, the La Guardia administration, severe as it was with the bigger houses, practically ignored this Bowery outpost. As a result, the entire cast of strippers at the Irving Place Theatre would journey down to the Peoples Theatre for Saturday midnight jamborees, wherein the principals of both shows would cavort in an endless procession of strip acts. It was an echo of gayer periods when two theatres under one management, such as the Star and Gayety in Brooklyn, would combine forces for a midnight gala. These Witches' Sabbaths lasted but a few weeks at the Peoples Theatre, but they provided the Bowery with the raciest spectacles it had ever seen since its decline.

As censorship finally closed in, Wilner and part owner and operator Tony Miccio relinquished control of the theatre. Yet, it lasted longer than most of the other houses, opening and closing irregularly, just as in the pre-Wilner days. Gladys Clark and Lola Pierce made their last stands at this house. A measure of life was given the theater, just before the end, when Babe Cummings, a roly-poly brunette, suddenly appeared as its operator in 1938. She had been a stripper at the Peoples in 1936, coming there from the chorus line at the Howard Theatre in Boston. Now an owner, as well as star, she had to protect her investment, which she did by seemingly performing without any G-string and letting the bunch at the Bowery know it.

But those days were gone forever. Paul Moss' vigilantes were very efficient. In 1939, the Peoples Theatre closed permanently.

But at least it was entirely fitting that the Bowery, which had been the first home of lusty burlesque in New York City, should also be the last to go in Manhattan.

HARLEM AND THE NEW GOTHAM

HURTIG & Seamon's Music Hall on 125th Street had started Harlem off as a burlesque center in the early 1900s. A little further north was Miner's Bronx. A few miles away in the other direction was the Yorkville Theatre. In the fullness of time appeared the Harlem Apollo and the Alhambra.

All of these claimed to be "class" houses. A few blocks east, however, on 125th Street, almost on the waterfront, stood a shabby hideaway, barely noticed, seldom recognized. This was the Gotham Theatre, and when all the other Harlem houses were gone, the Gotham persisted as the nudest of all burlesque theatres in New York City.

Before the 1930s, it had played the cheapest of stock shows intermittently and unsuccessfully for more than fifteen years. Ben Kahn had been interested in it before concentrating on his Union Square Theatre. As the New 125th Street Theatre, it was notorious for the incessant shimmying of its chorines, who were too decrepit even for Mutual. As a rule, the girls would climax their stint on the runway by lining up on the stage, backs to audience, still shaking furiously, and bend over as, with their hands between their legs, they waved goodbye, while the curtain descended mercifully on their distended rears.

The silent stag audience, Harlem counterpart of the Bowery scratch houses, stared moodily with the same unconcern they exhibited at the ancient Western movie "thriller" that followed.

During all these years, nobody had bothered to cut off the dressing rooms from the "Gents Room," which did not even have a door. The women in the cast had to run the gauntlet of an open, malodorous men's lavatory whenever they entered or left their dressing room.

At long last, in September 1930, after a usual six-month shutdown, George Katz, a real estate promoter, and Solly Shaw, burlesque booking agent, who had combined in the operation of the Werba's Theatre in Brooklyn, assumed ownership of the theatre. The lobby was swept free of accumulated debris. Posters, advertising "See Our Girls in Tandarlizing Poses," were replaced with more literate decorations. The room marked "Gents" was still without a door, but a new stage entrance for the performers was built at the 126th Street side of the theatre, just a few steps away from a police station. It was now renamed the " New Gotham" and in 1931 it was honored with a raid.

The new owners, subduing the cooching somewhat, but emphasizing the strip, in the current trend, were moderately successful for a time. In the meanwhile, Shaw and Katz lost the Werba's Theatre to the Minsky-Weinstock interest, and when they introduced Hirst Wheel shows at the New Gotham, they lost that too.

In the spring of 1933, Charles Schwartz, operator of the Oxford, tried stock there for a few weeks, but gave it up. Then, in August 1933, Abe Minsky, having definitely severed connections with his brothers, assumed ownership of the New Gotham as an opposition threat to the fading Apollo, showing hated Minsky-Weinstock productions.

In contrast to the lavishness of his younger brothers, Abe Minsky operated the New Gotham on a low budget with minimum-wage strippers and twenty-dollar-a-week chorus girls. He was able to draw competent talent at low prices because his theatre was one of the two remaining oases playing leisurely two-a-day shows, instead of the now prevalent grind policy—a reverse twist to the early days when only the New Gotham was a grind house.

Abe Minsky's line of action proved thoroughly correct. The theatre needed neither star names nor pretentious scenery. Surpassing even the Irving Place in nudity, the bits shortened and glossed over, the ensemble numbers simple and snappy, there was presented what License Commissioner Levine's inspectors called, in November 1933, "A parade of anatomy." As *The Billboard* stated in 1934: "Abe Minsky knows what they want after twenty years of the business."

The featured women, six or seven of them, including one chorine who also did a strip specialty, simply removed their clothing, with or without cooching, and then walked off the stage. No brassieres were worn to start with, and the shoulder straps of the dress went down at the end of the first strut. There was no applause the first three or four times the stripper went off the stage. It was known that she would be back, as a routine part of her act. After the fourth appearance, there was a roll of drums, and the stripper, now down to a G-string, took a bow. Then came a little applause, and it started all over again, at the point where in most every other burlesque houses it would end. The same unembarrassed obliging cutie reappeared again and again to a scattering of applause, progressively removing the G-string, then dangling it in one hand while using the other for protection, and at the last encore, playing hide and seek with her hands.

When the lights were raised to permit the playing of the next bit, the men sat back patiently, knowing that another similar strip would be due in about ten minutes. There was no limit to the number of the encores. The audience was the judge and it had to be satisfied. After intermission, all the strippers repeated.

Yet, the strangest part of this strange procedure was the absolute decorum that prevailed. There was no shouting, no hilarity, no brassy orchestra noises, no revelry, no adolescent hooting. The main floor was filled with silent, cigar-smoking burlesque-wise men, the prototypes of the early Irving Place audiences. The strippers did not sing, as a rule, before they started the undressing process, as common in other houses, and when they cooched, did so unctuously, with appropriate and methodical smoothness. It was all conducted with quiet, well-mannered, almost somnolent distinction. Compared to the yowling atmosphere of a Mutual show, the New Gotham was a Sleepy Hollow. Only, as it chanced, every few minutes, a starkly nude, well-proportioned young woman would undulate from one side of the stage to the other.

The ensemble numbers were produced by Billy Koud, a Columbia veteran, assisted by Abe's son, Harold. Though uninspired and monotonous, they never were too long or involved, as in most of the other houses.

The strippers who performed so assiduously for the New Gotham trade were, as might be expected, efficient and personable, but generally lacking the showmanship of the publicized stars. Teasers were not tolerated here. Mimi Lynne, whose enticing routine was that of "strip" above the waist, and "tease" below, was hurriedly substituted one week for an ailing principal. She was booed off the stage for failing to deliver according to the New Gotham standards.

The usual quiet of the theatre was somewhat disturbed by the gymnastics of Rose La Rose, who not only played peekaboo but fully exercised her hips and breasts in the process. She also was a talking woman in the bits and featured opening dresses, for ten successive weeks. Both Rose La Rose, a former box-office girl at the Republic, and Betty Rowland, appearing here after graduation from the Irving Place chorus, emerged from this Harlem experience as full-fledged and, then, top star strippers.

Thus, unadvertised, except by word of mouth—with hand over it—never overcrowded, but doing very well financially at a minimum of production costs, the New Gotham, with Sam Kraus, house manager since 1932, might conceivably have lasted forever. "Current show is the kind the customers go for," said one discreet critic in 1935. "Differing from the majority, Abe Minsky's Harlem location is strictly a man's world," said *Variety*.

Apparently, it was felt by the owners that for all the nudity displayed, the shows could not legally be considered obscene since they were conducted in so quiet and gentlemanly a fashion. Abe Minsky, who introduced his son Harold to burlesque via the New Gotham, certainly was not ashamed of it. His wife, Molly, like Max Wilner's wife, took a keen interest in the business end of the shows, was Secretary and Treasurer of the Burley Amusement Corporation, technical lessee of the theatre. She often conducted benefits there for the women's auxiliary of her local synagogue.

Nevertheless, of all the theatres, the New Gotham aroused the most condemnation and was the first to have its license revoked. Commissioner Moss would not even wait two weeks until May 1, 1937, the official expiration date, when he could merely have refused to issue another license, as in the case of all the other houses. He revoked it immediately. That act marked the end of the New Gotham Theater and in its wake the end of all burlesque in New York Ctiy.

BEYOND NEW YORK

THE pattern and behavior of the burlesque theaters in New York were duplicated throughout the country. Most large cities had one or two "class" houses and occasional mushrooming shoestring undertakings which were as pathetic as the New York or Chicago scratch houses. After the Wheels, many of the more substantial operations continued on a rotary stock basis, alternating two or three productions from theatres owned by the same management. Many played Supreme Circuit shows of the Minsky-Weinstock group, just as in New York. When the Supreme Circuit folded, they, too, joined the Hirst Wheel in a loose arrangement wherein they supplemented their stock shows with Wheel units under options permitting them enough flexibility to either continue with or discard the Wheel, as circumstances warranted. In the Midwest, Arthur Clamage organized the Western Burlesque Association, covering houses from Ohio to Omaha.

In 1933, just before the burlesque boom, there were about fifty burlesque theaters scattered throughout the United States. New York had the greatest number by far, eleven. Detroit was next with five, and Chicago with four. Los Angeles, at this time, had only one burlesque house, The Follies, and there was an exodus of West Coast burlesquers to New York, where the theaters were multiplying.

The more important operators and producers of the Middle West were represented at a conference in 1934. They included Arthur Clamage running the Gayety and Avenue Theatres in Detroit; Warren Irons of the Empire, Toledo and Roxy in Cleveland; Harry Hirsch of Minneapolis; N. H. Barger for the Star and Garter and Rivoli in Chicago; and Meyer Lantz of Cincinnati.

New York operators often went beyond New York City with more or less indifferent success. Max Wilner experimented with the Hudson Theatre in Union City, New Jersey, for a while, the Raymonds with the Orpheum in Paterson, New Jersey. The Wilner interests tried to buck the entrenched operations of Issy Hirst in Philadelphia, the profitable Bijou and Troc Theatres. They opened the Shubert Theatre for "glorified" burlesque, starring Ann Corio. They were unsuccessful. I. H. Herk went all the way to Chicago in 1931 to reopen the famous Star and Garter Theatre, which had been closed for about two years. He was not there very long, and the Star and Garter, after a few years of intermittent operation, shuttered its doors for good in 1935, leaving N. H. Barger's Rialto as the only "class" house in Chicago. The Rialto featured a popular group of male favorites, comedian Charles (Klutz) Country, straight man Jack Buckley and tenor Buster Lorenzo. The Mutual shimmy-shaker Jerri McCauley, now married to a wrestler, Ray Steele, was an ace female attraction there.

In 1936, the resurgence of burlesque in New York City was echoed by a revival on the West Coast. Nudist queens, headed by Zorita, were all the vogue in Los Angeles and San Francisco. In contrast to the East, where sheer stripping as practiced at the Wilner and Minsky houses in New York was the norm, the West Coast strippers embellished their routines with erotic specialties, including special boudoir and dream sequences. These novelties were just reaching New York in 1937. Popkin and Ringer led the West Coast operators with the Burbank and Million Dollar Theatres in Los Angeles and the Capitol and Moon in San Francisco

Just as in New York, the burlesque boom led many long-time operators to climb out of their shells and boast of their affiliation with the industry, as they regularly did when times were good and there was no censorship wave. In the early part of 1937, when all was as yet serene, Harry Hirsch celebrated his fifteenth season at the Gayety in Minneapolis. Hon Nichols, owner of the Baltimore Gayety, put in his bid for fame, boasting of thirty years of burlesque operation. Jimmy Lake, proprietor of the Gayety in Washington, D.C., covered the lobby of his theatre with clippings of his illustrious career, including his appointment as Boxing Commissioner. He had his detractors, however. They insisted that he was appointed to such high honors as compensation for the free passes he gave the influential members of Congress. In Boston, the ancient Howard Theatre went right on, effectively competing with the Park Theatre there, disregarding the persistent rumors that it was about to be torn down.

The managers passed through the same stages experienced by their New York colleagues. Starting on a small scale, they gradually expanded, became somewhat pompous and pretentious, wavered continuously between the erotica that brought in the customers and the yearning for respectability that comes with affluence. Their shows had to be geared to the tempo of the New York houses, and when the censors, led by the New York City authorities, bore down, they too were seriously affected, and many of them were forced out of business.

THE CANDY BUTCHERS

THE burlesque theatres might gilt-edge their façades, scrub clean the lobbies, and adorn them with a uniformed doorman. They might situate themselves in central, conspicuous locations, put tuxedos on the box-office men and present burlesque that was "glorified." But, omnipresent just the same, and all but omnipotent, were the candy concessionaires. Their pitchmen ballyhooed their meretricious wares before the burlesque show commenced and during the intermissions; and even before the curtain came down, at each finale they were already in front screaming their spiels in direct competition with the performers. They sold dirty pictures that were not dirty, French novelties that were neither French nor novel, and five-dollar prize boxes of candy for a quarter that were worth about a nickel—and all on the customers' time.

Their exhortations were time-proven mixtures of cajolery, outright begging, concealed knavery and open insults. When the candy butcher was severely heckled, as happened frequently, he looked quickly to spot the miscreant. If this culprit seemed to be alone, he was assailed as a "lowlife" or a "punk." If he was part of a truculent group, the pitchman was conciliating: "How would you like it if I stopped you from making a living?" This particular audience he was addressing was unusually fortunate: "Since there are just a few people here," or vice versa: "Seeing we have such a large crowd tonight . . ."

He was very frank and honest: "These beautiful gifts—I'll level with you—are not worth twenty-five or fifty dollars, but they are easily worth five to ten dollars at the very least. . . ." There may not have been a sale in the house, but no sooner had the pitchmen started to pace the aisles than the spieler jubilantly shouted: "There goes the first of the ten-dollar watches. Hold it up, please, so that we can all see it. Thank you. Oh, there goes the first of the genuine leather wallets and there's another—this time with a one-dollar bill. Hold it up, please. Thank you." After several moments, the leather-tongued, raspy-voiced candy butcher might dramatically order the sale stopped. After accusing some anonymous offender of calling the sale a fake, he would repeat his first spiel with additional and climactic fervor, finally commanding his salesmen to put aside "special for the next twelve lucky people with an ounce of sporting blood in their veins, twelve of the heaviest, twelve of the biggest, twelve of the costliest gifts, . . ." etc., etc.

Concessionaires have always been a part of burlesque. They were a holdover from the carnivals which gave the industry its first managers. Somehow, they have been indissolubly associated, as far back as one can remember, with tent shows and hootchie-kootchie dancers. From the 1890s on, advertisements such as the following regularly appeared:

> Mighty Hoag Shows—the Pride of Dixie
> Wanted—Candy Butchers
> 3 Oriental Dancers

In their early manifestations, in fact, the concessionaires provided an authentic masculine atmosphere to the shows. A portion of the theatre would be set aside for the sale and consumption of beer and the dispensation of pretzels and similar delicacies. Many an otherwise routine performance would assume glittering and riotous proportions when enjoyed under the benign influence of foamy suds, sawdust and a free lunch.

As burlesque gradually veered away from the beer hall and honky-tonk type of entertainment, the concessionaire simultaneously wheedled his way from the rear to the front of the house. During the sway of the two-a-day, he would appear about ten minutes before the opening curtain and at intermission to herald his wares. Then, there was no time wasted and no harm done. No time wasted, anyway. They always promised novelties and pictures 100 percent more ribald than what they actually sold. It was all done in the spirit of mild trickery. The police seldom bothered the peddlers. The censors were more concerned with the hypothetical morals of burlesque audiences than with their pocketbooks. Their money might be swindled with impunity, but their thoughts must remain virgin.

Naturally, the tougher and wiser the audience, the more difficult it was for the spieler. Hence there was the paradoxical situation whereby the candy butcher with his insulting persuasions flourished and was concentrated in the more refined, class theatres catering to the transient and sightseeing crowds, rather than in the rowdy slum spots.

The American Wheel, relying on regular neighborhood patronage, restricted the candy butchers and ordered their spiels to be brief, after complaints from harassed listeners who heard the same nonsense week in and week out. On the other hand, the Columbia Wheel, despite its self-proclaimed dignity, played welcome and liberal host to the candy butchers in all their cheapness. In fact, Sam Scribner himself was reputed to hold a financial interest in the candy concern that had the Columbia concession.

As they became firmly entrenched as part of the burlesque scene, the candy butchers, sometimes selling everything but candy, became more brazen and insistent in their eagerness for sales. The sexual allusions of their spiels were often bolder than those of the regular comedians. At the same time, they dignified their trade with an organization that bolstered the morale of the younger employees, pointed out the opportunities for advancement to master candy butchers—in which exalted state they did not peddle but only talked—and periodically held dances and socials for its membership. This was known as the Theatre Candy Concessionaires Association, and later as the Theatrical Concessionaire Managers Association. Further prestige came when one of its members, Al Corsky, married a soubrette and stripper, Syd Burke.

Under the grind policy of one-act shows lasting one and a half hours, continuous with movies, there was no necessity for an intermission, and the candy butchers could, ordinarily, have been eased out on the ground that there was no time for their services. Unfortunately, however, the owners, in too many cases, were bound over financially, hand and foot, to the concessionaires' interests. The latter sometimes were the real forces that kept a theatre open. When the Hurtig & Seamon Theatre on 125th Street was given up in 1929, for example, Oscar Markowitch, the man controlling all the concessionaires, not only took over the stage property but also the rights to the shows operated by Joe Hurtig and Harry Seamon.

By the time the grind policy came into practice in most of the houses, Oscar Markowitch was so inextricably tied in with the operators, and they with him, that leaving out his concessionaires in their theatres was as unthinkable as forgetting the first mortgage in a realty transaction. The operators rationalized that the butchers would, in any event, serve two purposes. First, they could fill in much of the surplus time that would be available if the five hours allotted to movies during each day were reduced. Inasmuch as the movies shown in burlesque houses were pretty hard to take, consisting of antiquated travel shorts, educational thrillers on deep sea diving, Andy Clyde comedies, etc., it would be just as well to reduce the number of shorts shown, and pad out the time with the spiels of the concessionaires.

Secondly, it was felt that a combination of movie shorts plus the harangues of the butchers would serve to drive away the "lodgers" who could and did stay through two shows and more. The owners were not touched by such flattering attention. They wanted the house cleared to make room for the later comers.

The result of such strategic cogitations was a timetable for the stage shows usually set for 12:30, 2:30, 7:00 or 7:30, and 9:30. The rest of the time was filled in with movies and spiels. There was a spot for the candy butcher before each burlesque performance and each movie showing including the time when the house first opened. This made eight opportunities in all before four different audiences. Under the two-a-day system, there were possible only four spiels a day before two audiences. And the audiences were, necessarily, captive audiences.

So, regardless of all pretense to any theatrical dignity, burlesque, by surrendering to the candy butchers, lowered itself again to the level of the wildcat gyp companies from which it originated. Only where, to quote the hawkers, "something hotter, something you can't get nowhere else" was anticipated could a paying audience tolerate such insults and such chicanery.

But the depressing fact was that the burlesque theatre owners were more captive than their audiences. Not only was Oscar Markowitch a top financial officer of Hirst's Independent Circuit, but in 1936, the heyday of modern burlesque prosperity, *The Billboard* observed: "Oscar Markowitch . . . probably has more invested in burlesque theatres than any other individual."

THE COMEDY AND THE COMICS

BURLESQUE humor is divided into two parts—old jokes that are dirty and old jokes that are clean. Burlesque comics have no particular aversion to clean jokes. All is grist to their mill. Even if burlesque were not a sexually based entertainment, the comedians would have to resort to suggestive dialogue and bits, because a whole new world of humor is thus open to them. The demands of burlesque, especially in stock, with new shows every week—in scratch houses every few days—were naturally too enormous even if the industry, like other entertainment media, could maintain large retinues of writers and editors, continuously grinding out new jokes. The comics in burlesque have always been desperate for material—of any kind and nature. Nor could they afford the luxury of emotion or satire or opinion in their routines. There was only one purpose in mind—to make their audiences laugh, no matter how.

Burlesque humor is a receptive vacuum. It has never thought for itself. If all its Jewish characters are depicted as mercenary, its Irish as drunkards, Germans as simpering simpletons, if all men are considered licentious and all women susceptible to a two-dollar bill, if all men with red neckties are effeminate and all middle-aged women madames, it is so for the simple and only reason that these clichés in the bits are convenient, handy methods for building up laughs. There is no more malice, meaning or deliberate reasoning in such characterizations than there is in the screechy repetitions of a parrot.

With the possible exception of the policeman type, under whose tyranny and petty grafting all burlesquers have groaned at one time or another, the "anything for a laugh" motto is the basis for all burlesque caricatures. "Anything for a laugh," says the comic to himself as routinely, without thinking twice of the implications or obscenity of his act, he distends the front of his trousers toward the corresponding anatomical portion of the talking woman in the bit, who is quite likely to be the wife of the straight man in the same scene.

Burlesque comedy, at the very beginning, even before it had a chance to get stale, was seldom anything to laugh at. Lydia Thompson's *Ixion* could never have survived without the Blondes. Typical of its wit was the following:

> Apollo: I've darted my last ray.
> Ixion: I never knew
> That you were both the son and darter, too.

Then, the Rentz-Santley shows and their prototypes initiated the type of laughgetters that have never changed, and are part of burlesque even today. These included mock courtroom trials, slapstick with the perennial bladders, racial caricature, and all sorts of horseplay. Billy (Beef Trust) Watson and his Krausemeyer's Alley typified this vogue. In the occasionally licentious afterpieces such as "The Sultan's Harem," "The Sultan's Dancers," etc., there was evolved that never-failing source of superior, knowing laughter—the eunuch. The eunuch, in the days of the Wheels, was transformed into a "sissy," then "nance" character; and in modern stock burlesque, particularly after the appearance of the Broadway play *The Captive,* the modern equivalent, the "fairy," became a burlesque staple. In its most advance manifestation, the male characters would group themselves around a circle and pat one another on the rear. Gus Schilling, after such a session, would truck off the stage, hand upraised, singing softly "Romance, romance . . ."

The Columbia Wheel nurtured, in addition to the finest comedians burlesque ever had, gifted writers, including among others Billy K. Wells, Leon Errol and Herman Timberg. Of more recent years, Eddie Cantor's script writer, Sid Fields, was in burlesque. But there never was, even then, and there never could be enough satisfactory material to satisfy the voracious demands of audiences which saw a new show every single week of the year.

The two basic comedy sources with the Columbia Wheel were rampaging husbands and racial caricature, both holdovers from the turn of the century afterpieces. Also standard in all burlesque shows was the use of odd descriptive names for the cast of characters, borrowed from musical comedy. *The Politician,* a Broadway musical, for example, produced in 1907, had in its cast A. Grafter, I. M. Wing, Stockson Bonds, Lotta Bonds, Ima Peach, Hiram Short and Seth Long.

During the entire duration of the Columbia Wheel, the only time when humor in burlesque had at least a chance, disappointment at its lack of comedy values was commonplace. Immediately after the formation of the Eastern Wheel, *Variety,* in 1907, lamented that burlesque humor was precisely like that of 1900, with stolen lines and stale devices, such as picking pockets, silly bets and throwing money on the floor. The "throwing money" gag was perfected by Al Reeves in 1908. According to tradition, he walked into an Elks Club and produced a bunch of $1,000 bills. "Boys, here's what I made this season," he boasted. Then, noticing a five-dollar bill, he flicked it off with his fingers. "How did you get in here? That must have been Reading." This version is more or less the one since used by all burlesque comics, up to and past Abbott and Costello.

In 1908, the following modern props were already decried by *Variety* as too stale: ". . . ill-smelling cheese, rubber-band comedy, money changing and pummelling with bundles." The courtroom scenes then and now would invariably commence as follows:

> "I'm Justice."
> "Justice what?"
> "Just as good as you are."

Bang! the bladder.

> "I object."

Squish! the seltzer-water.

> "Your Horror."

Bang! the bladder and so forth, ad infinitum. As early as 1908 Sime Silverman was already deploring "a lot of unnecessary horseplay with the bladders."

In 1912, the following familiar dialogue took place between Billy Arlington, the tramp in *The Golden Crook,* and soubrette Jeanette Buckley:

> Arlington: Will you give me a nickel for a cup of coffee?
> Buckley: Sorry, all I have is a ten-dollar bill.
> Arlington: Fine. I can change that.

The Sculptor's Studio bit, the favorite of Steve Mills, and shown in 1964 in *This Was Burlesque,* was already a favorite sketch way back in 1907 when it was featured in Hurtig & Seamon's *Bowery Burlesquers.* At that time it was labeled a "musical farce." In 1917, *The Billboard* declared that the following bits had "earned a pension":

1. Table scene where one player is drugged, the other is wise, feigns stupor, and comes out of it as the vampire takes his money.
2. Comedian makes love by instructions from book.
3. Comedians bet each other that they can pick up greenbacks without saying "Ouch."
4. Whiskey in the ice-cooler.

No wonder that in 1922, Fred McCloy, the peerless apologist for Columbia, had to admit that even he was "tired of bits." Before the coming of the strip act, which is usually blamed for audience indifference to comedy in burlesque, Nelson stated, referring to Columbia audiences, no less: "After sitting through *Gaieties of 1928* with its familiar bits and numbers, we are further convinced that patrons of Columbia Circuit shows want burlesque, and nothing else but burlesque."

"Not one new burlesque skit has been written in the last twenty years," exclaimed the attorney for the New Gotham Theatre in 1937 at a License Commission hearing.

The bane of burlesque, of course, is not the jokes themselves, which were funny the first dozen times around, but their inevitable staleness through repetition. These hackneyed clichés *are* burlesque humor, take it or, better still, leave it. Only the naïve bemoan it, since there never was a solution in the inherent nature of burlesque. One can only assume a superior condescension to it and go along with *The New York Times,* which summarized the situation in 1931:

> In twenty-nine other esthetic capitals of this nation last night a first comedian (some unheralded Bert Lahr) kicked a second comedian very decisively in the trousers, got his laughs and prepared to move on with his colleagues to the next town for another opening tomorrow evening.

On those occasions when the comics tried to be inventive and serious, the results were catastrophic. Dave Marion's *Stageland* in 1920 featured a depressingly long skit wherein the beggar, standing forlornly alongside a fashionable church, is ignored by all except the streetwalker with the heart of gold. The National Winter Garden, despite its raciness, went in for serious, intense dramatic playlets. Typical was the moral tract conceived by straight man Leon De Voe in which the sailors, on shore leave, accost the society girls whom they mistake for women of easy virtue. Thundered the police captain dramatically at the climax:

> When our best society dares go forth in the street with rouge and lipstick like any common prostitute, can we wonder that the pillars of society are falling apart? Can we blame these young men for the natural, honest mistake they have innocently made?

The weightiness of this harangue was sometimes lifted by the sailor's request to use the phone in the midst of the lecture. Permission granted, he asks for "Minnie's Place." Other literati of the National Winter Garden, Ray Paine and Tom Bundy, continued this melancholy trend, and when they passed on, Jack Linder, former associate of Mae West, was engaged to write similar serious disquisitions.

After burlesque discarded the olio and afterpiece sequence for the revue pattern, the comedians got into the habit of interposing "bits of business" to bolster the sketches. These "bits of business" were unrelated to anything in the show or in the bit itself. They could vary in nature from pawing at the women in the act to spitting in the straight man's eye. In this manner, a basically clean bit could be roughed up or dirtied at will, as circumstances dictated. If a bit needed lengthening, or time had to be killed for one reason or another, the action of the sketch could be preceded by comments about the "best part of a woman," a money-changing sequence, a "fairy" impersonation, or any of the multitude of timeworn routines that the comic and straight man might recall.

Two of the most common bits of business included the following:

> 1. The comic makes a pass at a girl. The girl says: "Say, you, be careful with that hand." This brings the never-failing retort, with the comic showing his other hand and crooking a finger: "Don't worry about that hand, baby. This is the one you wanna watch."
>
> 2. The French flirt keeps repeating: "You kiss me, ye-e-ss?" The comic in mock indignation: "What's that you said?" The French girl repeats: "You kiss me ess?" The comic: "I should say not. I never did and I won't now." The straight man: "Why that's nothing. That's just a custom in her country." The comic: "Well, that may be a custom in her country but that's the way you keep your job in this country."

With this as an apertif, the comic would finally proceed to the main course—the bit itself and its ageless plot. As often as not, the scene would have a bed in it, leeringly referred to as the "workbench." The action could involve a honeymooning couple or a lover and husband farce with dozens of familiar variations. Next in order of regularity on the program was the doltish policeman. His arrival was invariably greeted with, "Hey, boy, get me a policeman."

"Yeah, sure," responds the cop after making a false start to get one.

After a few moments of badinage, the cop will point to his badge.

"See that? That's headquarters."

The comic points to his backside.

"See that? That's hindquarters."

Double entendre was often provided by unsubtle use of the policeman's nightstick. Sometimes, the cop would be a woman, pleasantly swinging her club between her legs and proudly displaying a badge attached to the back of her tights or the thigh. The comic would, naturally, bend down to get a good look.

"Did you get the number on her badge?"

"Yeah, it was 0."

The ensuing blackout reminded all and sundry that this had a deep double meaning.

The third most repetitious scenes involved restaurants. The two comics would try to bluff their way into not paying the check as they have only twenty-five cents between them. Or the climax of the scene would be the preparation of some abominable malted, the ingredients of which were slop, sawdust and spit. For a straw, the comic selected a piece of broomstick and handed it to the guest. These colloquies were "musts" in all burlesque restaurant scenes.

> Waiter: Would the lady like some tongue?
> Woman: Sir, I'll have you understand I never eat anything that comes out of an animal's mouth.
> Waiter: Then, how about a couple of eggs?

The eggs were always asked for as follows: "Fry one on one side, and one on the other."

Also this:

> Woman: Waiter, I want one order of chicken soup.
> Waiter, calling to kitchen help: One order of chicken soup.
> Woman: Oh, I changed my mind. Make that pea soup instead.
> Waiter: Hold that chicken. Make it pea.

Then might come the numerous hotel scenes in which there was always a honeymooning couple, consisting of an old groom and a young bride, with all the characters peeking through the keyhole to see "if he can make it."

Next in order were the courtroom bits with the stupid judge, the lazy, dumb cop, the lady defendant crossing her legs to reveal her thighs, the never-failing bladders, and the judge's stand, which was always thrown down during the hot and heavy thumping of bladders. In the climax, the defendant admits that she shot her husband "between the coffeepot and the buttered toast."

The judge is enraged at this. "Imagine, if she had come one inch lower, she would have shot him right in the percolator." Blackout.

Sanctified by decades of continuous usage, the bits were as varied as they were numerous—the Love Books, the Woman Haters Union, the Buzzing Bee (where everybody is "buzzed" with water from the mouth), Jekyll and Hyde Change, Dentist's Office (filling a cavity), Sleeping in Room with Little Boy (No, thanks, I'd rather get wet in the rain), Kissing Vampires, Gasson (sic) the Lover, Tailor Shop (measuring the outside and inside seams), Slowly I Turned, Fluegel Street, Essence of Magic Perfume or Poppy, Parking the Car (Look, Joe, I found a place to park the car, as the girl bends over and lifts her dress), the Garter Bank (open day and night for deposits), Joe the Bartender, Not Yet Henry, etc., etc.

And in all burlesque shows, the following words were always sexually suspect: personality, scrutinize, Chevrolet, Queen's Box, machacha, Cleopatra's asp, tomb, mantilla, gondola, credentials, India, peace, cognomen, etc., etc., as well as practically all other words of more than two syllables.

As can be readily deduced, neither intelligence nor thought was necessary for comprehending the bits. What was helpful was a thorough grounding in suggestive gutter jargon.

Despite the general disparagement burlesque comics had to endure, they were considerably better than their material. Most, if not all of them, possessed a certain degree of professional competence, and many of them alternated burlesque with vaudeville or musical comedy engagements. They resembled the lower rank in any trade or profession, who are just good enough to be in it, but not quite good enough for anything better.

In the old days, the comics were infused with an excessive zeal for horrendous facial make-up. Billy (Beef Trust) Watson's putty and red nose was followed by the sideburns and whiskers of Joe Welch and the racial mimes and the grease-splattered tramp characters. The best of the modern comedians worked with little or no make-up, though they were sometimes given to outlandish costumes. In this respect burlesque humor did change, as slapstick gave way to the blackout, and the ear became more important than the eye.

Many comedians overcame the weakness of their material by proficiency in some specialty or characterization. Dave Marion was always remembered by his admirers as "Snuffy the Cabman." Clark and McCullough were renowned for their hotel room escapades. Lester Allen made famous the "Kiss Necessary to Get to Pearly Gates" bit in the *Bon Tons* show. Joe Freed established his specialty, in 1921, as a mock female impersonator with a red-wrapped balloon bosom. Joe Yule was never able to get out of burlesque for any length of time to keep company with his famous son, but in burlesque he was very well known for his "Hospital Sarah" bit. Jack Greenman was the one-man band who beat a drum, got a medal, then missed a beat and voluntarily returned the medal. Country and Buckley wowed Chicago audiences with the "Find the Lemon" bit. Harry (Hello Jake) Fields would present a dramatic sketch, "The Shoemaker," at the slightest provocation if one weren't careful, and Bob Carney always got a big hand by introducing two chorus girls as his daughters. Jack Diamond could make the antiquated Fluegel Street bit seem funny.

Often comics, long past their prime, would manage to hold on by virtue of their proficiency in one or two favorites. Cress Hillary, an aging wheelhorse, persisted in stock burlesque with his country bumpkin bit in which he turns the tables on the city slickers by adroit gunplay and then comes back to retrieve his lemon drops. Bob Nugent, after his descent to the Bowery, still amused with a skit which he had down to a timed science. It began with his arrest for a minor traffic violation during Prohibition. The following dialogue ensues:

> Cop: Here's a ticket for you.
> Nugent: Thanks, I wanted to see the fights.
> Cop: Well, this is a ticket to see Judge Murphy.
> Nugent: Who's he fighting?

At the conclusion Nugent was hauled to jail for having wine in a jug that he had been conspicuously swinging all along.

Many comics teamed up with a straight man as a permanent act. The most prominent of these were Abbott and Costello. No doubt, other experienced straight men who worked with Lou Costello consider themselves as able as Bud Abbott. But for the quirks of fate, it must seem to them, they too would have been among the nation's toasted stars, playing at the White House through invitation performances, instead of languishing in side-street dumps.

Lou Costello, who called himself the "Bad Boy of Burlesque," was a typical slapstick comedian ever since he was co-featured with Mutual's ace shimmy-shaker, Peaches Strange, in the *Laffin Thru* show in 1929. In 1936, paired with Abbott, he appeared at the 42nd Street Apollo. Also in the cast was Bud's wife, Betty, a veteran Mutual soubrette. After thirty weeks at the Apollo, they went to the Steel Pier in Atlantic City, and in 1938 were guests on Kate Smith's radio program. Thereafter, their rise was phenomenal. Their acclaim, resulting from the use of the oldest bits and hokum in burlesque with new audiences, is further proof that it is not the quality of burlesque humor that is at fault, but the endless repetition thereof.

At the 42nd Street Apollo, known for its lavish strip policy, the big attraction was the girls, not the comedians, even though they were Abbott and Costello. And when censorship banned the strip, the Apollo, regardless of its vaunted comics, was unable to draw enough customers to stay open. Indeed, nobody was more aware of their subordination to the strippers than the comics themselves. A favorite bit had the comic seated in a box, pretending to be part of the audience, and heckling the straight man on the stage: "Get the hell off the stage and bring on the women. That's what we want."

Phil Silvers first appeared in burlesque in 1936. He attracted attention at once, and Joe Bigelow of *Variety* advised, "The worst mistake he can make is to remain in burlesque longer than necessary." However, for lack of any place to go, he knocked about the humblest houses until eventual recognition. He was able to rise above the environment of stock burlesque, laughing at it as in his withering parody of the candy butchers. Similarly, Red Buttons, in burlesque for even a shorter period, ridiculed with exaggerated effect the standard bit of business in which the girl momentarily lifts her dress over her hips. "Hold it," he would admonish the girl. "Don't put the dress down yet. Make sure everybody has a good look."

Rags Ragland was another comic of modern burlesque who seemed talented enough to go beyond it. He did, time and again, but somehow always found himself back in burlesque among his old cronies. He began as an eccentric dancer in Joe Catalano's *Flapper Follies,* a Mutual show. A tall, gangling personality of decided mannerisms both on and off the stage, he drawled his lines in a slow, hesitant, ironical tone that contrasted sharply with the bawling bombastic style of his colleagues. He appeared in Broadway musicals, on the radio, and even had a Hollywood contract at one time. But to the day of his death he was primarily known as a burlesque performer.

There can be no doubt that many who attended burlesque shows in the past recall with the charity of nostalgia occasional hilarious episodes of enjoyable slapstick or engaging hokum. Such moments did exist, and nobody would have preferred this type of appeal more than the burlesque operators themselves. Unfortunately, the paying customers who kept the theatres open, the patrons who attended week after week, did not go for the jokes. They soon got tired of that. The owners had to cater to the "regulars," who paid the bills. Whether they liked it or not, and regardless of the consequences, the modern producers had no choice but to "strip" both the girls and the comedy.

MORALITY AND UNIONISM

WHEN all other theatrical crafts were strongly unionized, the burlesque performer alone remained outside the pale. The general notion persisted that an actor or actress in burlesque was ipso facto a queer duck, outside the fringe of the respectable world, a derelict personality of the demimonde to whom the ordinary privileges of decent hours and decent wages need not apply.

From earliest times burlesquers have segregated themselves from the rest of the theatrical profession. Like fellow sufferers in misery, they tended to become a clannish, suspicious group sufficient unto themselves. So much of a closed corporation was burlesque that even the professional reviewers hired by the trade magazines were usually not aloof critics, but actually part and parcel of the industry themselves. Alfred Nelson and Sidney Wire came to *The Billboard* from burlesque and then returned to it. Charlie (Uncle Dudley) Daniels, also of *The Billboard,* became manager of a burlesque theatre when his writing days were over. Sid Rankin, another professional commentator, was the father-in-law of a burlesque comic, the husband of Columbia prima donna Jessie Rice. Charles M. Feldheim, widely read author of U-Notes, a column of gossip about burlesque players, and also supervisor of the Sunday burlesque page for the *Morning Telegraph* for seventeen years, had been intimately connected with the industry first, and the press second.

This estrangement on the part of the burlesque people was not entirely of their own doing. Performers in more artistic fields often expressed their disdain of burlesque as cheapening the entire profession. Burlesquers were usually excluded from theatrical shindigs to which even the horses from Cain's warehouse were invited. Stage benefits traditionally included personalities from every possible sphere, except burlesque.

In 1910, the Actors Fund made a gesture of rapprochement toward the burlesque actor, stating: "The burlesque people may call upon the Actors Fund of America for assistance just as freely as any branch of the profession," adding this comforting note: "The last six persons to be buried by the Fund were burlesque performers."

In 1912, Sidney Wire lamented: "There are even more ignorant performers who look askance at burlesque and imagine that its very name is a joke and that the very thought of the word burlesque is to be discreetly shunned and banished."

Lacking a Lambs Club or The Friars, burlesque managers and advance agents organized their own Burlesque Club in 1915, excluding performers, however. In 1918 Henry C. Jacobs reorganized the Burlesque Club, and this time performers were permitted to join, but only if they were of top caliber. The rank and file were still unwelcome. Nelson made it a point in *The Billboard* that the members of the Burlesque Club were all "Men of Morals." Active members included the prominent figures of I. H. Herk, Billy Minsky, Emmett Callahan, Rube Bernstein, W. S. Campbell and Henry P. Dixon. There were no women members.

With the almost complete identification of burlesque with the shimmy and the strip, the Burlesque Club became a rather embarrassing stronghold for "Men of Morals." In 1936, after a partial liquidation, Emmett Callahan remained as president. Bobby Clark, of Clark and McCullough, a former president, was still loyal to it. But now there was a new vice president, candy concessionaire Oscar Markowitch.

For the average performer, there was no Burlesque Club and no union. Working for minimum wages under the most rigorous traveling conditions, forced to dress and undress in barns, crowded into one-night stands devoid of the most primitive sanitary facilities, subject to rain and frost, humiliation, contempt and occasional arrest, the burlesquer necessarily had to be a hardy, self-sufficient trouper. As the comic might say with bland acceptance of his lot: "I don't have to do this for a living. I could starve."

The entertainers in burlesque were too intent upon making a living to indulge in the luxury of deep moral evaluation. They shook their bodies and spewed forth their blasphemies routinely and unthinkingly. More often than not, they married conventionally among themselves, just like ordinary folk.

To a stranger to burlesque, the lines delivered by the performers might seem unspeakably vile and perverted when heard for the first time. They could be mouthed only by the degraded. To the burlesquer, however, as often as not a husband, wife or parent in good standing, these bawled obscenities were an ancient glib ritual so often heard and repeated that they fell from the tongue as easily and as thoughtlessly as a child reciting Mother Goose. David Dressler expressed it aptly: "Burlesque performers act vice, but they do not live it."

Though there has always been the tendency to deprecate the current players in burlesque, in contrast to the "good old days," the sad fact is that among the early burlesque troupes, according to Sidney Wire in *The Billboard* (October 12, 1919), "Every other show had a smoker or 'hop field' among the members . . . other members of the company attending the smokefests or hop parties at the hotel after the show every night."

Nevertheless, at least when the Wheels dominated the industry, the average burlesque performer was not the happy-go-lucky, don't give a damn, B.S. Pully type of character that one might envision. On the contrary, he was more likely to be a cautious, scared family man who preferred the security of a Wheel season contract to the vagaries of the more hazardous forms of show business.

Many stories have been circulated throughout the profession about the adventures and misadventures of the chorus girls. In 1919, for example, two chorines of the *Follies Frolics* went out on an automobile trip with three male acquaintances who became quite troublesome during the course of the ride. The girls, evidently too tired to walk back, called the police. As a result of the ensuing charges and countercharges, the girls submitted to a physical examination, which to everyone's pride, and perhaps astonishment, disclosed that they were virgins. The incident led Nelson to depose that as an editor he knew the executives of the Wheels to be "men of intellect, refinement and integrity." As a patron and reviewer, he added, he had closely observed the feminine members of burlesque, in the line of duty and "from what I have seen and heard I conscientiously believe that their moral standing is equal to any other in the world of arts and science."

In 1936, Buddy Wade, a chorine at the Boston Howard, burned to death backstage when her costume caught fire. Yet, at the cost of her own life, she kept away from the rest of the cast lest their inflammable costumes also catch fire.

The rescue of Frances Clare from an excited audience by her comedian husband Guy Rawson in the early days of the Columbia Wheel was paralleled in 1938 when Brownie Sick, straight man, retrieved his wife, stripper Toots Brawner, from an overstimulated mob which overran the stage of the Republic Theatre on a "Milkman's Matinee," New Year's Eve. The two then locked themselves in their dressing rooms for protection.

The parent-child combination has been ever present, from the days of Pop and Ida Siddons to Lillian Dixon and Vinnie Phillips. Kitty Madison sheltered her son in a military academy and, in the best sentimental tradition, visited him regularly during her travels on the circuit. Tiny Huff, a Columbia chorine and then a stock stripper and coocher, was inordinately proud of her daughter who auditioned on the radio. Joe Yule was a regular visitor to the movie lots to see Mickey Rooney, then known as Joe Yule, Jr. The prediction was then freely made by his burlesque colleagues that once movie directors saw Joe, Sr., "mugging" in character costume he would be lost to burlesque forever. Hattie Beall, through all her tempestuous years as queen of stock, mothered a precocious daughter, as did Agnes Nichols, another Mutual star.

In 1936, Lola Pierce had her fifteen-year-old daughter Rose at the Gaiety Theatre on 46th Street, New York City, as a special singer, following which Ma Pierce herself was engaged in her usual capacity as a stripper and shaker. The swivel-hipped Mlle. Fifi, hell-raiser of stock burlesque, anticipated Gypsy Rose Lee by five years in writing her own book during 1935. Though retired from burlesque, she appeared in the same year at a Philadelphia Food Fair, impersonating Mae West, while her seven-and-a-half-year-old daughter gave an impersonation of Shirley Temple.

Ethel De Veaux, hotcha woman of early rough stock burlesque—Kahn's Union Square Theatre and the National Winter Garden—herself the daughter of vaudeville parents, married comic Bennie Platt of the *Razzle Dazzle* show, continued in this show with him up to the very birth of her child, and then returned with her husband and infant to Sliding Billy Watson's show. When she married again, this time to comic Jack Diamond, she remained in burlesque as a talking woman on the Independent Wheel, serving as a foil for her husband in the usual smirking bits.

Vickie Welles was one of the stars in the last wild days of the strip era. Walter Winchell wrote of her: "She . . . doesn't drink, smoke, cuss or misbehave and goes straight home after each show to her mother." Vickie Welles' specialty, as one would never guess from this description, consisted in stripping nearly nude, rubbing the inside of her thigh with one hand, fondling an exposed nipple with the other, and all the time grinding and bumping.

When stripper Queenie King was interviewed on radio station WMCA about her craft, she received fan mail comprising "a pocket edition of the New Testament, a copy of the Gospel according to St. Matthew, several excerpts of Biblical passages and a four-page letter addressed 'Dear Sister,' exhorting Miss King to give up stripteasing." This did not reform Miss King, but gave everybody in burlesque a big laugh.

The aging, frowsy burlesque queen is not uncommon in fiction. However, when a burlesque performer does retire, usually when he can no longer walk, the same conditions prevail that are found elsewhere. A few—the big names—have put aside substantial investments to live on comfortably in their old age. There will be a few indigents who will require the benefactions of the other members of the profession. Many will, after a while, attempt to climb back into the amusement field, usually with pathetic results. A great many will set up business enterprises of their own. In 1912 Sidney Wire noted:

> There are few principals who have been long in burlesque who are not fairly comfortably independent and many of them own their own palatial homes at Freeport, Fairhaven or in some other Long Island or New Jersey suburb of Greater New York.

This happy circumstance, unfortunately, has not always prevailed. Al Reeves in 1914 was declared to be worth half a million dollars, but Harry Steppe had to be the recipient of a public benefit. W. S. Campbell and his wife, Rose Sydell, lived in comfort after their retirement, but Campbell's burlesque partner, Johnny Weber, died destitute. Mark Lea was a burlesque comedian for years. He was, to use one of his own expressions, "wined and dined." At the height of his popularity in 1918, he was producing director at the National Winter Garden. But in his later years he descended to the basement of a 14th Street sideshow doing eight or ten musical performances a day. And still clinging precariously to the coattails of his profession, he was last observed in a Coney Island peep show.

Too old to be a performer even at the last outposts, the Oxford and the Bowery, Evelyn Ramsey still clung to show business, literally by hook and crook. After employment as a wardrobe mistress, she was hired as a personal maid and then secretary to Tallulah Bankhead. In 1951, she was indicted for raising the amounts on checks given her by her employer. In a histrionic feat that would do credit to Miss Bankhead, this hard-bitten veteran of the Wheels and stock burlesque at its seediest, now appeared in the image of a gently bewildered, naïve matron. Fifty-nine years of age, she impressed *The New York Times* as "white-haired, motherly looking." However, this did not stop her from hurling vicious countercharges against her employer. She was finally found guilty of second-degree larcency and given a suspended sentence.

On the other hand, Kitty Madison saved enough from the earnings of her career as a torso-twister to withdraw luxuriously to her Flatbush residence when the Wheel was crumbling in 1931. The other runway favorite, Viola Elliott, opened up a millinery business in Des Moines, Iowa, during 1932. Mildred Cozierre, however, returned to burlesque after her proudly announced retirement to manage her father-in-law's apartment house. Margie Pennetti, who started in scratch houses and ended there, managed a kitchen concession in a bar and grill in midtown New York at the conclusion of her tumultuous career. Bert Carr, whose wife, Beverly, was a burlesque dance ensemble director, opened a delicatessen, but thought better of it after a while and returned to burlesque, still giving out with his specialty—a hearty, noisy belch in the midst of a solemn speech.

In the days of the Wheels, the summer layoff found the headliners relaxing in resorts like Lake Hopatcong which had housed a burlesque colony since the early days of the Columbia Circuit. More recently, burlesque performers would hasten to the Catskill Mountains in the summer, not for rest but for employment on the Borscht Circuit. There was no stripping, but the comics, for once, were in their glory. No bit was too ancient or too vulgar for Saturday night. On Friday night, the straight man donned a tuxedo and belted out the Prologue from *Pagliacci* with appropriate tremors and gestures.

Through it all, adversity, squalor, heroism, the burlesque performer, nonunionized, remained in a class by himself. In 1886, when burlesque was still classed with vaudeville, a secret organization, The AAB, Alpha Amusement Bureau No. 1, purported to cover all variety actors. This mysterious "Bureau" soon passed into oblivion. In 1909, the militant White Rats Actors Union was organized, a merger of the White Rats Union and the Actors Union. By this time, the cleavage between burlesque and vaudeville had become so marked that the new union concentrated almost entirely on vaudeville. Succeeding theatrical unions—Chorus Equity, Actors Equity and the Actors Betterment Society—similarly were indifferent to burlesque.

In 1933, the industry, to its surprise and gratification, was given official recognition as a legitimate enterprise in the formulation of the New Deal NRA codes. There was a great deal of discussion about minimum wages, reasonable working hours, etc., all of which gave impetus to the first burlesque union for the performers, the Burlesque Artists Association, known as the BAA. This was founded in June 1933 and was headed by Tom Phillips. Phillips had been a straight man, a rather unsuccessful producer of shows on his own, and a censoring doctor for Wheel productions in 1929.

It was brought out that some chorines were earning $10 to $12 weekly and working seven days a week for 82 hours. Though a good "top banana" could earn $150 a week, many principals received no more than $25 to $30 weekly. In 1934, claiming a paper membership of 1,300, the BAA was granted an AFL charter from the 4 A's (Associated Actors and Artistes of America). It then obtained a closed shop in the larger Eastern theatres, raising minimum salaries eventually to $22.50 weekly for chorines in stock, $25 if on the road. The minimum for principals was established at $40 weekly. Improved working conditions were obtained. Rehearsals, for example, were limited to fifteen hours per week and had to end at 2:00 A.M., with the exception of one night, when they could end at 3:00 A.M.

The BAA also attempted to correct the various booking evils that had arisen when the Wheels went out of business. The Columbia Wheel had maintained its own subsidiary, the Burlesque Booking Office, under the direction of Ike Weber, which placed both Columbia and American Wheel performers. Mutual had an "Engagement Bureau." With the rise of stock, the independent booker became very important. The top booking agency was that of Milt Shuster, a former burlesque comic, with offices in Chicago. His slogan was "Be a Booster for Milt Shuster." The BAA franchised only those booking agents who agreed to a 5 percent commission, including Milt Shuster in the West and Jack Beck, Phil Rosenberg and Lou Redelsheimer in the East.

At its formation in 1933, the BAA had one female executive board member, its secretary, Florence Naomi, a singer. Succeeding elections produced an all-male executive board. It was assumed that the interests of the chorus girls would be protected by Tom Phillips, whose wife was a chorine, but, significantly, nobody thought of giving the strippers any representation until 1936 when Carrie Finnell was elected to the executive board. In 1936, at its height, the BAA had jurisdiction over 40 to 50 theatres, 500 principals and 1,000 chorines.

It lost both prestige and most of its membership in the 1937 censorship debacle. It almost had its charter revoked, in addition, by the 4 A's on the ground that, under the new regulations, the theatres were presenting vaudeville, not burlesque. The BAA then changed its name to Brother Artists Association, eliminating "burlesque" in the fashion of the times, and continued to serve as sole bargaining agent with the surviving Hirst and Midwest Circuits.

Ironically, it had attained power and position in the industry immediately before its collapse. It had, at long last, invested the burlesque performer with a measure of human dignity.

Who could have foreseen that the censor was to take it away?

CENSORSHIP

BURLESQUE, having minimized the comedy and dulled the chorus line, was left with the strip act as its sole drawing power. In 1937, censorship took away the strip act and that all but ended burlesque.

Unlike other essentially illegitimate enterprises, burlesque theatres are open, in public view, and officially licensed. As a result they have always been fair game for the censors, professional and amateur, in the periodic waves of reform. The ". . . Comstockian trait in American psychology at periodic intervals becomes hysterical with the passion for reform," cautioned Rabbi Israel Goldstein, one of the more liberal of the clergymen, just a few years before the entire clergy pounced on burlesque.

Invariably, censorship on the legitimate or vaudeville stage has threaded its way down to the burlesque shows and, having no other place to go, remained there indefinitely. When Sally Rand appeared in the New York Paramount Theatre, she was ordered to wear panties. The fan dancer donned long flannel underwear, receiving some excellent publicity and a good week's gross at the box office. But the burlesque houses for weeks thereafter had to tone down their shows with correspondingly serious declines at their box offices.

Like burlesque itself, the routine of the censors up to 1937 had not changed much since Millie De Leon was grabbed by the scruff of her neck in the middle of her performance and thrown into a patrol wagon. Subsequently, the calmer procedure of waiting until the performance was concluded was adopted. But in either case the court trials were usually farcical and ludicrous, as a fat policeman would attempt an imitation of the cooch dancer on the witness stand. These raids, flamboyant and sensational, pleased everybody. They appeased the more superficial guardians of morality, on one hand, and provided some welcome publicity for the burlesque operators, on the other.

The technique adopted in 1937 in New York City of revoking or withholding licenses first and asking questions afterward was, by contrast, so directly effective, so forthright and efficient, that one might wonder why it had never been used before. The answer is that it had been tried before, but evidently the political power of the burlesque impresarios had been so well exercised or the censors had been so naïve that this dreaded device was discarded in favor of the simpler, easier, but futile methods of police arrests and court trials.

As early as 1909, *Variety* reported the anxiety of the owners over the renewal of their annual licenses on the fated May 1, this time because of the Sunday law: "May 1, the time for the renewal of theatrical licenses, is approaching, and this is said to be the reason for the renewed strictness of the policy in enforcing Sunday laws."

Since License Commissioner George H. Bell had availed himself of his privileges of license revocation in 1915, this drastic remedy had been practically forgotten. Skirmishes with the standard censoring authorities were routine and anticipated. However, as soon as the operators came out of hiding and marched up to 42nd Street, they met opposition of a sterner and more lasting nature. It took seven years after the opening of the Republic Theatre. The burlesque producers won many battles and their prosperity was remarkable, but they lost the final battle and with it almost the entire industry.

The scandal of three or four burlesque theatres concentrated in the heart of the Times Square district brought forth at first the wrath of the tabloids. Special observers were sent to the scenes of public iniquity. Lengthy and detailed reports were furnished to avid readers of the exact nature of the dialogue and the corruptive methods of undress one might see in these places. The New York *Daily Mirror*, particularly, was vehement in its attacks, all of which demanded, in effect: "When Will Somebody Do Something About It?"

The only ones who did something about it at the time were the Minsky-Weinstock interests, who posted the following on the backstage bulletin boards of the Republic, Harlem Apollo and Central Theatres during the last months of 1931:

Notice to All Performers

> We will not tolerate any indecent language or action on this stage. This refers particularly to the comics.
>
> All women must be decently covered, which means full brassieres and full net covering on backs at all times.
>
> Any violation means instant dismissal.

This self-imposed regulation, whether enforced or not, at least saved face for the police who had, thereby, an answer to the embarrassing crusades of the tabloids.

But, worse trouble was on the way. The 42nd Street Property Owners and Merchants Association, comprising most of the businessmen in the Times Square area affected by the prevalence of the burlesque houses, had never been especially noted for its zeal in reform. In the spring of 1932, however, it launched a bitter attack against burlesque in general, and the 42nd Street houses in particular, not because the theatres depreciated realty values but on the ground that they constituted a menace to morality. And with the eminent Ferdinand Pecora as counsel, the 42nd Street Association prepared for battle.

For the opening volley, the Association had the Eltinge Theatre raided in the routine manner, but the theatre was just as routinely acquitted in the courts. According to the decision, the dialogue at the Eltinge undoubtedly had double meanings, but it could not, from a sound juridical viewpoint, be considered indecent.

The 42nd Street Association took this setback quite calmly. It was obvious that reinforcements were needed, and they came quite readily in the form of the Society for the Suppression of Vice and the clergy. The Republic and Central Theatres were then raided. Again—court acquittals. Possibly, having seen the coming raids advertised for the past several weeks, the theatres had made their shows as clean as possible under the circumstances. They were unquestionably 100 percent cleaner than the burlesque shows in other parts of the city, which kept rolling along without any police interference whatever.

After the dismissal of charges against all the Broadway theatres, the 42nd Street Association started on a more ominous note. Proceedings were instituted before License Commissioner James F. Geraghty to have the licenses due for renewal on May 1, 1932, withdrawn. Prolonged hearings were then begun in April, and were not concluded until the middle of May. At the hearings, everybody seemed against burlesque, including the License Commissioner. The burlesque people were called loathsome and licentious. Cardinal Hayes led the attack of the clergy, branding the theatres as "Breeders of Vice." A license inspector testified that he had actually witnessed a card game for money backstage at the Eltinge Theatre. This time, also, emphasis was placed on the deterioration of the neighborhood as a result of the barkers and peddlers and steerers who were the "camp followers" of burlesque theatres. Commissioner Geraghty himself was reported ready to prove that the lobbies of the theatres were "loitering places for men who trade on the shady side of night life." A long-time foe of burlesque theatres, Reverend Joseph A. McCaffrey, of Holy Cross Church on 42nd Street, a police chaplain, branded 42nd Street "a cesspool of filth and obscenity."

After a mountainous array of alleged high crimes and misdemeanors, the burlesque people took the stand. As became theatrical folk, their testimony was more spectacular and dramatic, if less convincing. The ninety-three-year-old Mother Elm was brought forth to attest to the morality of the girls. Joseph Weinstock, sobbing and, according to *The New York Times,* "gesticulating with dramatic force," cried out that he was doubly accursed. First, he had begged the authorities to rid the sidewalks of pornographic peddlers and steerers only to be disregarded. Then he was blamed at the hearings for their very presence. It was all a conspiracy, he charged, on the part of Arch Selwyn and the Erlanger interests.

"We've been accused of everything except kidnapping the Lindbergh baby," he shouted.

Reginald Marsh, the famous artist and specialist in paintings of burlesque scenes, testified that in his opinion burlesque was "a part of American life." Cleon Throckmorton, the stage designer, arose to state that buresque was the poor man's theatre. Elias E. Sugarman testified that burlesque was offensive but not degrading. Brooks Atkinson, asked if he knew any way of remedying the situation since he disapproved of censorship, replied helpfully, "only by improving the human race."

Among the added miscellaneous witnesses trotted forth by the defendants were the mother of a burlesque chorine and the legitimate producer A. H. Woods. The female ushers and cashiers, it was pointed out, were never annoyed, regardless of how allegedly dirty the show or lecherous the audience. It was brought forth that such respectable personages as Maurice Chevalier, Horace Liveright and Otto Kahn had attended performances at the Republic. A real estate man estimated for the burlesque interests that as many as five to six thousand persons attended the Republic or Eltinge Theatre daily.

At this point, Commissioner Geraghty decided to become a spectator at a Republic show himself. In a ceremonious and majestic manner, due notice having been given of his arrival, the License Commissioner was treated to a performance which, it was later claimed, differed substantially from the usual presentations.

In the midst of the hearings a mysterious telegram purporting to come from Jane Cowl, to the effect that she dared not visit Woods' offices atop the Eltinge Building, was found to be a forgery, emanating, it was claimed, from the Selywn offices.

On May 11, the hearings were finally brought to a close with a plea from the National Council of Freedom from Censorship asking that the licenses be not withdrawn. Commissioner Geraghty then prepared to digest the voluminous testimony, and as no decision could obviously be made for some time in the face of all the work involved, the burlesque theatres were permitted to operate as usual pending the outcome.

Nothing happened. The cause célèbre was practically forgotten, until it was suddenly revived by Acting Mayor Joseph V. McKee in September 1932. McKee's first official utterance was to declare himself in favor of clean burlesque, and one of his first official acts was a conference with License Commissioner Geraghty who, presumably, was still reading testimony.

Coincidentally, following his conference with Acting Mayor McKee, the License Commissioner announced that he had just come to a decision. The licenses would not be renewed. And on September 20, the Republic and Eltinge Theatres were forced to close.

The metropolitan newspapers, in general, from the *Times* to the *Mirror,* applauded this new and sensational move, though a few opinions were voiced that it was all a political gesture. *The New York Times* editorialized (September 21, 1932): ". . . these performances have sunk to a level of lewdness never before tolerated in this city, and not to be tolerated now if any standards whatever are to be maintained."

Variety prophesied with undue optimism (September 27, 1932): "The strippers and shakers of burlesque have stripped and shaken for the last time."

The New York *Herald Tribune* was even more exuberantly mistaken, prophesying in its issue of December 30, 1932: "The year about to sign off will be remembered as the year when burlesque shows were forever stopped."

The Republic and Eltinge Theatres immediately went to court; and in their lobbies where once full-sized photos of girls in dishabille had been flagrantly posted, there now appeared argumentative posters expounding on the justice of their case and attacking the New York *Daily Mirror* and its publisher, A. J. Kobler, who in turn threatened to sue the burlesque owners for one million dollars libel. Above all, the Republic claimed, it had played to 800,000 men and women in the year and a half of its existence as a burlesque house. Apparently, Joseph Weinstock felt that 800,000 Americans couldn't go wrong.

But, notwithstanding these polemics, the theatres remained closed, and Max Rudnick of the Eltinge, particularly, lost heart after an adverse Supreme Court decision. He was all for giving up the fight, and reopening his theatre for "Musical Follies."

However, there are more ways than one to skin a cat, or peel a stripper, as the Minskys had learned from long experience. Before another month had elapsed, the public excitement and conjecture had died down, and popular interest was transferred to other transient objects. At this propitious point, Samuel A. Scribner was called upon to lead the procession to City Hall, and with remarkable ease and a minimum of publicity the licenses were quietly restored.

"Any objections?" asked the License Commissioner, looking around him cautiously. This time no one appeared to interpose any valid objections. That was all there was to it.

Scribner, back in the industry, became a semiofficial censor, paid, however, by the very owners whose shows he was supposed to censor. Herk, who in the face of the common peril had forgotten past differences with Weinstock and Herbert Minsky, was given credit for the master move in securing the intervention of the respected head of the mighty Columbia Wheel.

For a time, all was serene. There were occasional raids here and there, as at the Oxford in February 1933. But this was as it always had been. The License Commissioner would issue a severe order to the theatres to clean up in twenty-four hours. And they did. Only it would seem that they mistook the order to read "for twenty-four hours." Be that as it may, the public temper had noticeably changed. The moral indignation of *The New York Times* in 1932 had now given way to a sorrowful but tolerant note, as per the homily under Topics of the Times (May 17, 1933):

> The issue is, actually, not so much moral as economic and, possibly, political. The alleged obscenity of the burlesque shows is exceeded by their external frowsiness. The neighborhood of such theatres takes on the character of a slum.

In lieu of the unanimous outbursts of indignation of the previous year, the *New York Sun,* for example, printed the following letter from a subscriber (June 10, 1933):

> In spite of having attended burlesque shows extending over many years, I have never discovered any burlesque show impaired the morals of any of its patrons. De gustibus non est disputandum. Let burlesque live for the entertainment of its sophisticated patrons. No robust theatregoer should be bothered by touches of Rabelaisan or Decameronic humor.

And John Mason Brown, dramatic critic of the *New York Evening Post,* remarked (July 13, 1933): "What they continue to offer uptown is the same thing they used to offer downtown."

The 1933 licenses were renewed practically as a matter of course.

But troubles never ceased. In October 1933, Geraghty, who had supported the unsuccessful McKee against the new Mayor, John P. O'Brien, was superseded as License Commissioner by Sidney Levine, who at once proceeded to belittle his predecessor. The easiest way was through the burlesque shows, which he termed morally destructive. "Geraghty," the new Commissioner charged, "permitted obscene shows to go on running solely to embarrass Mayor O'Brien."

License Commissioner Levine served summonses on all the burlesque houses that he considered indecent, including practically all of them. He decreed that hereafter there would never be tolerated the removal of clothes on any stage in New York City in an indecent manner. But "immobile tableaux and statuesque presentations with distinctly artistic appeal provided the vital parts are clad in opaque raiments" were given the stamp of approval. This turned out to be a boon rather than a ban, for in practice it gave official sanction for the first time to the baring of breasts, whereas the verbiage about removing clothes "in an indecent manner" added nothing to what was already on the statute books.

There was a great deal more furore. The practically defunct Gayety Theatre in Brooklyn was fingered for special condemnation, and tirades against immorality emanated regularly from City Hall.

All of this dissipated into thin air with the election of F. H. LaGuardia as Mayor in 1934. The new Mayor appointed a new License Commissioner, Paul Moss, brother of the Broadway producer B. S. Moss and himself a former legitimate theatrical producer. He opened office with the customary preface that he was no censor, but nevertheless felt it his obligation to uphold the common decencies.

As a theatrical man who had never been associated with burlesque, Moss displayed a traditional suspicion, if not hostility, that many showmen had displayed toward the black sheep of entertainment. He was not fooled by glib platitudes about the glamour of the theatre, insofar as it applied to burlesque. One of his first utterances boded ill for the burlesque operators. He told the press that he was going to clean up not only burlesque shows, but the taxi dance halls as well. This gratuitous threat—or promise—proved that he knew much more about burlesque than he did about his new job. He had no jurisdiction over the dime-a-dance emporiums, a police function entirely. But his pairing of burlesque shows with taxi dance halls indicated that he had more than a superficial knowledge of what was going on.

These dance halls, including in addition a large cluster of so-called dance studios, gave the burlesque patron a certain measure of fulfillment for the erotic stimulation of the shows. Many were known to their connoisseurs as "rub joints." And they were more numerous than the burlesque houses. Most of the dance halls were located strategically near the burlesque houses, and as a logical corollary to the burlesque show, the steady habitué went directly from one to the other. This phase had barely been touched upon before Moss' arrival on the scene. His coupling of the two served notice that he was already viewing burlesque from its worst angle.

The new Commissioner did not waste time. In February, but one month after his appointment, the Irving Place Theatre was raided by the police. Ten performers and the house manager were arrested. The Irving Place had been going along pretty much as usual. Margie Hart, featured stripteuse, had been calmly separating the folds of her trick dress. Comic Mickey Markwood intermittently pulled up his trousers and projected the front thereof in the direction of the nearest female. One of the other strippers had prefaced her act with a classic burlesque lullaby, entitled "Hot Nuts." And so on.

When all seemed lost, Herk intervened successfully with Mayor LaGuardia. After the runways were removed as a "distinct fire hazard," the Mayor seemed quite amiable. "What do you want us to do?" he rasped when complaints of leniency were voiced. "Do you want to send all these performers to jail because one woman complained against them?"

Something new was added to the usual promises of reform and the anticipated evolution of "a higher form of the burlesque art" with the formulation of the new NRA Code especially for burlesque. Strippers would all wear brassieres from now on, and desist from encores. The dialogue would be refined, etc., etc. In an editorial headlined "Commendable—If True," *The Billboard* commented: "The burly barons have decided to immediately sterilize dialogue, tone down strips, eliminate strip encores, throw out runways and all other forms of audience mixing."

Even Georgia Sothern got religion in the frenzy of the moment and announced that in keeping with the times she was no longer a stripper. *The New York Times* found in April 1934 that, according to Minsky-Weinstock spokesmen: "Burlesque, in the last month, has so improved that it is now cleaner than any of the Broadway plays or revues and all hells and damns have been barred from the dialogue." And before the end of the month, Moss jubilantly exclaimed: "The day of 'filth' is past."

This happy state lasted but a few weeks, if indeed it could be said to have existed in the theatres outside 42nd Street and the Irving Place at all. As in times gone by, the fury of censorship soon spent itself, and the houses went back to normal.

In 1936, Moss made the mistake of attempting to revoke the license of the Republic Theatre, though no criminal conviction had been obtained against it. The law has always been that the License Commissioner has the right to refuse a new license or not to renew an expired one. But he has no power to revoke a license before its expiration unless a criminal conviction had been rendered against its holder in a court of law. With the National Council on Freedom from Censorship intervening on behalf of the theatre, the Court of Appeals of New York State affirmed this interpretation of the statutes, and the Republic Theatre continued on its merry way.

After this setback, Moss surrendered, or else he decided that the best strategy was to give the operators enough rope to hang themselves. At any rate, for the first time in years, no hearings were held on May 1, no restrictions of any nature imposed. To everybody's complete surprise the licenses were renewed almost as a matter of course. The Reverend Joseph A. McCaffrey issued his annual tirade, but that was about all.

However, in August 1936, the New Gotham Theater was cited by the police for indecency on the complaint of John S. Sumner, of the Society for the Suppression of Vice. The case was held pending until the spring of 1937 without any decision, and in the meanwhile the theatres, including the New Gotham, continued as always. In Los Angeles, a sudden series of startling raids culminated in the imprisonment of the manager of the Hollywood Goes Minsky troupe, and at the end of the year Popkin and Ringer's Burbank Theatre was given the same treatment. The principals, Jack Greenman, Sherry Britton and Ermaine Parker, were given jail sentences as a Christmas present. Eventually, their jail sentences were suspended, but reform was definitely in the air, and in 1937 it would not be denied.

The letters to the newspapers, and the editorials, this time did not condone burlesque shows as robust echoes of heroic humor and robust, hearty slapstick, but as depraved dens that should be wiped out. To add to the general outcry, a series of degenerate sex crimes occurring in New York City just before license renewal time, May 1, 1937, further inflamed public sentiment.

Without any connecting evidence whatever, the sex crimes were judged a logical development of moral chaos brought about by the burlesque shows. Actually, despite their nudity, the burlesque shows were less corruptive and rowdy than the earlier stock and Wheel shows of 1928 to 1932. There were no chorines writhing on rumbling runways, as adolescents hooted and bawled in sensual delight. The chorines, in their dance numbers, behaved as if they were in the Radio City Music Hall. And the strips were ushered in to the chaste strains of "A Pretty Girl Is Like a Melody," "Love in Bloom" and pseudo-romantic trappings.

But, adding insult to injury, the 42nd Street and Broadway burlesque houses continued, as ever, to parade their untoward exhibitions on the mainstream of the city. The city administration was thereby placed in the position of a wife who might condone her husband's infidelities, but is forced to sue for divorce when her spouse's misconduct is publicized by him in every newspaper that will grant him space, with interesting pictures of his mistress to boot. The BAA, through Tom Phillips, attacked the Minsky organization for this fault, and *The Billboard* restated the premise succinctly: "Overabundant, uncontrolled publicity, focusing civic eyes on decadent shows, became a thorny boomerang."

Almost a year after the original arraignment of the New Gotham Theatre, the case came to trial in the Court of Special Sessions in April 1937. The charges were brought to a head in an atmosphere of revulsion against burlesque which aggravated the offenses, rather than minimized them. The tactics of delay, normally very effective, now backfired. A jury trial was denied the defendants. A verdict of guilty was rendered against Sam Kraus, personally, as manager of the theatre. The Burley Amusement Corporation, legal operator, represented by Mollie Minsky, Secretary and Treasurer, was fined $500. "The evidence," according to *The New York Times,* "was that five young women went through 'strip-tease' acts to the accompaniment of soft music and softer lights."

The consequences of this heinous offense were farflung and severe.

License Commissioner Moss, having at last obtained a conviction, found himself with the legal power to revoke the license of the New Gotham. Though he could just as well have waited another two weeks, and merely refused to give a new one, immediate hearings were held on the revocation of the old license. The result was almost a foregone conclusion, especially when Abe Minsky lost his temper at the hearing. He refused to testify on the ground that he was not personally involved and was present only as a spectator. Exasperated, he told the License Commissioner that he, Moss, had not accomplished anything at all since he had assumed office—an accurate state of facts which Moss immediately proceeded to rectify. And then Abe Minsky added a parting shot that the License Commissioner was prejudiced because his brother, B. S. Moss, found business very poor at his new Times Square movie theatre, the New Criterion, following which heartfelt outburst, the portly Abe Minsky was ejected from the hearings room. Moss forthwith revoked the theatre's license, which still had about a week to run.

The portentous hearings on the applications for renewal of the licenses for the burlesque theaters began April 29, 1937. They were to mark the beginning of the end for the industry. But to the operators, at first, it seemed just another annual nuisance.

Churchmen of all faiths united this time in a common-front attack. Jewish and Lutheran spokesmen joined the usual Catholic opposition in the forefront of the assault. Rabbi Stephen S. Wise contributed a highly pertinent observation: "You cannot make these places decent. You might as well try to freeze hell." Cardinal Hayes' strenuous objections were echoed by the Lutheran Church and the Lord's Day Alliance. Organizations such as the Catholic Charities, which usually had remained aloof, now attacked burlesque on aesthetic grounds: "There is no element of truth in it. It has no element of goodness or of beauty, the three fundamental requisites of art in any form, whether it be literature, drama or painting."

The supposedly rampant sex crimes had a prominent place on the agenda. Reverend Brougher, of Brooklyn, arch nemesis of the Star Theatre, testified that a father in his neighborhood saw a burlesque show, then went home and attacked his own daughter. Three irate women swore that burlesque conditions were degrading, and their testimony seemed truly appalling until it was revealed that none of them had ever been inside a burlesque theatre. But the hunt was on.

Adding to the general hysteria, the District Attorney of Brookyn awoke from several years of lethargy and on April 30 led three raids against the Star, Oxford and Werba's, all of which he now decided were "largely responsible for the sex degeneracy and sex crimes of the city."

With this suddenly unleashed tide of abuse gaining new momentum hour after hour, the burlesque operators seemed at a total loss. They were completely unprepared for this overwhelming barrage. And only a year ago there had been no trouble at all. As usual, each sought at first to exclude himself from the pack.

"Not us," said the Minskys. "Not me," said Wilner. "We're clean. It's the others they're all talking about."

Moss had a different view: "Reports of inspectors of my department made during the last three years satisfy me that all burlesque theatres run practically the same shows."

By the time the burlesque owners decided to unite in one common cause, it was much too late. The best they could offer in rebuttal was Morton Minsky's assurance that he had fired a chorus girl at the Oriental Theatre because she lacked the necessary refinements for his productions, and Tom Phillips' asseveration that though he had been in burlesque all his life, though his wife was a chorus girl and his children had been reared in the atmosphere of burlesque, these children, notwithstanding, were now exemplary, decent, college graduates.

On May 2, 1937, Moss exploded his unprecedented decision refusing license renewals to all fourteen existing burlesque houses, and denying applications for three additional new licenses. In his opinion, the License Commissioner stated in part:

> After a hearing . . . and after listening to the many witnesses representing civic and religious organizations, and reading the letters of protest from citizens and organizations that have come to my attention, I am satisfied that the proof before me clearly indicates that the type of performance, the language used, the display of nudity, are coarse, vulgar and lewd, and endanger public morality in the welfare of the community and are a disgrace to the people of the City of New York.
>
> In 1934, I started to work with the burlesque people, as one who understands the theatrical business. I tried to make the burlesque houses family places instead of being largely only for men. . . .
>
> The lack of imagination and the lack of showmanship as well as the general calibre of the men running burlesque is such that they do not understand that clean entertainment pays and the vulgar, cheap performances do not.

The immediate reactions were varied and emphatic. Mayor LaGuardia, interviewed while attending, symbolically enough, a circus show, nodded his approval: "This is the beginning of the end of incorporated filth."

Cardinal Hayes announced: "I have seldom received news that brings more joy to my heart. . . . May God bless our Commissioner of Licenses."

The actors affected, estimated at about 1,000, as well as about an equal number of stagehands and musicians, did not share this joy. *The New York Times* (May 2, 1937) reported: ". . . the effect on the performers bordered on the hysterical."

The operators were stunned. They had anticipated something drastic —like another set of severe restrictions. But it could not be possible that the industry was to be abolished entirely. After all, the complainants were clergymen, religious organizations and professional reformers, who would be prepared to testify just as eagerly against nightclubs, cabarets and Broadway revues.

The burlesque operators immediately instituted a formidable legal barrage of stays, writs, mandamuses and superseding writs. But public opinion and the prevailing atmosphere were against them. All the legal maneuvers failed. In Brooklyn, a grand jury voted indictments against all the raided theaters in that borough. In Albany, a bill was introduced authorizing, in effect, an official censor for all theatrical exhibits. There were the customary personal acrimonious exchanges. Moss declared that the Minsky brothers "cannot be trusted with a license." The Minskys retorted: ". . . the two of us will match our private lives against the Commissioner's any day."

Then followed more conciliatory measures, and more effective planning by the burlesque owners. If only they could get their houses open, even under severe restrictions, they would manage to survive until the end of the year, when Mayor LaGuardia's term expired. In June the Mayor agreed to confer with them. He was expected to reopen the theatres by June 25. But nothing happened. On June 24, the New York *Herald Tribune* remarked: "Last vestiges of the once flourishing art of burlesque disappeared yesterday afternoon."

At length, after one or two false starts, the theatres were permitted to open. In collaboration with Gene Buck, President of the American Society of Composers, Authors and Publishers (ASCAP), working in behalf of Mayor LaGuardia, a new code for burlesque, or rather vaudeville, or rather vaudesque, as the presentations were first called, was put into force. Dancing to the tune, and pretending they liked it, the operators donned a set of false whiskers, and masqueraded as the Variety Revue Theatres Association. According to the Constitution of this august Association, its aims were:

> . . . to provide for regulation and supervision of the stage enter-

> tainment presented by members of the Association and to promote and uphold standards of decency with respect thereto, and to improve the artistic value of such entertainment.

As a more substantial guarantee that these high-minded resolutions would be kept in mind, the operators were required to post a bond of $1,000 and to agree to a forfeit of $500 for any breach of the faith. The owners also agreed in a written 100 percent restrictive covenant that they would obediently abide by the decisions of a censorship board, which would have complete jurisdiction over all the theatres, including labor relations.

The chairman of this board of censors was John F. X. Masterson, attorney, and Chancellor of the Columbus Council of the Knights of Columbus, an organization which had been among the most zealous in opposition to the burlesque industry. Masterson was a virtual czar over the entire burlesque field. Samuel Scribner was appointed executive secretary of this board.

As a further condition to the opening of the houses, the operators waived any and all civil rights, practically prostrating themselves with the attested statement that "this stipulation and agreement is entered into voluntarily on my part and is not the result of duress." The *World-Telegram,* in its issue of July 14, 1937, editorialized: "The text of this agreement seems to us one of the most shockingly dictatorial black-jacks we ever read. . . . It is a precedent for strangulation of almost any form of expression." And at that, the licenses were issued for only ninety days!

There were no ceremonies attendant upon the reopening of the theatres. There was an abundance of false hopes, illusory prophecies, inane predictions and overweening hypocrisy. In naïve jubilation over a new order that, based on the entire past record of the entertainment, was thoroughly impossible, extravagant, fanciful promises gushed forth.

The group of advisors to Gene Buck in the formulation of the new code of behavior was headed by such men as Charles Warner, superintendent of, and attorney for, the Society for the Prevention of Cruelty to Children; Dr. Francis McCaffrey, brother of burlesque's most articulate foe, Reverend Joseph McCaffrey; and Jerome Bentley, Educational Director of the YMCA. Under their benign influence, Gene Buck expressed the keynote of the futile hopes: "I believe that a wholesome forward step has been taken toward bringing back a new form of vaudeville and making possible the development of talent which is sorely lacking today."

Paul Moss stated that the theatres were on probation in the hope that "as these theatres prosper and new talent is discovered, it will lay a groundwork for the future stars of radio, motion pictures, musical comedies and legitimate plays." Heretofore, they had consisted, he declared, rightly enough, of "a hodge-podge of skits which the producers' grandfathers enjoyed, routine dance numbers and countless variations of the hootchie-kootchie."

David Dressler also joined the chorus, albeit somewhat more cautiously: "It has a chance again to develop entertainment based on the appeals that made vaudeville popular."

John Anderson, dramatic critic of the *New York American,* had a happy thought:

> It should, and I hope will, present a caustic and happy commentary on the affairs of Broadway, taking pokes at other shows in the old manner, making fun of public characters and spraying the acid of wit on political affairs.

The New York Times editorially asked for "boisterous and lusty humor."

It immediately developed, unfortunately, that instead of this heralded renaissance, the producers, with their customary great imaginative and creative artistry, were merely presenting the usual strip acts without nudity, and the usual bits without obscenity. *The New York Times* (July 13, 1937) reported one such strip act under the new regime as follows:

> One girl did take the center of the stage, but instead of singing a chorus, idling up and down and unfastening, she merely kicked and somersaulted. She wore a flaring organdie gown over a pink jumper when she started. She wore the same when she finished.

Ann Corio at the Apollo tried to keep business going at that house with "piquant" songs about her "striptease." The Republic, seriously taking an ironic hint from George Jean Nathan, put on a striptease in reverse, starting with a sparsely clad girl who gradually put on her clothes. The Oriental, finally permitted to reopen with colored revues, was more risque than any of the "Follies" shows, as they were now called, featuring for excitement typical off-color songs such as "You Better Get It While You Can," expounded by middle-aged female entertainers. The closest any of the theatres came to vaudeville was in the burlesque debut of the rough-and-tumble comics Arthur and Morton Havel, and the closest they came to "good old-fashioned burlesque" was the revival of comic Bobby Barry, whose last appearance in burlesque was in Scribner's *Maids of America* with Al K. Hall.

Disillusionment was evident at once. The *New York Evening Post* headlined: "Gilded Burlesque Dashes Lusty Hopes of Old-Timers." *The Billboard* summarized the proceedings at the Gaiety, and indeed of all the "follies" shows, as "Little business and little entertainment." *Variety* proclaimed what every burlesque operator had known all along: "Clean Burley Doesn't Pay—New York Finds." Its correspondent, Joe Schoenfeld, concluded: "It's not a vaude revival—it's just the pushing back of burlesque about ten years."

The most depressing thought of all to the burlesque strategists was the realization that for the first time in the history of censorship and license renewals, a license had not been granted for the full year. Moss, apparently, had been the first one to think of this very simple and extremely effective plan of control. In just ninety days, the theatres could all be shuttered again. In fact, His Honor, the Mayor, sounded a deeply ominous note with his blunt statement in August: "In my opinion burlesque is definitely on the way out, and it is by no means certain that the current ninety-day burlesque theatre licenses will be renewed."

With this Damocles sword perpetually over them, the strippers and comics had no choice but to "work clean." The result—as summarized by *The Billboard* in the fall of 1937: "It's the same old story, no biz." One by one, the theatres voluntarily closed shop and dropped out of burlesque permanently. All the Brooklyn houses, with the exception of the Star, collapsed.

The calamitous season in New York was echoed all over the country. "Burlesque business is terrible in all parts of the country," *The Billboard* reported in November. At that time, Chicago, once a robust home for robust burlesque, was devoid of a single standard theatre. The elaborate Rialto Theatre, facing a revocation of its license, as per New York procedure, discontinued operation. On the other Chicago extreme, the Folly Nickelodeon—admission only five cents—also closed. Just holding on were the National and State-Harrison, which were little more than scratch houses. In Boston, the old Howard was still open, starting its ninety-second season, but that was about all that could be said of that city. The only large city which could still boast of some favorable conditions for burlesque entertainment was Detroit.

In New York, the operators waited impatiently for Election Day. When the sad news came, however, that LaGuardia and Moss were good for another four years at least, the Oriental and the Apollo folded at once, before the end of the month. In 1938, there were five struggling survivals, precariously hanging on to ninety-day license renewals—the Star, Republic, Eltinge, Irving Place and Peoples Theatres.

Meanwhile, the Censorship Board, headed by John F. X. Masterson, buttressed by the bonds the producers had to post to insure their good behavior, was the most diligent and restrictive the industry had ever had to cope with. The Board was shrewd enough to avoid the pitfalls of other censorship bodies, such as setting up a "code," and then leaning back comfortably in the pleasant anticipation that the "code" would be automatically obeyed. Instead, Masterson's censors judged each performance on its own merits. Every theatre was subject to relentless observation.

A year later, there were only three "Follies" theatres left. Fortunately, for many performers, the 1939 World's Fair gave some opportune employment. And still there was some hope. After all, 1940 might see another Mayor.

In 1940, upon LaGuardia's re-election, Commissioner Moss decided that even ninety-day licenses were too long. He cut down the period to sixty days, then thirty, and even on a week-to-week basis. The end was now in sight. In March 1942, License Commissioner Paul Moss, acting under the orders of Mayor F. H. LaGuardia, unequivocally refused to grant any license renewals to any of the burlesque theatres. There were no hearings, and little protest. The burlesque ranks were now too thinned out to offer any effective resistance. Furthermore, even if they remained open, they could not hope to survive another four years, until blessed Tammany might come in power. Burlesque died in New York City, and with it any hope that burlesque might ever become again an established, large-scale enterprise.

To those few who had mildly protested these repressive measures, such as the American Civil Liberties Union, the Mayor had already given his answer. Burlesque, he exploded, was just so much garbage, and therefore he had as much right to censor or abolish it as he had to run a sewer system.

SURVIVAL

A WHIPPED dog, the burlesque industry retreated into the shadows. No more bright lights and Broadway. Most of the houses in operation in the rest of the country went back to the side streets and obscure locations. When these, in turn, were censored out of business, the operators withdrew still further—to Skid Row.

Many of the old-timers were dead, and many of the new operators were bankrupt. Bill (Beef Trust) Watson and his namesake competitor, Sliding Billy Watson, both died the same year—1939. Scribner's death in 1941 was followed a month later by the demise of his star soubrette, Rose Sydell, widow of W. S. Campbell, at her Brooklyn home, at the age of seventy-six. In 1939, Joe Hurtig, the last of the four Hurtig brothers, died. The Hurtig and Seamon partnership had long since been dissolved when Harry Seamon left to start life anew as a booking agent.

At the time of his death, Joe Hurtig had been managing the Shubert Theatre in Philadelphia. This was one of the few lavish burlesque houses left in the East. The Wilners, who had been operating the theatre, were evicted by a federal court, which found them in default of Social Security and Amusement taxes. In addition, Mrs. Stella Wilner, who from her vantage post at the box office had always assumed a supervisory interest in the financial end of the theatres, was fined

$1,000. She left burlesque to become a costume designer, and her husband, Max Wilner, went back to directing a Yiddish playhouse in Brooklyn.

Then, Rube Bernstein and Allen Gilbert, who had collaborated in an abortive seven-week operation at the Brooklyn Tivoli Theatre in 1941, decided to revive the Shubert Theatre with their own brand of publicity bombast: "We believe in the theatre, flesh and blood entertainment, burlesque, and the land we live in." They discovered that Philadelphians preferred the strippers of Issy Hirst and the equally prosperous Fay's vaudeville house and Carroll's nightclub to Allen Gilbert's dance numbers.

Joe Weinstock's son, Eddie, heir to the Minsky dynasty, left the Republic and burlesque to manage, without censorship troubles, a small movie house in south Brooklyn. Herk tried his hand in miscellaneous unproductive ventures before embarking on the most disastrous of all for him, a Broadway revue. Jean Bedini, the last of Columbia's actor-producers, periodically made conspicuously unsuccessful efforts to "revive" burlesque. Of all the Minskys, only Harold, Abe's son, eventually remained active in the field. Following the 1939 World's Fair, the performers fled to South America, federal theatre projects, and nightclubs.

In 1941, there was a modest recovery outside New York City, with the consolidation of the Independent Wheel under Issy Hirst, and the Midwest Circuit, dominated by Dewey Michaels, N. S. Barger and Arthur Clamage. The new Wheel was geared to a season of twenty-six to thirty weeks and stabilized the tottering theatres by furnishing talent and scenery at prices considerably below the costs to the individual owners.

So circumspect was the Independent Circuit at first that in the East the lobbies displayed pictures of men, rather than the usual undressed, voluptuous sirens. But the bits were the oldest Columbia routines greased with the smut of Mutual. At first there were only three strippers. A Girl in Blue unit was revived, with Ann Corio, and a Hindu Belles show for Hinda Wassau. Other headlined strippers were of top caliber, ranging from Georgia Sothern and Margie Hart to the newcomers who were skilled in the latest erotic novelties. These featured strippers drew the audiences, and the shows were named after them.

After a few years, the Wheel increased the number of its strippers, who also intensified the salaciousness of their specialties. However, unlike the stability of the big Wheels, the Independent Circuit found its ranks depleted by the continuing censorship throughout that followed in the wake of the New York restrictions. In New Jersey, the Hudson

Ann Corio—then and now. *Sy Seidman; Pictorial Parade Inc.*

Theatre in Union City and the Empire in Newark, both operated by Jules Leventhal, had been playing, quite profitably, Hirst Wheel shows to the deprived New York customers. They were joined by Harold Minsky, who opened his own stock burlesque theatre in Newark. At all three theatres, the headliners shook like those of Mutual and stripped like those of stock. When permitted, the combination of nudity and the cooch was the rawest yet seen in the East. However, there was no firm "rapport" between the theatres and the officials. The managers never were quite sure, from one week to the next, how to proceed.

George Jean Nathan, who believed that even musical comedy should aim at the stimulation of the sex impulse, was rather disappointed on one of his periodic pilgrimages to burlesque. Gloomily surveying the situation in New Jersey in 1956, he lamented that "everything was in good order, so good, in fact, that it was like going to a Sunday School picnic, minus only its occasional wayward hilarity." The Hudson Theatre in Union City was, he found "as innocuous as a women's bridge-whist party in Sandusky, Ohio. . . . Everything was as clean as a whistle, if a lot louder."

Evidently, the eminent critic had chosen a "bad" week. Normally, as the word had gotten round, "anything goes" in Jersey. This was given further public exposure by some dialogue to the same effect in Sammy Davis' show on Broadway, *Mr. Wonderful.* The publicity was not appreciated by New Jersey officialdom. Shortly thereafter, all three theatres were closed permanently by the authorities. The Independent Wheel lost two highly profitable spokes. Harold Minsky transferred operations to Las Vegas, taking with him his star comic, Irving Benson. The other featured comedian, Joe De Rita, emerged from it all to become a children's favorite as one of the Three Stooges.

Los Angeles, after the New York havoc, seemed on the verge of becoming the new burlesque capital. But severe raids liquidated many stock theatres in that area. In Indianapolis, the Mutual Theatre tried to defeat the censors at their own game. It posted on its walls, with erudite bravado, the Latin proverb "Omnia Perversas Corrumpere Mentes"—"Anything Can Corrupt a Mind Already Tainted." The censors were not diverted. And Chicago, the Midwest burlesque center, was left with but two scratch houses operating on a grind movie policy, the pattern for those theatres outside the Independent Midwest Wheel.

In 1956, Tom Phillips, the prototype of the "good and the clean" in burlesque, opened up a burlesque house in New York City, the first since 1942. Phillips apparently took seriously the usual thoughtless banalities about the virtues of "old-time" burlesque. There were plenty of old bits, slapstick and inoffensive routines. There was no stripping and no cooching. Instead there were replicas of the ancient tawdry production numbers. Typical of these is the scene where the chorus girls huddle around a dilapidated teakettle on logs, as the juvenile or prima donna sings, "Play, Gypsy, Play," or the chorines wave red pieces of cheesecloth to the strains of "Red Sails in the Sunset." This was supposed to meet the competition of movies and television, when vaudeville couldn't. The show was laughed off the boards. It did not last a week.

Much shrewder in conception is *This Was Burlesque,* starring Ann Corio and featuring comic Steve Mills. It opened in 1963 on Second Avenue, New York City, and in its third year moved uptown in the heart of the theatrical section. It is currently on tour. A successfully slick confection of old bits and new strippers, this show is not quite burlesque, not musical comedy, neither fish nor fowl. It is an exercise in glib showmanship. Ann Corio's sense of humor lies along the low, leering lines of Mutual, but her sense of publicity values matches that of the Columbia Wheel. It is billed as "Burlesque at its rowdiest," "Leave the kids at home if you want to see something startling," and the "Show that was too hot for the World's Fair." But at the same time, it is let out that Ann Corio, who is of a different mold from the reckless modern breed, belongs to "old-fashioned" burlesque, and the severest professional censors were her admirers.

The hoary bits, skillfully unfolded by the ancient Steve Mills, seem delightfully quaint to the new audiences who have made *This Was Burlesque* an "in" spot. Steve Mills is assisted by at least two other comics. One of them is usually someone like Charlie Robinson or Harry J. Conley. These are top burlesque performers, who are acknowledged to be really too good for burlesque. The only trouble is that audiences smile appreciatively at their droll cleverness, but seldom laugh. For balance, there is also someone like Mac Dennison, a down-to-earth, raffish character who learned his trade well in the stock burlesque houses of New York City during the thirties. When Charlie Robinson left the show to manage a competitive production on Second Avenue, starring Blaze Starr, there were actually two quasi-burlesque houses in New York. But Blaze Starr was comparatively unknown in New York, the special brand of Ann Corio hoopla was lacking, and the new venture folded within a few weeks, dashing the hopes of some who thought burlesque was about to be revived.

Ann Corio, now looking for all the world like the President of the Ladies' Auxiliary of the Knights of Columbus, is narrator of the show and is aided and augmented by three younger female principals new to burlesque. Since they are not permited to strip with any degree of effectiveness, they make up for it with some indecorous cooching—all executed, however, with tongue prominently in cheek, the favorite tactic of self-conscious non-burlesque performers.

With off-Broadway prices, which are still much higher than those of regular burlesque houses, scaled down from $4.95, the production avoided the usual infirmities of burlesque. Even more leisurely than the old two-a-day, there were in New York only three matinee performances a week. For the first time in history, the performers were not overworked. There were no rehearsals each and every week for the following week's new show, the bane of normal stock burlesque. No additional routines had be dug out every single week of the season. And, most important of all, admission prices were just high enough to permit the hiring of chorines who were typical of Broadway showgirls. The professional reviewers, who were merciless to Tom Phillips and Charlie Robinson, were only slightly derogatory of *This Was Burlesque,* in effect praising it with faint damns.

Ann Corio's *This Was Burlesque* is a publicity coup, not a burlesque revival. But after her troupe left New York City, a procrustean revival of sorts was introduced by a newcomer, Leroy Griffith, a former candy butcher. His shows are devoid of any glitter, frills or other such trivia. There are no chorus lines, no production numbers, no scenery to speak of—just strippers, a comic or two, and a straight man.

Since there has been no influx of new male performers in burlesque, the old faces, and they are really old, are now reappearing, one after another, in harrowing procession. The comics look as ancient as their jokes. Age has withered and custom has staled their infinite vulgarities. To see these men in their sixties and seventies pretending to an uncontrollable concupiscence and a puissant wolfishness in the same grooved routines that were preposterous even when they were young, is not conducive to laughter—at least not as intended. The occasional younger comics are more presentable, though, with the passage of time, they have become quite fat. Where and how they secured employment during these long lean years for burlesque is uncertain, but at least they've been eating.

The girls are mainly new. However, a "name" like Georgia Sothern will still be occasionally featured with younger and later headliners ranging from Lili St. Cyr, tall and patrician in appearance, whose specialty is taking a bath onstage, and the curvy Blaze Starr—both highly publicized—to the most recent crop of busty favorites diligently advertising the exact dimensions of their billowy breasts, which they are not averse to displaying in slow and rapid motion, up, down and sideways.

Blaze Starr: 48-24-36. *James J. Kriegsmann*

The old scratch houses which charged ten to twenty-five cents for matinees had a larger cast than these presentations which reach a top of $4.20 for a matinee performance. With such a setup, this latest mode of burlesque operation, designed to give the customers what they presumably want—and not a whit more—is surviving financially.

Finally, burlesque without comedians, straight men, singers, chorines or scenery—just the strippers—has managed to survive in all-girl nightclubs as "Burlesque After Dark." In these "strip-clip" dives, the show, such as it is, merely serves as a background to boost the sale of drinks.

The price of admission is nominal, usually one dollar or so for a glass of beer. If the customer has the legs to stand at the bar that long, and the stomach for the nonchalant parade of dreary, interminable strip routines, he can remain until closing time, 3:00 or 4:00 A.M., for the price of his one beer. Performances are continuous, as a rule, since an intermission would drive the patrons out. A continuous show demands a large platoon of strippers, virtually the only entertainment offered, except for a mistress of ceremonies and an occasional singer. The stage itself is so small that it cannot accommodate more than one or two performers, in addition to the two or three musicians.

Since, often enough, there are not enough strippers on hand to go around continuously, the time is padded out by the mistress of ceremonies, whose main requirement for the job is an ability and a willingness to recite glibly every dirty joke ever known. If there is still too much time, the strippers will stall for an additional fifteen minutes before getting down to the bare essentials. Usually, a performer does her act about every two hours. Since this is too short a time for her to leave the club, and too long a period to remain idle, what could be more appropriate than for her to double as a B-girl, sitting with the customers and wheedling them, one way or another, into buying drinks—to the financial betterment of herself and the owners? In the more advanced places, there are booths as well as tables, cozily described as "love nests."

Unfortunately for this convenient design for drinking, it leads to obvious abuses and is illegal in many states where "mixing" is prohibited. As a result, these burlesque nightclubs, which cannot exist financially without "mixing," any more than a burlesque show can survive without strippers or coochers, are usually closed down as soon as they get too flourishing and notorious. In New York and Miami they were banned after many years of successful operation. In Chicago, where they prominently line the Loop area, severe jail sentences were meted out to clip-joint bartenders and operators. Nevertheless, they constitute today's most conspicuous reminders and remainder of the burlesque industry. And the nightclub strippers themselves blithely continued the "sophisticated" trend becoming prevalent in burlesque just before censorship stepped in, embellishing it with their own improvisations—the "Radio Dance" number in which male prop hands clutch every part of the dancer's body; symbolic liaisons with a snowman; inventive suggestions of perversion, etc.

But the gaudy strip era is dead, and with it most of burlesque as it has been known for over seventy years. The epitaph was written in this obscure notice in *The New York Times* (May 19, 1942):

> Herbert Kay Minsky, who described himself as a theatrical manager, "presently unemployed," but who once was producer of burlesque performances, filed a petition in bankruptcy in Federal Court here yesterday.
>
> Mr. Minsky listed liabilities totaling $64,837 and only one asset, a $5,000 insurance policy naming Mrs. Juanita Minsky as beneficiary. The largest single creditor listed was Oscar Markowitch, whose address was said to be "care of the California Candy Company at 721 Broadway." Mr. Markowitch's claims totaled $30,000.

REPRISE

THE GOOD old days of burlesque, alas, never were. Before 1900, the shows were, according to Fred McCloy, "a conglomeration of filthy dialogue, libidinous scenes and licentious songs and dances." After 1900, there was the Empire Circuit which accommodated the "gang," who "wants it as raw as it will come." The Columbia Wheel toned down sex, but otherwise it was a triumph of exploitation, not of theatrical values. It fitted in with Brooks Atkinson's description of "clean" burlesque:

> Nothing is quite so pathetic as the insincere gesture toward artistic refinement—the dinner jackets into which the comedians squeeze themselves, the tawdry production numbers, the coy bird cages and sylvan glades and pastoral sentiments, the formal duets, the tired orchestral flourishes. Like a lady of easy virtue, burlesque makes a blowzy attempt to keep up appearances.

The Mutual Wheel, just before the modern strip act, was the rowdiest Roman of them all. Then came the strip act, which, deplored though it was, also gave the industry its greatest prosperity since the Columbia Wheel.

It is a paradox that when nudity was supreme in all its theatres, burlesque thrived, and was dignified with a multitude of newspaper and magazine articles on its "striptease contribution" to art and drama, something Scribner in all his years was never able to accomplish. Only then was burlesque flattered by imitation, even in Paris, where the Alcazar's *Revue Nu* was advertised as being "in the manner of the burlesques of New York." But when the strip was banned, and the theatres could not survive, the same pundits complained, "What Is Wrong with Burlesque?"

The lamentable shortcomings of the entertainment, obvious to the most casual patron—from the presence of the candy butchers to the lack of applause—were inherent in the first barnstorming troupes seventy years ago. When an audience did applaud an afterpiece in the *Bon Ton Burlesquers* of 1898, the *New York Clipper* remarked that the cast was thereby "receiving something that has heretofore been unknown in the burlesque sphere."

Burlesque, at its most prosperous, could not appreciably improve the chorus line. When a chorus girl in an early Columbia show bothered to smile, *The Billboard* rushed to print with the hope that this smile "might well be imitated by many a surly-faced member of the 'merry, merry' with many a burlesque troupe on both wheels." "The chorus . . . had become a negligible factor in the proceedings," wrote *The New York Times* of another Columbia show in 1925, a strange twist indeed for "girlie" shows. If the atmosphere of many burlesque houses was such that it accorded its paying customers the same scant respect they in turn gave the performers, 'twas always thus. The bouncers ever present in the shows of the Wheels were thus reproved by *The Billboard* in 1911:

> . . . over-officious preservers of the law become a worse nuisance than the original evil itself . . . the slightest noise or louder than usual applause is the immediate signal for a thunderous rapping of a heavy club or stick upon a wooden floor or steel post.

And the humor of burlesque is convivially commemorative only in nostalgia, not in fact. As early as 1903, *Variety* epitomized all burlesque comedy with the devastating comment that "comedians try very hard to make the audience laugh, but it is no use."

Any hope that burlesque might resume, sometime in the future, the supposed greatness of the Columbia Wheel—putting aside its basic gullibility—is obviously futile in this age of television. In 1938, Scribner himself admitted that Columbia could not possibly compete with the movies:

> . . . the ability of movie palaces to provide not alone talking pictures but ballets, choruses, specialties and great orchestras at far lower prices than traveling shows proved killing opposition. Burlesque's family trade was invaded wholesale. In every big city there were big theatres, big shows and low prices—opposition that traveling burlesque could not meet, let alone overcome. As far as Columbia burlesque was concerned, there was nothing to do but capitulate. It would have required unattainable millions to equip and conduct effective competition with the big cinemas through the medium of traveling attractions. It simply couldn't be done.

Again, burlesque is left with only sex as its attraction. When permitted by the authorities, there will aways be customers. When not, the only audiences are the Saturday night parties of giggling slummers. The future of burlesque is mirrored in the fate of the Palace Theatre in Buffalo which decided to reform after the New York City censorship in 1937. It went in for expensive and meritorious talent, lavish scenery and widespread publicity. What happened? Let *Variety* tell the story (November 3, 1937). "So the net went up and the gross went down."

Then, the theatre, facing severe losses, returned to stock and to strip:

> There are shakers and tossers in the raw and without embellishment. Comedians wouldn't even rate a gong on an amateur hour. So what? So the net is down and the gross is up in four figures. It's what they want here and the mob is back, with standing room for supper shows, midnight shambles, Sunday performances and so on.

The perpetual dilemma of burlesque was exposed: "Operators are out on a limb because they can't please both censors and dyed-in-the-wool fans."

Burlesque, finally and consequently, has crawled back into the honky-tonk crevices from which it first emerged. To give burlesque its due, it was not a particularly immoral force, even at its dirtiest. The proof is in New York City, which went without burlesque for more than twenty years. When banned, burlesque was blamed for "sex degeneracy" and the cheapening of New York, particularly 42nd Street. But New York is no safer now. The sex crimes have not diminished. 42nd Street is worse than ever. Burlesque, in its normal lumbering fashion, is usually behind the times, not ahead of them. The vicarious evils that trailed burlesque were not brought on by the burlesque shows. They were symptoms of more basic deficiencies.

American burlesque has given a livelihood to thousands upon thousands of performers, musicians, stagehands, ushers, producers, candy butchers and censors. It has provided countless hours of unmitigated boredom, and many other hours of genuine pleasure. It has served as a proving ground for talent. It may have given some surcease to the lonely, the derelict, the sexually driven. Beyond that, one cannot and should not hope for more, or expect less.

BIBLIOGRAPHY

Brown, T. Allston. *A History of the New York Stage: From the First Performance in 1732 to 1901*. Vol. 3. Bronx, New York: Benjamin Blom, Inc.

Dressler, David. "Science Looks at Burlesque," *The New York Post,* July, 1937.

Freedley, George, and John A. Reeves. *A History of the Theatre* (rev. ed.). New York: Crown Publishers, Inc., 1956.

Gilbert, Douglas. *American Vaudeville: Its Life and Times*. New York: Dover Publications, Inc., 1940.

Green, Abel, and Joe Laurie, Jr. *Show Biz*. New York: Garden City Books, 1952.

Leavitt, Michael B. *Fifty Years in Theatrical Management*. New York: Broadway Publishing Co., 1912.

Sobel, Bernard. *Burleycue*. New York: Farrar and Rinehart, 1931.

The following three publications are valuable chronicles of the changing burlesque scene:

New York Clipper, 1870 to 1910
The Billboard, 1897 to date
Variety, 1905 to date

INDEX

Note: References to shows and troupes such as May Fiske's English Blondes, Gus Hill's Aggregation, *etc.,* will be found under the surnames of producers or stars, *i.e.,* Hill, Gus. Names of performers beginning with titles—Countess Nadja, Princess Olga, Madame Celest—will be found as Nadja, Countess; Olga, Princess; *etc.* References to teams will be found, for the most part, thus: Gallagher and Shean (not as separate references to Gallagher and to Shean).

THE AUTHOR AND HIS BOOK

IRVING ZEIDMAN received his B.A. from the College of the City of New York in 1928, at the age of nineteen. Four years later, after earning an LL.B. from Brooklyn Law School, he was admitted to the New York State Bar. Besides practicing law, he has been a social worker, a schoolteacher, and an inspector for the Department of Labor.

In order to write THE AMERICAN BURLESQUE SHOW, his first book, Mr. Zeidman read almost everything ever written on this historically obscure phase of show business. He says, furthermore, that no burlesque theatre has opened or closed in the New York metropolitan area in the past thirty-five years that has not been subject to his personal scrutiny.

At present a partner in a New York concern which manufactures and sells institutional equipment, Mr. Zeidman lives in Brooklyn with his wife and two children.

THE AMERICAN BURLESQUE SHOW was set into type by the Harry Sweetman Typesetting Corp., South Hackensack, New Jersey; printed by Mahoney & Roese, Inc., New York City; and bound by The Book Press Incorporated, Brattleboro, Vt. The text is set in Times Roman, a type face designed for the London *Times*. Chapter titles are set in Lydian, a face designed by Warren Chappell.

A HAWTHORN BOOK